Publisher

Publisher

Gene Pulliam,
Last of the Newspaper Titans

Russell Pulliam

Jameson Books
Ottawa, Illinois

Publisher
Gene Pulliam, Last of the Newspaper Titans

Copyright © 1984 by Russell Pulliam.

Copies of this book may be purchased from the publisher for
$16.95. All inquiries should be addressed to Jameson Books,
722 Columbus St., Ottawa, IL 61350. (815) 434-7905.

Distributed by Kampmann and Company, New York City. All returns to Kampmann and Co.
warehouse.

ISBN: 0-915463-02-4

Printed in the United States of America

5 4 3 2 1

Contents

Preface

REMEMBER THE DAYS of old, consider the years of all generations. Ask
your father, and he will inform you, your elders, and they will tell you.

Deut. 32:7

My earliest recollection of my grandfather, Eugene C. Pulliam, was
when I asked him, incredulously, "You mean, you really own a
newspaper all by yourself?" Some years later, my eighth-grade
teacher told us that everyone had someone over them—no one
escapes a chain of authority. I objected, proudly proclaiming that
my grandfather didn't have a boss; he was the boss. The teacher said
no, he too had a boss, in a sense more than anybody: all of his
newspaper readers.

But it was not until I went to college that I became aware of my
grandfather's place in the newspaper and political world. It
prompted me to ask him on vacations about the age he had lived
through and helped to shape, the days which lay now in the books I
was studying. For instance, what about Robert LaFollette?
LaFollette, he told me, was ready to run for president in 1912 until
Teddy Roosevelt stepped in; a man who, with his liberal ideas, was
ahead of his time. And Theodore Roosevelt? Teddy Roosevelt he
looked on as his boyhood idol—a fighter, who busted the trusts, took
on big business, the kind of man we don't have around any longer.

He had met, and known to various degrees, the presidents of his
lifetime, a roll call of historical figures: Roosevelt, Wilson, Taft,
Coolidge, Hoover, FDR, Truman, Eisenhower, Kennedy, Johnson,
Nixon, Ford. He was easily the most interesting man I ever talked to,
a man who had seen so much, done so much, a man who knew so
much.

In one letter which impressed me particularly, he cautioned me against the arrogance of youth, at a time in the sixties when we were inclined to think we were something special:

> I think you are inclined to believe your generation of youngsters is somehow different and set apart from youngsters of other generations. Of course every generation has its characteristics, but frankly, Russ, there is very, very little difference in the actual performance of one generation after the other, except that in the last fifty years succeeding generations have been better educated than the previous one. I think you are too much inclined to discount the things that your parents believe in and the things they do. It is a very fine and useful exercise in "thinkology" to mull over these things, but you shouldn't allow yourself come to the conclusion that your father's generation or my generation weren't worth a damn and that it is up to your generation to save the world. We didn't save the world and you are not going to save the world. All you can do is do your best, and I think that is what you are doing—except I would be very unhappy to see you get a cynical or ultracritical attitude toward older people.

I learned about my grandfather from other people, too, and heard some describe him as a reactionary who was holding up the progress of liberalism in Indiana and Arizona, a close-minded conservative who wanted to turn the clock back a century or so. But that didn't fit the man I knew. He was a conservative, it seemed, but you could never box him in. I remember telling him about the forcible occupation of a building by black students at Williams College in my sophomore year. He couldn't understand it. Why hadn't the college administration met the black demands before the blacks ever thought of them? They should have anticipated the grievances. Look how I did it with my newspapers, he said. No strikes for twenty-five years. I gave my employees the things the unions never dreamed of, after World War II; the recreation areas, the pension plans, the medical benefits. Those college presidents, they ought to know.

After I went to work for the Associated Press in New York in 1971, I read some journalism history, biographies of Joseph Pulitzer, William Randolph Hearst, Henry Luce, Henry P. Watterson, William Allen White, William Rockhill Nelson, Colonel Robert McCormick, and found many parallels to my grandfather's life. My job entailed an eternal search for a good story, and I covered demonstrations, murders, political campaigns. But he, I knew, was an even bigger story. I wanted to write it, but I had a problem. I was his grandson, and, as such, he almost always showed me his best side. Could I keep the sort of distance that an author needs from his subject? Could I write of his faults, his weaknesses? Would others tell me what he was really like? I began.

I had a number of long talks with my grandfather, primarily about the first thirty years of his life. And I interviewed more than 150 people who knew my grandfather, some of them several times. Obviously not all those interviewed can be named, but of special help were former *Indianapolis Star* editor Jameson Campaigne; the late Indianapolis lawyer Frank McHale; Indianapolis Newspapers Inc. president William A. Dyer; former *Arizona Republic* reporter Walter Meek; Davis Vandivier, who worked for my grandfather in Indiana and Oklahoma in the 1920s and 1930s; *Republic* political writer Bernie Wynn; *Republic* investigative reporter Don Bolles, who was killed a year after my grandfather's death; and the late newspaper publisher John S. Knight.

Several Associated Press executives were helpful, including former general manager Wes Gallagher, his assistant Harry Montgomery, and Webb McKinley, head of the AP's world services. My grandfather's secretaries were also of great assistance, Marge Tarplee in Indianapolis and Mary Freeman in Phoenix, and I was made welcome at the libraries at the *Star* and *News* in Indianapolis and the *Republic* and *Gazette* in Phoenix. My sisters, Debbie and Myrta, aided me in various ways, and my father gave special help in encouragement and comment. My thanks to him and Laurie McGinn for reading the manuscript, as well as editing by Jameson Campaigne. My wife Ruth deserves special credit for constant encouragement as well as for typing the manuscript.

Part I
The Newsman

1

Introduction

GENE PULLIAM WAS not a typical newspaper publisher. He once told one of his star investigative reporters, Don Bolles, that he, not Don, would go to jail if the Arizona State Senate persisted in demanding that Bolles give up his notes and reveal his sources. Yet he also killed stories on a deal he made to give the Republican nomination for the U.S. Senate seat from Indiana to Richard Roudebush. State treasurer John Snyder, Roudebush's competitor for the nomination, later got a job offer from the Nixon administration.

Gene Pulliam ordered his Indianapolis newspapers to cut down on news coverage of Senator Robert F. Kennedy's presidential campaign in the crucial Indiana primary in 1968 because he wanted to block Kennedy's bid for the presidency. Yet in 1964 he was one of the first publishers in the country to start full opposite editorial pages in his newspapers.

He would pick up the telephone, ignore any chain of command and threaten to fire someone if his orders were not followed, only to call the same employee the next day to play golf later in the week. When an employee had a real need—a daughter's foot caught in the lawn mower—Pulliam was always there to help. He would pay all the medical expenses, arrange first-class medical treatment, pick the doctors, the hospital, do everything but the operation itself.

He was the last of his kind—the self-made man, the Horatio Alger of newspaper publishing. Starting with no financial resources, he bought and sold newspapers, and played a powerful part in politics. He used the news coverage of his newspapers for his political efforts. He developed an independent, belligerent crusading attitude toward corruption in state and local government. By the 1960s he had become the major force in Indiana and Arizona politics and journalism.

His father was converted to the Christian faith and became a Methodist preacher. Because his parents moved from year to year, Pulliam's boyhood was itinerant, restless. He showed a flair for newspaper work at a young age. As a student at DePauw University, he helped start the nation's leading journalism fraternity, Sigma Delta Chi, as well as a daily newspaper. He spent a year as a reporter at the *Kansas City Star,* in 1910, after which Pulliam was usually his own boss, buying and selling newspapers over the next forty years until he had established a solid chain of eight papers in Indiana and Arizona in the late 1940s.

He developed a knack for reviving a small-town newspaper, giving it new life and vigor and financial success. His newspaper purchases took him all over the country, from Massachusetts to Florida, Arizona to Kansas, Oklahoma to Georgia and various states in between. With vast reservoirs of energy and ambition, he had a quick mind for business as well as unusual vision of how a newspaper could serve and mold a community. But he had to wait until after World War II to have his greatest impact on two communities, Indianapolis and Phoenix, having acquired the major morning and evening newspapers in both state capitals.

His hero, mentor, and model, his one-time boss, William Rockhill Nelson, publisher of the *Kansas City Star,* died in 1915. After World War I, William Randolph Hearst was dying and his vast publishing empire had shriveled. Joseph Pulitzer died before World War II. Nelson, Hearst, Pulitzer had been a new breed, part of what journalism historian Frank Luther Mott has called "The Rise of the Independent Press."

These men moved daily journalism away from the purely personal approach of the past, the party newspapers. They put a new emphasis on accurate news, independence of political party, and crusades for what they perceived to be the public interest. Yet they still had a powerful personal impact on their newspapers and their communities, and, in the case of Hearst and Pulitzer, on the entire nation. These new publishers, and the others who followed them, were usually not easily identified as political figures, in contrast to the previous generation of editors. Most of them, except for Hearst, moved behind the scenes. They used their news coverage to promote their goals but also established new standards of truthful and aggressive reporting.

Colonel Robert McCormick was president until 1955 of the *Chicago Tribune.* McCormick was the same kind of individualistic publisher, and, like Hearst, he inherited his journals from his family.

Gardner Cowles, Sr., who built up the *Des Moines Register* and *Tribune,* died in 1946. Like Pulliam, he had been a Methodist minister's son, moving from town to town every year or two in Iowa.

Roy Howard, who became the head of United Press in 1912 and entered a partnership with E.W. Scripps in 1922, survived with Pulliam after World War II, living until 1965.

Oscar Stauffer, Pulliam's fellow reporter at the *Kansas City Star* under Nelson, went on to build up a smaller media empire in Kansas and several other states. Stauffer's newspapers were never as large as Pulliam's, nor would he develop the two-state political clout that Pulliam had for more than twenty years.

William Mathews, a preacher's kid like Pulliam, was a copy of the old-fashioned editor and publisher, plunging into Arizona political battles with his *Tuscon Daily.* He was eventually eclipsed by Pulliam as the major publisher in the state. Mathews lived until 1969, occasionally engaging Pulliam in old-fashioned editors' duels, as they fired at each other in front-page editorials.

John Knight, who like Hearst and McCormick had been born into a newspaper family, outlived Pulliam after building the Knight newspapers into a major chain. He was blunt and forceful like Pulliam, and they enjoyed arguing with each other.

At an Associated Press meeting in Phoenix, January 1963, *Washington Post* publisher Philip Graham, who was then suffering through manic-depressive phases and committed suicide a few months later, let loose at other publishers in an embarrassing scene that included a compliment for Pulliam:

> Gene Pulliam's the only publisher here that has made it the hard way, the only one that really has blood on his hands.

Pulliam's feet were planted between two different eras of

journalism. He tried in the 1960s to use his newspapers decreasingly as his political instruments, to have the news coverage balanced and fair. But at heart he was still an old-fashioned editor who went into political battles with both fists swinging. He could remember the old days when competing editors had fist fights in the streets, as well as brawls on the editorial pages. He could never forget how hard he had sweat to build his own newspaper empire. His first flatbed press cost $3,700. By 1971 a new press for his Phoenix or Indianapolis plant cost $1.5 million and each plant had several presses.

He embodied some of the paradoxes of many strong, powerful men—tremendous bitterness, jealousy, and insecurity, brilliant insights in news judgment and politics, yet with odd lapses in his perspective.

He was somewhat similar to Henry Luce, another postwar Horatio Alger figure in journalism, also a missionary's son. The two became friends in Phoenix after Luce retired from the Time-Life empire he built. Pulliam never had the national impact of Luce, but both took the Christian zeal of their parents and applied it to journalism with substantial success. They never lost their rough social edges that could be embarrassing in polite company. Both used their media empires for their broader political and social goals. Both hated corruption with the zeal of Protestant reformers. Conservative, anticommunist, they ironically abandoned Republican Barry Goldwater in his 1964 presidential campaign. Both thought some critics of the Vietnam War effort in the 1960s, the Walter Lippmanns and William Fulbrights, were weakling sissies.

One difference was that Henry Luce would retire in 1964, three years before his death. Pulliam never retired.

2

Boyhood

IN 1880 WESTERN Kansas had barely been settled by the white man. The Indian wars were over. It was a barren territory, dry, dusty, the ground covered only with short buffalo grass. A few rolling hills broke up the flat landscape. The prairies were ruled by wild horses, antelope, coyotes, bobcats, rattlesnakes, and sand rats. Small ramshackle towns were developing along railroad lines. Farms could grow only wheat. There was no irrigation. Blizzards would wipe out entire cattle herds in the winter. Dreaded prairie fires endangered everyone in the summer. Progress was economic growth of any kind. Every town wanted to be the county seat, to bring more commerce and money. There were deadly gunfights during a county seat election, with lynchings and murders when one town won out over another in the competition. Six had been killed when Wichita County picked its seat. Killing was common anyway in the saloons where disputes over gambling and manhood broke out regularly.

Grant County, twenty-four square miles in the southwest corner of Kansas, had a population of nine in 1880. Five years later, the town of Ulysses was created with the help of Wyatt Earp's brother, George Washington Earp. The first white child born in the county arrived in December, just before Christmas 1885. Farming started the next year under homesteading laws. By 1888 Ulysses appeared to be booming. More than two thousand settlers had come by covered wagon, usually settling in dugouts or sod houses. In the county seat election Ulysses beat Appomatox, 578 to 268, after a few gunfights. Ulysses was on a stagecoach and mail route from Hartland in nearby Kearny County, which was located on the Santa Fe Railroad.

Ulysses was supposed to grow into the "Wichita of the West," and New York bankers sank $150,000 of their bonds into new town waterworks and a streetcar system. The boom didn't last. A recession hit in the 1890s, but bond payments were met. The crunch came in the recession of 1908, when the town could no longer scrape up the cash to make the payment. The bondholders could now seize much of the town—at least the land which had been put up as collateral for the bonds. But the country boys outwitted the city boys. The town, with only one hundred people left, literally moved three miles away across the prairie, leaving some useless land, the schoolhouse and courthouse, for the bondholders. It was that kind of territory.

Somehow it attracted Irvin B. Pulliam, Eugene's father. In 1888 he left a lucrative job and a nice home in Danville, Illinois. He brought his wife and two daughters, Zella, four, an invalid, and Corinne, two, to Ulysses. He had been called by God. The Hound of Heaven had tracked him down. He had run from God as best he could, but he couldn't escape him.

I. B. Pulliam had come from a line of Baptist preachers and he was expected to be one too. At LaGrange College, a Baptist school in Missouri, he lasted only one year. He didn't want anything to do with it. He went his own way. The family story was that he "went out and raised hell" before his conversion.

Then he met Martha Collins, a student at Asbury Academy, a Methodist school in Greencastle, Indiana. They met in Danville through some mutual friend. Martha's father wanted her to marry a preacher, not a businessman like I. B. Pulliam. But I. B. Pulliam and Martha were married anyway on March 30, 1881.

For seven years I.B. continued to work as a salesman for wholesale grocers in Danville. Somehow during that time he "got religion," as some say; he was saved, born again. Apparently he was influenced by a Methodist preacher named Banner Shawhan, who ran Operation Helping Hand for tramps in Kansas City. Shawhan held a series of revival meetings in Danville, preaching the gospel that I.B. Pulliam ultimately accepted. He saw his shortcomings before God's perfect standards, he saw he could never satisfy God's requirements by his own efforts, so he put his trust in the work of Jesus Christ on the cross at Calvary.

He had intended to live his life his own way. Now he had a new course to chart, seeking the will of God for himself and his family.

Perhaps through Shawhan's influence, I.B. joined the Methodist ranks, and he and his wife were given a trial run as missionaries in western Kansas in March 1888.

Life was not easy for anyone in western Kansas. Part of his job was to identify with his people and comfort them in the misery and sorrow that came with pioneering the West. In the midst of his ministry, he once reminisced about the life of a circuit rider:

> The Methodist Episcopal preacher has been an important factor in this state-building business. He has eaten from pine tables, slept on the homemade bedstands, kneeled on the bare floor of the sod house and dugout, and carried to the throne of grace the destiny of the struggling state. He has faced the blizzard to meet a few heroic souls in a sod school house. He has wept with mothers at the lonely graves of children, and with children over the graves of mothers whose form reposes in the virgin soil surrounded by the wide expanse and death-like silence of the plains. He knows what it is like to endure hardness like a soldier of Jesus Christ.

The move to faraway Kansas, apparently by stagecoach, must have shocked the rest of the family. Zella, born in 1883, had been crippled at the age of eighteen months by spinal meningitis and would never be able to walk without help. Corinne was not quite two when it was time to move. But there was a wanderlust tradition in I.B.'s family background. The Pulliams had followed Horace Greeley's advice to go West. They came to Virginia from Wales, in the British Isles, around 1700; some moved west to Tennessee and Missouri; others went south to North Carolina. A Tom Pulliam reputedly helped Andrew Jackson win the battle of New Orleans. Harry Pulliam became president of the National Baseball League.

I.B.'s parents had seven children. His older brother, Eugene, whose name would be passed on to I.B.'s only son, went to California in 1859, soon after I.B.'s birth, to work in the gold fields.

Family records reveal little about I.B.'s upbringing in Palmyra, Missouri. He recalled in later diaries that Abraham Lincoln's Emancipation Proclamation had some impact on his own racial prejudice. He saw a neighbor's slave go free and he noted, "Did not then realize I was also emancipated by the same proclamation—transformed from a prejudiced provincial to a citizen of the world." His father, the Reverend William H. Pulliam, was born March 1, 1827, in Virginia and his family moved to Palmyra seven years later.

Somewhere he met and married Maria Elizabeth Singleton. He died December 16, 1893, a few years after seeing his son go into the Methodist ministry.

In Ulysses, Kansas, I.B. and his family may have lived in one of the few houses, but more likely in a dugout. Ulysses history indicates some sort of Methodist parsonage built in 1887. But the ordinary home was a sod hut, which could withstand the weather, the cyclones and tornadoes, better than wood frame houses. His son, Eugene C. Pulliam, always claimed that he was born in a mud hut, May 3, 1889.

With or without the mud hut, the beginnings were humble. "Another day, another dollar" had a very literal meaning for I.B. Pulliam. His salary averaged about $1 a day those first few years as a missionary. The family also received an occasional "missionary barrel," a happy occasion for the children.

Often he didn't know where the next meal for the family would come from. Waiting for the missionary barrel to come back from Illinois increased their faith, as I.B. once wrote:

> Such a barrel came into our home one day. It was not expected, but had been longingly waited for until we had almost given up hope. "Hope deferred maketh the heart sick" and the missionary barrel delayed will sometimes seriously impair digestion for lack of something to digest, but—it came! It came on the afternoon train. It was hailed with great joy. It came at supper time. The coffee pot was on the stove, the baby boy on the floor, the girls on the lookout. The barrel was hustled into the house, the head hurriedly removed and then dive, dive, dive and the process of unpacking began. The coffee pot was dancing a Sioux war dance on the stove; the baby boy putting forth a succession of Sioux war whoops on the floor, but let it boil and let him yell, we are going to the bottom of this barrel. At last it was unpacked and there we stood waist deep in the grandest aggregation of creation comforts that ever came out of one barrel since the world began.

"Times when the pastor's pay consisted of eggs, butter, potatoes, possibly a ham or side of bacon or even a quarter of beef," was how the *Ulysses Republican* recalled I.B. Pulliam's days as the first Methodist missionary in Grant County.

Eugene C. Pulliam seemed alternately to resent and take pride in his childhood poverty. It drove him to seek wealth for himself and his family. But it also helped him to identify with others who had struggled to overcome the odds and to respond with personal compassion and charity when he saw someone in need. He had learned it at home. Tramps, always received at the Pulliam home, put a sign outside to let other tramps know there were welcome and food available.

It was an unsettling existence, in the tradition of Methodist pioneer John Wesley. Each year the assignment changed during Eugene's childhood. Ulysses, Leoti, Syracuse, Hutchinson, Nickerson—those were Eugene's home towns in the first three or four years of his life. In every place I.B. had several towns to minister to—he was what they called a "circuit rider," traveling from one town to the next. Eventually they would settle down a little and move only every three years.

It put a firm stamp on Eugene's later political and social views, as well as on his friendships. He was always attracted to poor boys who made their own way—in national politics, Herbert Hoover and Lyndon Johnson, in Indiana politics and civic work, Frank McKinney and Frank McHale, and in newspaper circles, Roy Howard and William Rockhill Nelson. He resented those who came from a wealthy background, the Franklin Roosevelts, the Kennedys, whose liberal politics and generosity with the money of others seemed to him to reflect their own lack of experience of making it in life the hard way.

His father, always a more reflective person than his son, reminisced after his retirement in 1920 about the homelessness he endured.

> Now I think next to a soldier overseas—the Methodist itinerant appreciates home—Homecoming has a pathetic note in it for him—He is merely a tenant in somebody's house—What a procession of huts and handsome residences he occupies in the course of thirty years! A Preacher's home is the heart of his people.

The wandering lifestyle had a permanent impact on Eugene Pulliam. He would always be a restless wanderer. His childhood friends changed from year to year, and in some ways it was that way for the rest of his life. He always had to prove himself in each new town—by the age of fifteen he had lived in at least ten towns. The new guy, a preacher's kid at that, didn't get a break in the schoolyard. He had to fight to prove himself, year after year after year. He never had an identity in a home, in a neighborhood. So he spent his life establishing himself in other ways, in his work, in his accomplishments. Like many preacher's kids, he seemed driven by the restlessness of his childhood wanderings. And when he came to town as a newspaperman, again the new guy, he often wound up in fights, one or two with his fists, the rest with his pen. "Preachers' kids were picked on often," he told me. "My first day, they told me the initiation was to eat Indian root. It burned your mouth. I ate some and during the afternoon recess they tried to make me eat some more and I got in a fight with the kid who tried to make me eat it again.... Being a preacher's kid was a hard row."

A psychiatrist might have a field day with all the problems that could have or should have developed from this sort of childhood. But Pulliam's mother was the balancing influence. She had the dominant impact on the family, as I.B. was riding the circuit so much of the time.

Raised on a farm, Martha Collins was the organizer in the I. B. Pulliam family. She was a doer, with a practical business mind, a gregarious personality, and a welcome for all strangers. She understood children, their need for encouragement, for someone who believed in them. She provided the security and warmth that her son was unlikely to find anywhere else in western Kansas.

Eugene's mother saved him from many of the tribulations of his childhood. And she saved him, to some extent, from himself. He was always hyperactive, suffering later in life from related stomach disorders. Along with energy to spare, he had a bad temper. A neighbor once called him a name after Eugene had chased a ball into the man's yard. Eugene retaliated, hit him with the bat. Though the injury was not bad, his mother extracted a promise from Eugene never to seek revenge again.

His fondness for his mother was expressed in his own editorial when she died in 1932. Part of it provides insight into the life of a preacher's wife in Kansas at the turn of the century.

> This semi-public range of mother's activities seemed only to make of her a more devoted mother. In fact she was mother to all the children who came into her life. Our house was always full up and running over with neighbor youngsters. She loved all of them, made all of them always at home. Ministers' salaries in those days were meager and usually in arrears. How father and mother managed to give their children a college

education and still continued among the ten top contributors to the local church budget was a miracle in home management. One summer while I was on vacation from prep school I had a job helping run a grocery store. The owner became ill and I was left in charge. I made enough of a success of it that the owner offered me a steady job as manager. I was immediately fired with business ambition and wanted to accept. However, mother set her foot down so firmly that the matter was discussed only once. She was determined that her children should have a college education and she won. We children always were well dressed. Mother was an expert designer with both dresses and hats. Dress materials were used and reused for years. Hats that had seen several seasons were made to look like the latest creation from a Kansas City hat shop. Most of the clothes I wore as a boy mother made. Even my first long pants were made over from a pair of my father's. They were so good looking I strutted with pride the first night I appeared at a party in them. And during all these years mother gave day-and-night attention with tenderest devotion to my invalid sister whose illness became progressively worse with the years. She was too busy ever to think of complaining. She was too sincerely imbued with the spirit of service ever to consider that her lot in life was hard. Her children frequently longed for the soft comfort which wealth afforded many of their friends, but mother apparently learned early in life that the way to happy living was along the road of useful work, kindly service, sympathetic understanding and devotion to those ideals which gave a spiritual rather than a materialistic aspect to the atmosphere of her home.

There were other stories he told about his childhood, perhaps embellished as the years went by, but nevertheless giving some sense of life on the prairie. One of his favorites was about the pet coyote he kept tied by a rope. He would tease it, run with it. Then one day the coyote broke loose and went after him. He had a scar on his leg to show his grandchildren when he told the story of how he was "bit by a coyote." Another adventure he recalled:

When we lived in Humboldt, Kansas, and I was not quite eight years old, I was playing with some friends in a wheat bin—not a hay silo—owned by the father of one of the boys. All at once workers, not knowing we were in the bin, began dumping in a load of wheat. We could easily have been suffocated, had we not been able to attract their attention and get out.

His mother helped rescue him from the materialism of his time. He always wanted to make up for the poverty of his childhood, but he never joined the ranks of the robber barons, the men who sought wealth and power and the lavish trappings that come with it, the Jim Fisks, the J.P. Morgans, the Cornelius Vanderbilts. He was tempted to join their ranks, but a formal Methodist education gave him the intellectual and philosophical framework to stand against the cold commercial way of life. His mother was also there at crucial points to encourage him away from devotion to mammon. He remembered his infatuation with a cowboy's daughter when he was about eleven years old. He decided he wanted to be a cowboy too, until his mother suggested the possibility of a college education. Martha Pulliam was a rare breed on the Kansas prairie at the turn of the century, a woman with a college education.

She never sheltered him. With his father away so much of the time, he had to be the man of the house. He could never understand why other mothers sheltered and pampered their boys. His own rough-and-tumble boyhood seemed good enough to him.

She encouraged him to work. He always had a job—the family could use the spare change. He sold hot tamales at a train station, popcorn at county fairs, the *Saturday Evening Post* and the *Rams Horn*. He organized a cow route with the help of a black friend. He was already applying the drive and organizational ability that would later be used for buying and selling newspapers.

3

DePauw

METHODISM WAS NOT just another church denomination when Gene Pulliam was growing up. It was a worldview, a philosophy, an ideology, that had implications for every area of life. With its roots in the Bible and the writings of John Wesley, Methodism stood in firm opposition to another dominant philosophy of the nineteenth century, the crass materialism and commercialism of powerful businessmen like John D. Rockefeller.

Pulliam would be pulled back and forth between these competing values throughout his life. The influence of his mother combined with a Methodist education kept him from sliding into a totally materialistic way of life. When he stood up for the public good ahead of newspaper profits, when he developed his sense of public servanthood and boldness as an editor—these characteristics could be traced to old-fashioned Wesleyan Methodism.

In 1904 Pulliam's father had risen in the ranks of the Methodist Church in Kansas. No longer was he a circuit rider with seven churches in seven towns to look after. He had been assigned to a larger church associated with a major Methodist school, Baker Academy and University in Baldwin.

Methodists had traditionally scorned formal education and academics. As the old joke ran, ask a Methodist why his church had no doctor of divinity and the Methodist would explain that the divinity of the church was not sick. But in the nineteenth century the Methodists began to see the need for academic training and established schools like DePauw University in Indiana and Baker University in Kansas.

Preachers' kids were supposed to be models of good behavior, but Pulliam never followed the model. He like to tell a story of how he wound up in Baker Academy, a refugee from the public schools.

I started in a public high school in Baldwin and this professor had it in for me. I liked being the eraser boy because it gave me the freedom to move around, but I got demoted. Then a little, mischievous, blackhaired girl got her hair pulled by a boy behind her, and she yelled, "You stop that, Gene Pulliam." The professor, his eyes blazing, told me to leave and he got to the door before I did. I ran to the corner and the professor started yelling, "Take your seats." I got to the pile of erasers and started throwing them at him, and he turned down an aisle, giving me a chance to escape. I ran out and never returned.

He felt wronged by the teacher, and his father took his side, arranging for him to enter Baker Academy. His behavior did not improve much. He was always restless, quick to join in a prank.

I never was expelled from school, the academy, or college, but I had a very close call when I was in the academy. A very dry-as-dust professor came out from Drew Theological Seminary for a scheduled series of five lectures.

We listened to the first lecture on a Tuesday morning and the student body was very courteous and very attentive, but it was the driest, dullest talk I have ever heard in my life. That afternoon after basketball practice, three of us decided that we should really do something about relieving chapel service of such monotonous routine.

That night we took a Big Ben alarm clock—one of those intermittent clocks which rings for half a minute, is silent half a minute and rings again, and keeps that up for about fifteen or twenty minutes—and put it down in the very lower inside of the piano where we didn't think anybody could get at it quickly, and set it for five minutes after this speaker was supposed to speak. We timed it perfectly. He had just begun his talk when Big Ben went off. He smiled a big grin, turned around and looked at the piano and smiled, and just then, of course, the alarm stopped. He smiled and started on with his talk. He talked for half a minute and Big Ben went off again. The same thing happened again. Each time he would try to maintain his poise but he was becoming rather annoyed, so the president of this college got up to go over to the piano to see what he could do about the nuisance. Just as he put his hand inside the piano Big Ben went off again and the president jumped clear back and almost fell off the platform. Well, of course, the student body was in an uproar. Everybody was howling and laughing and even the faculty couldn't restrain themselves. The president showed excellent judgment and good common sense when he went to the platform and announced, "This chapel service is recessed until tomorrow morning at 8:30. You are dismissed."

The president and other college officials made every possible effort to find out who was responsible for the prank. We three boys had pledged solemn secrecy to each other that we wouldn't tell anybody, under any circumstances, no matter what happened. Well, we never did and nobody found out. However, I have often wondered how it happened that my father and mother—neither one of them—never asked me if I was mixed up in the alarm clock prank. I just wonder what I would have told them. That was the nearest I ever got to being expelled from school.

When he was not pulling pranks, he began to get the academic side of the education he had received informally at home from his mother and father.

As a freshman at Baker Academy, I soon realized that I was in a different world where money and personal possessions were not the important yardsticks of life. There was an enthusiasm and genuine eagerness for education. Teachers, students, and townspeople unconsciously creating an atmosphere of near reverence for learning. They were not trying to learn how to make money but how to live useful lives.

Pulliam did well in most of his subjects, making the equivalent of As and Bs, in subjects like history, rhetoric, Latin, geometry, and American literature, but he ran into difficulty with German, physics, and astronomy. In chapel he learned about the Methodist sins of the modern world, which included some he would preach against in later editorials: dishonesty, graft, racketeering; ignorance, prejudice, bigotry; cowardice, fear, preaching to please the powerful; intemperance and drunkenness. Life after school included a range of normal activities, corn cob fights, skating, pony rides. "He came to our farm a lot," recalled a boyhood friend, Wilbur Counts. "They'd fight with corn cobs, soaked in water, and when it hit you, you felt it."

He finished prep school at Baker in the spring of 1906 and started Baker University in the fall. But his mother had attended DePauw University in Greencastle, Indiana, when it was Asbury College, and he followed in her footsteps the following January along with his sister, Corinne.

He joined the Deke (Delta Kappa Epsilon) fraternity. "They

were the outstanding men on the campus," recalled Mrs. Susan Ostrom, a DePauw student who knew Pulliam at the time. "They were the high-powered prima donnas."

Soon after he had come to Greencastle, he met Myrta Smith and before long they were a twosome. "It was what he called a college case, a college love affair," Mrs Ostrom said. "She wasn't like him, not so rambunctious. She was refined, very much a lady, not a gladhander, not an extrovert. He was all extrovert. She was a stabilizing influence on him. His life would have been different if she'd lived."

Myrta's social background was a contrast to his. She had been born in McCordsville, Indiana, in 1887. Her father, J.W. Smith, managed real estate. Her half-brother, Frank Littleton, was an attorney and former Republican speaker of the state House of Representatives in 1899. She had literary talent, later writing for the *Sunday Indianapolis Star,* which her husband would buy thirty years later.

They were not to marry for five years, after he had worked for the *Kansas City Star* for a year and then bought his own newspaper. He was never a good student at DePauw. He did well in English and history, but he failed some other courses and never graduated, leaving school after his junior year in 1909, the year Myrta graduated. He turned most of his attention to other activities on campus. "He went to get something," recalled a fraternity brother, Felix McWhirter. "He wasn't just marking time." Some of his activities helped him make money, a pants pressing club he started, a supper club. He was already an entrepreneur. But most of the activities involved journalism of some kind and DePauw, at the time, was an excellent place to learn journalism, not from the faculty but from fellow students. He was part of a remarkable group of young journalists, including Leroy Milliken, Foster and Gilbert Clippinger, L. Aldis Hutchens, Marion Hedges and Paul Foster Riddick. Most of them were preachers' sons, like Pulliam, taking their parents' driving missionary zeal and applying it to other areas of life like newspapers and business.

At DePauw this group started a daily college newspaper, a remarkable task in those times, and started the oldest journalism fraternity in the United States, Sigma Delta Chi. One of their goals was to make journalism respectable on campus, especially among the faculty. The University of Missouri had only recently started the first journalism school in America when Pulliam entered DePauw. Columbia Journalism School would be established a few years later. No editorial organization had been started to set standards for the profession, except for local press clubs. Most newspapers were merely political propaganda sheets, and few well-educated people gave much serious thought to a career in newspapers.

Another journalistic tradition was emerging—at William Rockhill Nelson's *Kansas City Star* and Joseph Pulitzer's *New York World*—the idea that a newspaper should be an independent force in politics, not bound to any political party, with a quantity of news and information about the local community. Pulliam and his group were trying to work out this new idea at DePauw. They took the college newspaper out of school politics—it had been controlled by the reigning political party—and transformed it into a daily. Pulliam was the assistant business manager, later business manager. But in actual practice, he was remembered by others as the key figure in the enterprise. "As I remember, he was the driving force and I looked up to him. He was it," said Henry Ostrom, also a business manager. "He was the one who guided. I didn't know anything about it."

From Foster Clippinger, Pulliam inherited a "stringer" or correspondent's job with the *Indianapolis Star*, sending in stories about DePauw to the newspaper he would buy thirty-five years later. Before starting Sigma Delta Chi, the group had a Press Club, with Pulliam as vice president, and organized the Indiana Collegiate Press Club to hold dinners with speakers, charging admission and making a profit.

The stories differ on who first had the idea for the journalism fraternity, but the ten founders included Pulliam, who proposed the name. The fraternity was a logical outgrowth of their discussions about journalism. "They longed for a 'better journalism,' both amateur and professional. They talked of a truthful honorable press, one not dominated by commercialism," Charles Clayton wrote in a history of the fraternity, *Fifty Years for Freedom.*

The founders may not have realized they were starting what would develop into one of the nation's leading journalism societies, as well as one of the first national organized efforts to raise the standards of the profession. But they were idealists and were aiming for the stars. Their story in the *DePauw Daily* noted that:

In the course of years, it is hoped that the role of alumni will contain the names of many prominent journalists and authors. By binding such men together in the true fraternity spirit and inspiring them with common ideals, a larger spirit of idealism will be injected into the press of our country.

The preamble to the first ritual sounded like a combination of the fraternity spirit, a Methodist sermon, pre-World War I optimism, and Bull Moose progressive politics.

Stranger, you are on the threshold of a great and mystic Brotherhood; a Brotherhood grown out of world movements; the result of our highly complex civilization, built upon the lofty principles of light. Today, the race has reached its greatest achievement. This is the golden age of which Plato and John More dreamed. This is Utopia realized, and yet men revel in their wantonness. There are world evils to be corrected, there are moral faults to be mended, there are local cesspools to be cleaned. The nation is steeped in men whose souls are dead to patriotic feeling, who prostitute their sacred offices to selfish ends; false counsels are heard in the courts and in the senate halls. Therefore, the national pulse must be quickened, blow must be met with blow; thieves must be scourged from the temples; our ears must not be given up to false witnesses. But where is the Titanic force which can accomplish these reforms? It is at hand! It is that servant of national opinion, the public press. The hope of our nation is in the education of its citizens. The institution to which all citizens are put to school is the public press. How boundless, then, is the influence of this institution; it becomes the educator, the protector, the disseminator, the evangel of our nation. How necessary the press, that this institution be controlled by men of acumen, of patriotism, of vision. To this high purpose, the control of the national press by practical idealists, Sigma Delta Chi looks. To inject idealism into the commercialized institution, and to make it awaken to its opportunities to shape this nation after the plans and purposes of the righteous God, the Brotherhood of Sigma Delta Chi was established.

Stranger, in you we see the blended elements which will make you a leader among men. We would secure you to the profession of educators and evangels, JOURNALISM! Let us, bound together in this higher circle, strive for this dim goal. So that, when the flood of years has carried us afar from these college halls, you will not be forgetful of the precepts you have learned this night. Remember these your brothers in Sigma Delta Chi, who have likewise vowed her vows, and her lessons.

Some of the founders went on to journalism careers. Marion Hedges became the editor of the *Electrical World,* and a leading labor editor; William Glenn held various editorial positions in Florida newspapers; Laurence Sloane worked for several New York City newspapers before he became head of Standard Statistics Company; Paul Riddick ran two weekly newspapers in northern Indiana; Charles Fisher worked at the *Kansas City Star* with Pulliam after his graduation in 1910 and later went into teaching. Pulliam would go on to eclipse them all in the field of journalism.

4

Kansas City Star

W ITH THE FRONTIER closed and a business career ruled out either by distaste for commercial routine or by the feeling that the adventures there were all over, journalism offered one of the last vocations for the young man who loved to travel, to be independent, to make a quick reputation, to move mountains. Around the turn of the century journalism recruited a new college-bred generation of men spoiling for exertion against the odds.

As author Otis Graham had noted in *An Encore for Reform,* newspaper reporting was one of the few fields left for adventure when Eugene C. Pulliam was growing up in Kansas and thinking about a career. The West had been pioneered and settled. The Indian wars were over. His father and other missionaries had brought the gospel to the West. If you wanted to be at the top of the journalism profession in the Middle West around 1900, you chose William Rockhill Nelson's *Kansas City Star.* Pulliam had his sights on the *Star,* but he had to prove himself elsewhere first. He found a reporting job at the *Atchison Champion* in the summer of 1909, having worked at the *Chanute Sun* in previous summers.

At the *Champion,* Pulliam worked under Sheffield Ingalls, whose father, John, had been a U.S. senator from Kansas. Sheffield Ingalls had been a Progressive Republican in the state legislature and, like many editor-politicians of his time, enjoyed attacking other politicians in print. Ingalls wrote that the Republican boss of Atchison was robbing the county blind, according to Pulliam's story. So the boss came in drunk the next day and demanded to see Ingalls, threatening to kill him. Pulliam led him around town, making sure they didn't find the editor, and eventually sent him home. Sobered up later, the boss thanked Pulliam for preventing a homicide and in gratitude gave him tips, including one that led to some news stories on lost towns on the Missouri River.

Pulliam stayed at the *Champion* only a few months, long enough to impress a *Kansas City Star* editor who decided to hire him after he wrote a colorful story about some women who got in a fight during a dishpan sale at a local store.

By 1910 Kansas City was no longer just an "overgrown country town," as William Allen White had described it in 1891 in his autobiography. Kansas City had been modernized after William Rockhill Nelson came in 1880 and established the *Star*. Blessed with an unusual vision for city planning, Nelson had led successful campaigns for boulevards, paved streets, parks. But Nelson had never been able to clean up Kansas City politics to his satisfaction. He had driven out saloons, sometimes buying up their property, and refused to advertise whiskey. Yet the political machine run by the Pendergast brothers, Tom and Jim, still dominated Kansas City, despite the *Star's* efforts.

Nelson was a firm individualist, independent in politics, not owing loyalty to any political or financial backers, unlike most of his contemporaries in the newspaper world who were just as loyal to a political party as any Democrat or Republican. Many papers were owned or controlled by a utility, bank, or other financial interest.

But Nelson and others, Joseph Pulitzer and William Randolph Hearst in New York, and William Allen White in Emporia, Kansas, were developing a new style. They promoted whatever they considered the public good without regard to party politics, but still used their news columns to promote their personal political and community goals. Nelson backed Grover Cleveland, a Democrat, while still attacking the Democratic machine in Kansas City. He promoted Progressive Republican Theodore Roosevelt for president in 1912. He was a national committeeman for TR's short-lived Bull Moose Progressive party, but otherwise he refused to hold public office. "He belonged to the age of individualists—the fire-eating, hell-bent-for-wealth group," *Star* reporter Icie Johnson wrote. He had tried to run an independent newspaper in Fort Wayne, Indiana, but encouraged so much opposition and controversy that he left for Kansas City where he started the *Star* in 1880. "Nobody ever accomplished anything in this world without arousing somebody's anger," Nelson liked to say.

Nelson's personality permeated the *Star* and its staff. He was called Colonel Nelson "just because he looked coloneliferous, without any reference to a war record," William Allen White observed. Pulliam didn't meet Nelson when he first joined the *Star,* but before long he was called into the editor's office after writing a story about a family fight. The family was sitting in Nelson's office, complaining about the story. White had described Nelson as "a great hulking 260-pounder, six feet tall, smooth-shaven, with a hard, dominating mouth and a mean jaw, high brow, and wonderful eyes, jade in color, which opened with wide frank cordiality or squinted like the lightning of Job."

"I was scared stiff, wondering what I'd done wrong," Pulliam wrote years later. Nelson asked the nervous young reporter if the story was true. Pulliam replied, "Yes." Nelson said, "Bully for you!" and ordered the family out. "I left thinking you would die for a man like that," Pulliam said. At the *Star* Pulliam picked up the same Progressive, Bull Moose principles he would later advance in his own newspapers. Nelson was always campaigning for paved streets, parks and boulevards, lower utility rates, using his newspaper to promote the Bull Moose program that was reaching the peak of its popularity.

Nelson attracted a large number of talented young journalists to the *Star,* despite low salaries. Pulliam started at $15 a week. The *Star* became a training ground for writers like Ernest Hemingway and Edgar Snow, the first Westerner to meet Mao Tse-tung, for playwright and producer Russel Crouse, for Roy Roberts, Oscar Stauffer and Walt Disney. Roberts, who roomed with Stauffer, later became editor of the *Star* and joined with Pulliam and others to promote Kansan Dwight D. Eisenhower for president in 1952. Stauffer, like Pulliam, left the *Star* and went on to build up his own chain of newspapers, including the *Topeka Capital-Journal* and several others in Kansas.

Pulliam's year of reporting at the *Star* was the kind that reporters remember with nostalgia, forgetting the hours of fear, boredom, and loneliness. Kansas City was a big place for him. He had grown up in smaller Kansas towns such as Ulysses, Nickerson, Chanute, Garden Plain, Baldwin, Hutchinson, Garnett, Iola, and Pleasanton.

At first he was a police reporter at night for the morning edition of the *Star*, the *Kansas City Times*. He worked under Marvin Creager, then the night city editor who later became editor of the *Milwaukee Journal*, "the best all-around newspaperman I ever had contact with," Pulliam commented years later. He always recalled a lesson he learned from Creager after writing a story about an auto accident. "The *Star* newsroom was a great big open room with no partitions of any kind and everybody from managing editor down worked in that room." Across this room, Creager's Kansas nasal twang called out, "Pulliam, you say this woman's eyesight is impaired. Did you inquire about her ear hearing?"

The police beat exposed Pulliam to the parts of Kansas City that the moralistic crusades of the *Star* had not reformed. The district around the police station was called Hell's Half Acre. Houses of prostitution flourished, many of them owned by Annie Chambers. "I was a preacher's kid and of course I was prejudiced against prostitutes," Pulliam once wrote, reminiscing about his encounter with Annie Chambers. She had sent champagne over to the reporters' room at the police station, and Pulliam had refused to drink it. She came into the pressroom the following night, demanding to meet the upstart young reporter who wouldn't touch her gift. Pulliam, who was in charge of the pressroom, ordered her to leave. Charging down to see a police captain, she threatened to have him thrown out of the newsroom.

The captain faced a dilemma. Annie had some good connections in the police department and the Pendergast political machine. But here was this young, rather harmless-looking reporter telling him he would write an embarrassing front-page story in the *Star* about how he had been thrown out of the pressroom for not drinking a prostitute's champagne. That wouldn't look too good. Annie raised the stakes. She threatened to have the captain fired if he wouldn't follow her orders. Pulliam went one up on her, saying he'd have her house shut down if she carried out her threat. The captain decided in Pulliam's favor, realizing it was wiser not to risk the wrath of the *Kansas City Star*.

Reporting for the *Star* was sometimes dangerous. Courtney Riley Cooper, who covered the political beat with Pulliam, was stabbed and wounded one night in apparent revenge for a *Star* series on the municipal courts. On the police beat, Pulliam joined a raid on an opium center that turned out to be the distribution headquarters for the Southwest as well as a gambling place. Awed by it all, he wrote, "It's a dark hole, that place on West Sixth Street, and a dirty one, too." Pulliam's story read more like a novel than a newspaper story as he described each step of the raid in meticulous detail.

> The air was heavy with the pungent stifling odor of opium. The contents of those buckets on the stove were bubbling hard with the concoction which the detectives were seeking.
> Anderson and Love whistled their amazement as they looked around the room. As revenue officers, they had raided many places where opium was kept or where opium was made on a small scale. But this was a well-equipped factory for the making of the drug that makes beasts of men and women.

On one assignment, he met John L. Lewis, who was just starting to organize coal miners in Illinois. "I met him once when I was a reporter for the *Kansas City Star* and went down to Centralia, Illinois, where he was doing a helluva strike job. He was very personable and very smart and later became head of the union."

After several months on the police beat, Pulliam was assigned to write feature stories about his father's missionary territory, the sprawling plains of Kansas, as well as Nebraska and Oklahoma. It was an assignment about as romantic as the slums of Kansas City. The Republican boss of Atchison, grateful to Pulliam for calming him down when he was threatening to kill Sheffield Ingalls, gave the young *Star* reporter a tip about one of the old towns on the Missouri River that had dissappeared, apparently during a flooding. Doniphan, in the 1870s, had supported seven newspapers. "Doniphan was wiped off the river map and erased from the river log," Pulliam wrote in one of his Sunday *Star* feature stories. Another town, Sumner, was an antislavery community started in opposition to the proslavery sentiments of Atchison in the 1850s. Pulliam found the old town only after a difficult hike through the underbrush.

> So completely had nature healed over the wounds made by the inroads of
> a few years of civilization that the townsite proper is now accessible only
> by a most difficult tramp through underbrush and thick chaparral.

Sumner's decline began after it lost the county seat contest to
Atchison. And the Missouri River helped wipe out that the town,
too.

> The Missouri River with its bends and curves entered that struggle for
> municipal existence in the role of Dame Fortune and lavished its smiles
> upon Atchison and Leavenworth. The reflex action of those smiles
> resulted in Sumner's natural but romantic death.

As a roving correspondent, Pulliam met his first three
presidents. President William Howard Taft, Woodrow Wilson, and
Theodore Roosevelt were all gearing up for the 1912 campaign.
Three-time loser William Jennings Bryan also was in the race, and
Pulliam interviewed him on a train, writing the story across Bryan's
back. "He insisted that since he had been misquoted so often by so
many reporters, I should write out my story right there," Pulliam
said. "And so I sat scribbling it out in longhand with my copy paper
balanced on his broad back. Then I read it back to him and got his
okay."

He remembered President Taft as the candidate who couldn't fit
through the bathroom door of a train, and the reporters couldn't
figure out a way to write the story. "We tried to think of some way we
could tell this story so it would get into print, but none of us could.
Newspapers were pretty conservative in those days. Why, women
never had 'legs'—they walked on 'limbs'."

In central Kansas, he was awed and thrilled by the emergence of
a motorcar capital in Hutchinson, where he had lived as a boy. Born
and raised in the horse-and-buggy age, Pulliam discovered that
"Hutchinson, though the 1910 census gives it only 16,364, has more
motorcars than most towns of double that size, and is in a very real
sense a 'motorcar capital.' It puts gasoline and electric vehicles to
more uses than the average first-class city, owns something over four
hundred of them, and now has even a motor factory of its own."
Hutchinson had changed drastically.

"To walk down Hutchinson's main business street is to see dozens of instances of the commercial uses of the motorcar. Here is one being loaded with sacks of flower. Here is another whizzing by loaded high with bottles."

He also visited the ranch of Frank Rockefeller, the brother of John D. Rockefeller, who had the reputation of being the richest man in the world. Rockefeller would not allow motorcars on his ranch. "Motorcars are to Rockefeller as the liquor traffic is to the WCTU (Women's Christian Temperance Union). Even in Cleveland, Ohio, the millionaire ranchman rides in a carriage drawn by a handsome team of blooded horses in preference to the modern motorcars," Pulliam wrote. But he found plenty of cattle there, including prize bulls imported from England.

The *Star* provided other romantic opportunities also. Roaming the West looking for stories, Pulliam claimed he received a marriage proposal from an eager young lady, who eloped with another reporter a few days later. Pulliam turned her down because he wanted to marry the Indiana girl he had fallen in love with at DePauw.

5

Atchison

T HE *KANSAS CITY Star* was a great place to learn journalism. But it wasn't a very good place to earn a living. To get married, Pulliam figured he would have to earn more than the $20 a week he was getting at the *Star*. "There wasn't anything as important as getting married then," he reminisced later. He also wanted to be his own boss, and he was impatient at the *Star*. "He wasn't satisfied to be a reporter," recalled fellow *Star* reporter Oscar Stauffer. Pulliam, looking for a chance to buy his own newspaper, kept in touch with his former boss, Sheffield Ingalls, in Atchison.

His father was assigned to the Atchison church in 1910, and then became the conference evangelist for the area in 1911. Pulliam left the *Star* to have an appendicitis operation, and then, for a time, he joined his father's evangelistic ministry as his secretary. His father was a fundamentalist in the original sense. He believed in the fundamentals of the Christian conversion and commitment to Jesus Christ. But he never accumulated the excess baggage that fundamentalism picked up in the twentieth century in America, the legalism, the rules about smoking, drinking, card-playing, and dancing.

He had a blunt and outspoken manner that his son would pick up, a manner that carried him, and later his son, into public controversy time after time. In Boulder, Colorado, he refused to go along with the Ministers' Union and Women's Christian Temperance Union in their call for prohibition for the lower class only. He denounced them in a sermon as the controversy heated up.

Why let the white-collar, cut-away, patent-leather-pump, automobile crowd have beer by the case, and deny it to the crowd by the schooner? Class legislation is reprehensible in a free country, whether enacted and administered by a prohibition party or by a party of booze-boosters.

The preaching style, the exhortation, the emphasis on right and wrong and eternal values, his son Eugene would incorporate into his own editorials and speeches, preaching from a different pulpit, and, eventually, a different message. But for a few months in 1911, he joined his father's cause. Then he had an opportunity to become editor of the *Atchison Champion.*

The *Champion* had been started as the *Squatter Sovereign*, a proslavery paper before the Civil War. Later it switched to a free-state Republican paper under John A. Martin, a Civil War hero who became governor. The *Champion* faltered after Martin died toward the end of the nineteenth century. In the meantime, Ed Howe had come to Atchison and started the *Atchison Globe*, which became the top paper in town by printing gossipy local news items. Like William Allen White in Emporia, Howe had a national reputation, and his articles were widely reprinted in other newspapers. The various owners of the *Champion* had never been able to compete with the *Globe*.

Pulliam was named editor in May 1911, one of the youngest in the country, with a $140-a-month salary. He and Myrta were married in February 1912. In May, her father, J. W. Smith, and half-brother, Frank Littleton, bought the *Champion* stock that Pulliam did not already have, providing money for new equipment. It was the one exception to his later claims that he had made his own way in life without any help from his family.

Pulliam took on big odds when be became editor of the *Champion*. Henry Allen, then editor of the *Wichita Beacon* and later governor, predicted that the *Champion* would return to its glory days of Martin under Pulliam's leadership. But Allen, a Bull Moose Progressive like Pulliam, apparently wasn't reckoning with the Howes and the resistance of the Atchison establishment to an outsider like Pulliam.

Most of Kansas was Progressive, following the Bull Moose programs and opposing the Stand Pat position of the regular William Howard Taft Republicans. *Atchison Globe* editor Ed

Howe and his son, Gene, stoutly resisted reform and new ideas. To Pulliam, the town seemed aristocratic. For their part, many Atchison natives regarded Pulliam as a young whippersnapper with a college education who thought he was anointed to reform the town.

The Howes were tough competitors. Gene Howe, angry about a *Champion* story that hinted that Howe's wife was living it up at a party, assaulted Pulliam on a street in Atchison. "He hit me in the nose before I could tell him I didn't write it," Pulliam recalled sixty years later. "I hit him back and then the two [men with Howe] stepped in." Pulliam came back with a table-thumping front-page editorial the next day, accusing the Howes of running dozens of similar articles.

> Everybody knows that for the last thirty years the *Globe* has been publishing "hint items" about anybody and everybody who "wouldn't come through." It has slandered and abused almost every family in town. You know how it persecuted old Captain John Seaton; and how it blackmailed the Fowler Packing House out of Atchison, how it hurled vile article after vile article at Charley Brown's father, how it has insinuated that some of the cleanest and purest women in Atchison have been guilty of immoral conduct.

The battle was on. It was a marvelous spectacle for the fight fans in Atchison and editors in Kansas who followed it. Pulliam, a Bull Moose Progressive, was warming up for the 1912 battle with the stand-patters in the Republican party. Ed Howe and the *Globe* were practically apolitical compared to Pulliam, and Howe was cynical about progress, making fun of all reform and opposing the women's movement. Although he claimed he was above the partisan politics of his day, Pulliam openly promoted Roosevelt's Square Deal in the *Champion.* The *Globe,* Pulliam charged in his editorials, had "a dilly-dally, do-nothing policy," whereas "the *Champion* has but one political policy and that is to advance the Square Deal in every phase of municipal and national life."

Pulliam said he strived for "more than just news and gossip" that dominated the *Globe:*

> The policy of the *Champion* long has been in accord with enlightened journalism, which considers it to be within the province of a newspaper

to expose corruption to public view and strike at evils, which threaten the healthy growth and progress of a community.

A newspaper should be something more than the mere purveyor of news and social gossip and a reflector of the everyday habits and customs of the people among whom it circulates. We believe that a newspaper should constantly address itself to social, economic and political problems, and in a determined fearless and unprejudiced way endeavor to awaken among its readers a conscientious desire to lend their thought and effort to the upbuilding and strengthening of a healthy, wholesome public sentiment in the community in which they live.

The competition was especially intense for city or county printing contracts, which the *Globe* had monopolized for several years.

Then Pulliam won the county printing contract with a lower bid in 1912. The flavor of the battle could be tasted in his front-page editorial the next day.

In last night's *Globe* there appeared one of those mean little articles— which only the *Globe* knows how to write—bemoaning the fact that Atchison newspapers are paid starvation rates for legal printing. The *Globe* knocked the *Champion* for taking the county printing at the present rates. The *Globe* lost the county printing contract yesterday, and that is the reason they were so peevish last night....

Finally the *Globe* has discovered that the *Champion* is not "going to the wall," and that the *Champion* is just as firmly established and just as solidly financed as the *Globe*.

There is no one but the *Globe* to blame for these low rates. It was their own selfishness and folly and poor business judgment which brought about the present condition. The *Champion* had no other course to pursue but to meet the competition it encountered.

The *Champion* made no complaint when the *Globe* landed the county printing last year but now that the *Champion* has been made the official paper the *Globe* bawls like a spoiled baby. Let them bawl! They threw the sand in their own eyes.

At the height of the Bull Moose movement, Pulliam was an ardent supporter of judicial recall, a method of removing judges who stood against Bull Moose principles. Judges were out of touch with reality, Pulliam complained. They should be made to visit jails and factories and see for themselves the other half of life so they would not always favor the wealthy in their decisions. He wanted "old-fogy judges" removed from office, to "restore to the people the inherent right to run the courts." He opposed former President William Howard Taft's nomination to the Supreme Court because Taft distrusted democracy and "would only add to the toryism that already makes the Supreme Court a menace to human freedom hardly less than in Dred Scott's day."

The Bull Moose movement was a reaction against the crass materialism of the post-Civil War era, which saw the growth of a kind of big-business aristocracy. Pulliam was a typical Square Dealer, a small businessman, the common man who resented the advantages big business received from legislatures and Congress. Favorite targets were John D. Rockefeller, senior and junior, and their Standard Oil Company, symbols of wealth and favoritism. John, Sr.'s $10 million gift for a study of white slave trade, Pulliam argued, was unnecessary, since everyone knew the trade was caused by low wages. And Rockefeller, "the Pharisee," came under the gun after John, Jr. ordered the infamous massacre of strikers in Colorado in 1911.

> The irony of it all is that these wretched men are fighting for a chance to earn bread and butter. They demand an opportunity to engage in the very hardest kind of manual labor. But Rockefeller sitting in his mahogany furnished office in New York handing out platitudes about the evils of White Slavery says "No."
>
> Of course Rockefeller's monumental inconsideration for his fellow-man does not justify the drastic measures which have been taken by the Colorado strikers. But when poverty and starvation begin to stare men in the face and they see their families in want and distress Reason no longer sits on her throne....
>
> Can anyone wonder that there is an alarming increase in the number of socialists in this country?

The Square Dealers were the reformers of their time—"the history of progress is the history of protests," Pulliam wrote. Their protest was aimed at special interests and privilege, at judges who let the rich criminals off with light sentences but were hard on the poor, and at bossism and political spoils that gave special favors to party workers. Big business and utilities came under attack. "It has long been known to the American people that their public utility corporations get into politics so they can control cities and legislatures in order that they may continue to milk the public." But the major thrust of the Bull Moose movement in national politics

came in 1912 as Robert LaFollette and then Theodore Roosevelt
tried to impose the Bull Moose stamp on the Republican party
controlled by President William Howard Taft. Laying out the
themes of the Bull Moose campaign, Pulliam wrote:

> Day is just dawning upon a momentous struggle of great import in this
> country. On one side are arrayed the brains, the money, the power and
> the prestige of men who believe—or claim to believe—that property
> interests have supreme priority over all other rights. On the other hand
> are allied the will, power, persistency and fierce determination of a
> unique group of industrial and political leaders, representing millions
> of Americans who believe that the people's rights have been woefully
> and wrongfully neglected in the development of our national life.

As the Progressive campaign got under way against Taft and
his allies, who dominated Atchison politics, Wisconsin Senator
Robert LaFollette carried the banner. Pulliam defended LaFollette,
who, he said, was not a "radical, wide-eyed reformer," claiming that
his "worst enemies are the paid and kept newspapers of the East."
    LaFollette had a breakdown in the early months of 1912, and
Roosevelt jumped into the race against Taft, drawing the backing of
LaFollette's Progressive supporters. He dramatized the Bull Moose
issues and made himself the charismatic leader of the movement.
Roosevelt won the party primaries, but Taft controlled the
convention and won the nomination in Chicago. Pulliam forecast
the death of the GOP and the rise of the Progressive party unless
Roosevelt received the nomination.

> The rank-and-file of the Republican party has asked for Colonel
> Roosevelt with overwhelming voice, and unless the National
> Convention hears and heeds that voice the Republican party—the party
> of Lincoln, of Blaine, of Garfield, of McKinley—will be no more
> because out of the chaos and storm of popular disapproval will be born a
> new party, with progressive leaders impelled by progressive principles,
> and it will take up the right for the rule of the people and by the people.

The Bull Moose party led by Roosevelt ran ahead of Taft in the
presidential race, split the Republican vote and handed the election
to Democrat Woodrow Wilson.
    Wilson's victory, a victory for the Bull Moose principles but not
for Roosevelt personally, was welcomed by the *Champion*. "The

new president is like a reborn Lincoln." Pulliam wrote after Wilson's inauguration, "For the first time in our generation, the nation is asked by its elected head 'to count the human cost' of greed and reckless ambition; to put men and women and little children before mere dollars. Thus does the counsel of William Jennings Bryan, rejected with seeming scorn in 1896, become in 1913—a very brief time as time is measured in history—the will of the majority."

Pulliam kept up his attacks on various private utilities and his demands for municipal ownership. He charged that the private companies were keeping their books and profits a secret while buying franchises with public money. "At the present time, Atchison is paying over $6,000 a year to the McKinley syndicate, a corporation owned by foreign capital, for furnishing us with a few dingy street lights."

On a statewide level, Pulliam added, "The state of Kansas should make an example of the Kansas Natural Gas Company.... The Kansas Natural is probably the most conscious and best example of a gigantic stocks and bond swindle that was ever perpetrated on the people of a good state.... The Kansas Natural pipe lines are full of hot air and its stock is soaked with water."

Although he never got the municipal utility ownership he sought, Pulliam did manage to persuade the city government to lower utility rates on several occasions. His other local reforms—commission government to replace the spoils system, mayor-council form of city government—were turned down in several referenda, although they were adopted in many other cities. Commission government, he wrote, "takes city government absolutely out of politics and places it in the hands of five men, who are elected regardless of party affiliations. The professional politicians all oppose commission government because it puts an end to their ability to prey upon the municipal exchequer."

The voters did not agree. They turned it down 962–935 a few days later.

The *Champion*'s financial fortunes paralled the political career of the Bull Moose movement. Pulliam managed to bring the paper's circulation from 2,100 in 1911 to more than 5,000 during the 1912 campaign, prompting the *Globe* to observe that "the *Champion* is here to stay all right." But a newspaper that threw so much of its heart and soul into a passing political movement could not sustain the long-term interests of readers. Circulation dropped back to 4,043 in 1913. At the time Pulliam claimed his business failure was a result of moral and ethical success, an independent and stubborn refusal to go along with the Atchison establishment. When the Atchison Street and Railway Light & Power Company refused to advertise in the *Champion*, Pulliam explained that "the *Champion* cannot be 'bought off.' It wants to win or lose as a fearless, independent newspaper and as a result of this policy it does not have access to the funds offered by certain local interests who wanted things 'hushed up' and 'smoothed over.' "

In later years he said his inexperience had hurt him. "I didn't know enough about the business end to come in out of the rain," Pulliam recalled. "But you learn a hell of a lot from necessity." He also valued the Atchison experience. When he returned in 1952 during the Eisenhower campaign and was interviewed by the *Globe*, he said,

> Although as an editor of the Atchison *Champion*, I made a rather amateurish effort to compete with the *Globe*, I learned more about the value of local news and how to write from Ed Howe than from any other newspaperman I ever knew.

6

Crash

Now PULLIAM'S WORLD, the Progressive world, was falling apart. Roosevelt's loss to Wilson took the steam out of the Bull Moose movement. The *Champion* could challenge the *Globe* in 1912 because the *Champion* had a vibrant cause, and Ed Howe did not believe in fighting for causes. But the cause was dying in 1913 and 1914, and the *Champion* died with it. There were other factors.

A city printing contract went to the *Globe* in August 1913, although the *Globe* bid was 25 percent higher than the *Champion*'s. The city power brokers were telling Pulliam to get out of town. He kept hammering away in his editorials.

> The *Champion* has been informed time and time again that it could have the city printing contract in a minute if it would not stir up trouble when the council put a crooked deal over on the people. But the *Champion* will close up shop before it will accept bribes from councilmen or anyone else.

A year later he did have to close shop.

"I worked day and night and almost had a complete breakdown so I sold out and took off about six weeks and then went right back into the same thing," he later recalled. Ed Howe had whipped the young whippersnapper. Maybe he did not do it fairly and squarely, but he had beaten Pulliam and had beaten him badly. He, his father-in-law and brother-in-law, gave up control of the newspaper, selling it for some land in Colorado and $11,000; the paper folded in a few years.

One of the brightest spots in his life came at the same time. His only son, Eugene S. Pulliam, was born, September 7, 1914, as he was selling the *Champion*. They moved back to Myrta's home in Indiana in Noblesville and lived with her parents. Gene, Sr., took a few months off to recover from the hectic pace of life in Atchison. He started looking for a job in Indiana. He had a chance to work for the *Indianapolis News* for $20 a week. Foster Clippinger, one of the preachers' kids from DePauw days, told him of a better job offering $35 a week as managing editor of the *Franklin Evening Star*. He took it in January 1915.

His experience at Atchison had been sobering. He didn't go crashing into Franklin, ready to reform the whole town right away. But other harsh personal blows were coming. Myrta became pregnant again. She had a miscarriage, topped with asthma. He received some bad medical advice. In early September 1917 she died—just thirty years old.

It was a devastating blow. He had waited and worked for five years in order to marry her. "He was like another person after that," his younger sister Helen recalled. He couldn't sleep, he had indigestion. "It is so dark for Gene," his sister Corinne wrote to their parents in Kansas. "We just all must bear up for Gene, it is just killing him," his father-in-law wrote. He sold the small cottage they had bought in Michigan. He never wanted to go back. "Too many things to open the wounds afresh," he wrote to his parents in Kansas. Now he was left alone to care for his three-year-old son. He was confused: why had God let her die? He gave money to missionaries. He drew closer to his own family, went to Kansas to visit them. It was a sad trip without Myrta, he wrote them afterwards. "We must not let distance make any difference and do all we can to make our homes the real center of our lives." He considered the ministry for himself. His father advised against it, suggesting:

> That must be absolutely a matter of conscience—From my viewpoint I think there is a freedom of action in your work that you would not find if related to any ecclesiastical or semi-ecclesiastical body on earth. Your friend Burkhardt is an example of how a man's wings may be clipped, his spirit broken by the dumb reactionaries with whom he must labor and in a sense give account. The journalist is the freest force in this free land today. In spite of government censorship, the press of this country make and unmake, set standards and take them down, and direct the destiny of the nation.

World War I had started April 6, 1917, for the United States, as Congress declared war on Germany. Reverses soon began to jolt the country out of its romantic optimism. Pulliam tried to get into the military service, but he was rejected because of his intestinal troubles and poor vision. The next day he wrote an editorial about how the only happy young men were in the military service. The rest, he said, were restless and impatient. His fifty-eight-year-old father wrote reflectively in some random notes:

> I have made my contribution to the common cause—Eugene anxious to get into the service—to have some part in the conflict—to fight the good fight.

Pulliam now plunged into the war effort, selling bonds under Will H. Hays, Indiana's war bond chairman, joining the Johnson County Council of Defense, and serving as general chairman of the County War Conference Organization. He was optimistic about the mission of the war, the common hope that the war would settle international problems forever. "This is a war to win Christian liberty for all and forever," he declared in a July 4 speech in 1918.

> Johnson County believes in a just God and has an abiding Faith in the ultimate supremacy of the Divine right of right over the cruel right of might.

He traveled in the southern part of the state, making speeches, promoting the bonds and the war effort in the *Evening Star*.

Then came the loss of two of Pulliam's heroes. Theodore Roosevelt and William Rockhill Nelson passed away during this watershed period, 1914–1919. They symbolized the end of a special time in his life and an era of American history. Nelson died in January 1916, and Pulliam paid him tribute in the *Evening Star*.

> Could one man ever have accomplished so much? ... William Rockhill Nelson is dead in the flesh, but William Rockhill Nelson, the influence, will live as long as a city sits on the hills at the junction of the Big Muddy and the sandy bottomed Kaw. To have known him and to have been one of his "*Star* boys" is a heritage, priceless in its personal indulgence, undying in its vigorous inspiration.

It was prophetic. Nelson's influence would be lived out in the life of Pulliam. Nelson would be Pulliam's model and hero. If Pulliam imitated anyone as a newspaperman, it was Nelson. From Nelson he inherited his crusades against corruption, his fierce independence, his front-page editorials, his civic dedication, his political independence, his use of his newspapers, including the news reporting, for political and social purposes, and a very short blacklist of names that could not appear in his newspaper. Nelson hated the liquor-politics alliance that the Pendergast machine established in Kansas City. In a move that would baffle and dismay Indiana Republicans, Pulliam went after the liquor-politics alliance of the Indiana Republican party after he bought the *Indianapolis Star* in 1944. Nelson was never a party man. And neither was Pulliam.

Teddy Roosevelt died in January 1919. Pulliam wrote only a one-paragraph tribute, in contrast to his long eulogies and editorials on other subjects:

> Theodore Roosevelt was a great and fearless American. He loved his country with a zeal that could not be content except in service. His name will live as long as the spirit of America, which he so truly embodied, endures.

Roosevelt's death and World War I ended the progressive tradition in the Republican party. Nevertheless, Pulliam couldn't find a home in the Democratic party in the 1920s and 1930s. Al Smith and Franklin Roosevelt were identified with the political bosses, the machines, the very things that Bull Moosers detested. The New Deal appealed to blocs and classes; Bull Moosers were interested in the good of the whole. Pulliam later accepted certain parts of the New Deal; but he disliked the lack of direction and consistency and the increasing size of the government. Like most Bull Moosers, he didn't trust Franklin Roosevelt. "They found something shifty about the man, some indefinable quality of ambition and excessive flexibility, amounting ultimately to expediency in all things," wrote Otis Graham. Or, as Pulliam recalled Roosevelt late in life, he was "the greatest politician America ever produced."

He was charming, but the biggest liar that ever lived, arrogant; he capitalized on his polio, he was smart and had a good voice, used the radio well.

Nor could he find a home in the Republican party. Harding, Coolidge, Hoover, Landon could never quite stir him the way Teddy Roosevelt had.

At the end of his life he would always say the first Roosevelt was the best president of the century, with Lincoln getting the nomination for all time. And Albert Beveridge, chairman of the Roosevelt 1912 Bull Moose convention, a DePauw graduate and Indiana senator, would rank "by all odds the most brilliant senator Indiana has had in my lifetime."

7

Franklin

FRANKLIN WAS A small farm town, south of Indianapolis, a county seat with no manufacturing or dominant industry. When Pulliam came in 1915 there was no single influential and wealthy family like the Balls in Muncie or the Millers in Columbus. Retired farmers lived in Franklin, as well as people associated with the small Franklin College. Controversy came easily; you didn't have to wiggle too hard to rock the boat, as Pulliam would learn.

W. W. Aikens captured the spirit of Franklin. He was publisher of the *Evening Star,* which he had started in 1895. He was well liked in town, seldom started a controversy, and was able to smooth some of the waves that Pulliam started to make.

Pulliam was well liked by some because he was gregarious and friendly, with an engaging manner. But he had another side also—pushy, aggressive, strident—and it would alienate people. It was that way all his life. Some would adore him for his kindness, or for his bullheadedness if they shared his goals and purpose. Others would hate him because he trampled on them, or because they did not like what he was trying to do or how he went about it. But you always knew he was there, with his volcanic energy, his ability to articulate a vision, and his iron self-discipline.

He quickly became the talk of the town in Franklin, calling for this, demanding that. In another place, at another time, this would be ordinary civic drive, common to many newspapers. But not in Franklin. "He was controversial," said Raymond Blackwell, then a high school student in Franklin. "He pushed a little too much for the older ones." The town was not interested in progress and change. "There'd be some who'd even oppose the second coming in a small town," commented another Franklin native, Dave Vandivier.

But some liked him very much, including Vandivier's father.

> He [Dave Vandivier's father] often said, "Gene Pulliam is the best thing that ever happened to Franklin" in his lifetime. He said his drive and enthusiasm were infectious and affected everyone in Franklin.

Pulliam was constantly calling for a municipal gym, public parks, street lights, auto regulation, a city garbage system, a better poorhouse, public health for the rural areas of Johnson County, or a city library. He would personally campaign for some of the projects, by knocking on doors, for example, when a bond issue was about to be voted on.

He made all sorts of changes in the *Evening Star*, with its 2,500 circulation. He brought in an outside wire service, the United Press, with national and international news. He persuaded Aikens to buy a duplex press to replace the much slower flatbed. He started using headlines and modern makeup techniques.

He was an organizer. With Bill Bridges and Raymond Blackwell, he helped start the Indiana High School Press Association, which was designed to raise the standards of high school journalism. It still exists. "We couldn't have done the thing without Gene," Bridges recalled. "We had the idea and he knew how to do it." Blackwell, Bridges, Wayne Coy, Yandell Cline, Dave Vandivier were some of the high school and Franklin College students who worked for him, got a taste of the bigger and better world, and eventually moved on to horizons that extended well beyond Franklin.

"He was by far the most sophisticated person in town, not just a local homespun product like Aikens," commented Bridges, who worked for Pulliam and later went on to write for the *New York Sun*, the *Reader's Digest* and the Bronx Zoo. "He bought in better, real reporting for the first time. He was the only professional newspaperman I knew until a murder in Johnson County brought a *Chicago Tribune* reporter to town."

Wayne Coy later became secretary to Indiana Governor Paul McNutt during the depression and then went into Franklin

Roosevelt's New Deal administration. Yandell Cline and Vandivier later ran Pulliam newspapers in Oklahoma during the depression.

Pulliam also started a Rotary Club, a forum for spreading the message of service and responsibility to the community.

In a typical Rotary message, he would quote the Bible—"Where there is no vision the people perish," from Proverbs 29:18. He called Rotary an effort to apply the Sermon on the Mount to everyday living.

Rotary would help explain some things later in his life after he owned the Indianapolis and Phoenix newspapers. At times he seemed like an odd publisher; he would help smaller competitors. They couldn't understand it: a man with a reputation as an irascible, domineering, ruthless competitor, helping them out? It didn't make sense. But it was Rotary philosophy.

Or he would pay a huge medical bill for an employee in the 1940s, long before many companies were providing health insurance. Publishers were supposed to be cruel, hard-hearted, pennypinchers. He had a small-town, Rotary mentality about certain matters and he kept it all his life. He was quick to defend it, for example, when the *New York Call* editor complained that Calvin Coolidge had "the mentality of a small-town Rotarian." He fired an indignant letter to the *Call*.

> Some of the greatest achievements in industrial peace have been worked out in the small factories of small-town Rotarians. In his relations with his fellow businessmen he clings persistently to a policy of square dealings.... As a community man, the small-town Rotarian is an everlasting booster for better schools, better roads, better municipal equipment, better housing, better community life. With good common sense, he accepts conditions as he finds them and tries to leave them a little better than he found them.
>
> Some of the greatest minds and the biggest hearts America ever has known have come from Main Street, which is the small-town Rotarian's business home.

Although he was making waves in Franklin and stirring up controversy, he had toned down considerably since his Atchison days. He was more skeptical of reform and seemed to be making an effort to be more persuasive in editorials. His father wrote of him on his thirty-third birthday in 1922:

He has detached much excess baggage—mostly dreams and visions—
with which he began to race.

He once defended a Rotary Club invitation to Colonel Frank
White, a former North Dakota governor, arguing that White was not
radical or bolshevist, but merely wanted a square deal for the
farmers. He no longer saw primaries as panaceas, although he still
favored them and let loose at the opposition.

> The very fact that the men who make their living out of the
> manipulation of political machinery were lined up solidly against the
> primary is in itself an indication of the primary's effectiveness as an
> agency for representative government as against government by the
> bosses.... The same interests and the same men who manipulated the
> state highway commission to obtain control of the Republican party
> machinery in Indiana are now using the same power to destroy the
> primary.

In contrast to his optimism in Atchison ten years earlier, he now
concluded that "government ownership of any utility always means
a lot of meddling by bunglers and a lot of jobs for the politicians."

Elections no longer excited him so much. After the 1920 race
between Republican Warren G. Harding and Democrat James Cox,
he sounded like the cynical Ed Howe in Atchison in 1912.

> Now that the election is over and the county is overwhelmingly saved,
> Franklin can again give scientific attention to its pet hobbies, basketball
> and bridge.

He accurately forecast that Harding's success would depend on
his ability to keep the politicians from turning the government into
a "pie bakery." Harding didn't succeed. Pulliam was not entranced
with him anyway. He thought the country needed strong leadership,
a Republican Teddy Roosevelt or a Democratic Grover Cleveland.

Some of his loss of enthusiasm for politics must have been a
result of the circumstances. Indiana, unlike Kansas, really had no
strong Bull Moose tradition in the Republican party. The only
substantial Bull Moose effort in Indiana after World War I came in
1922, when Senator Albert Beveridge challenged the Ku Klux Klan.

8

Ku Klux Klan

THE KU KLUX Klan had become very powerful in Indiana. Starting in Georgia on Stone Mountain, the Klan sprang up in various parts of the nation after World War I, capitalizing on postwar fears, racial hatred and religious bigotry. Indiana led the nation in Klan membership. In terms of political influence, the Klan was more successful in the Hoosier State than anywhere else in the country except perhaps Oklahoma. Klansmen attacked some Carroll County German farmers, complaining that the farmers had refused to buy war bonds, shaving the hair and beard of one man, killing a dog and painting the house yellow at another farm. Pulliam defended the indictments of the Klansmen in the *Evening Star:*

> The KKK is too Hunnish for Hoosiers and the Carroll County grand jury is doing its duty in indicting men who are known to have been guilty of malicious white capping. Those Dunkard farmers may have lacked patriotism but the KKK plan is not the proper method to use in inspiring patriotism in their heads.

The 1922 election marked a rather quiet beginning of Klan political influence. Klansman D. C. Stephenson was running for Congress in Evansville, in southern Indiana. Within two years he was the boss of Indiana politics. Samuel Ralston was the Democratic candidate for the U.S. Senate in 1922, drawing support from the Klan. Ralston's opponent was Albert Beveridge, who denounced the Klan throughout his campaign.

Beveridge, a former senator, was the only major Bull Moose Republican in Indiana politics. He had been chairman of Teddy Roosevelt's 1912 convention, after the Bull Moosers stalked out of the Taft-controlled Republican gathering. He ran unsuccessfully as the Bull Moose party candidate for the U.S. Senate in 1914. By 1922 he had come back to the Republican party and managed to beat the incumbent Republican senator, Harry New, a party regular, in a primary. This gave him his chance to go after Ralston and the Klan. Gene Pulliam promoted Beveridge in editorials, but Ralston won the election and carried the heavily Democratic Franklin area. Pulliam mocked and complained about the Klan in editorials, but he did not seem to be taking it too seriously until near election day.

> The much press-agented Ku Klux Klan has been loudly heralded for its "American principles," but there is a strangely yellow sound about the name of the Klan's high mogul.

He tried to see some merit in the Klan:

> There is always some good in everything. For instance, the KKK with its mysterious contribution visits is getting a lot of men to church who probably haven't been inside a church for years.

But as the election drew near, he wrote a long editorial, entitled: "Americans Need a New Birth of Sensible Toleration," a call for racial tolerance.

> In recent months orators have dwelt with eloquent emphasis on the need of a rebirth of devotion to old-fashioned liberty in these United States. Undoubtedly such a rebirth would be a wholesome influence but what we need even more is for individual Americans to have a new-birth of sensible toleration for the other fellow's beliefs and viewpoint. The aftermath of the war seems to have nourished with uncanny care all of our old racial prejudices and religious animosities.

He complained of prejudice against Jews, Roman Catholics, Moslems, and blacks, arguing that:

> The Negro problem never will be solved in a spirit of hate and contempt. Neither will it be solved by Utopian schemes which would force

> absolute social equality even among white people, which fact makes
> such an effort on behalf of the colored race a silly and absurd mockery.
> Economic justice and interracial cooperation, mingled with sensible
> toleration, will eventually bring emancipation to the race.

He dismissed racial fears as ungrounded and forecast that:

> The Ku Klux Klan will die out and disappear just as all orders of
> fanaticism have done.

Ultimately he was correct, but the Klan took a heavy toll first.

The Klan's dramatic ride to power came in 1924. By then, Pulliam had bought the *Lebanon Reporter* in a railroad town of 6,000, northwest of Indianapolis. In Franklin, the Klan was more of a joke. There were no Jewish or Catholic merchants, very few blacks—the enemy was far away. But in Lebanon it was serious business. Two of Pulliam's best friends were Jewish merchants, Mark Adler and Isadore Eichman. They also were advertisers in the *Reporter*. The Klan tried scattered boycotts against Jewish merchants, and under Klan pressure a few advertisers pulled out their ads. Two Klansmen came to Pulliam's home one night and demanded that he run an item about a Klan march, including an order that Jews, Catholics and blacks were to stay off the streets during the march. He refused—anyone could walk the streets, he told them. They threatened to burn down the *Reporter* building. Pulliam told them to wait a minute, went back in the house and grabbed a gun he had had since his reporting days in Kansas City. Back with gun in hand, he told them he would kill them both if his plant burned down. Gun in hand, he sat in his office all night, ready for them.

The plant didn't burn, and the two men never went near Pulliam again. If they were coming down the street toward him, they would invariably cross to the other side. Later he recalled:

> When those two guys came that day, I told them, if anybody does
> anything to the plant, I'll kill both of you. I loved to fight in those days.
> My two best advertisers were the Adlers and Eichmans. If was amazing
> that some of the men who joined wouldn't mention it five years later. It
> made them feel important, one of those crazy movements.

Usually Pulliam tried to stay out of local political fights in small towns like Franklin and Lebanon. He didn't want his newspaper to join in partisan fights for the mayoralty, or council seats, unless there was something crucial to fight about. The Klan, however, fit the criteria; it was the only issue that provoked him to take sides in local elections in the 1920s, particularly in 1924.

He gave extra publicity to anti-Klan candidates and their supporters. He reprinted a speech by Father Charles Marshall of a local Catholic school urging tolerance. He attacked Senator James Watson, then considered an Old Guard Republican, for waffling on the Klan issue, calling him "the nation's champion fence-straddler." He ridiculed Klan organizers for making themselves rich as they recruited followers. He wrote editorials about examples of Negro success, citing a particular case and concluding: "White men may not love a black man because he makes money, but it makes them respect him."

The Klan's most successful year was 1924. That year another Bull Mooser, William Allen White, ran unsuccessfully for governor in Kansas in order to fight the Klan. Pulliam's opposition to the Klan in the *Reporter* had mixed results. Fred Purnell, a Republican congressman who opposed the Klan, lost to the Klan-backed Democrat James Davis. But in Boone County the successful and Klan-supported Republican candidate for governor, Ed Jackson, ran behind the Democrat, Dr. Carl McCulloch, who opposed the Klan.

For the first time since Lincoln's Emancipation Proclamation, blacks began switching to the Democratic party in Indiana. The Republicans had tried to hold the black vote through patronage promises, which drew protest from Pulliam in a long editorial, "Baiting the Colored Vote in Indiana."

> In other words, the colored voters must stand together and vote the straight Republican ticket or suffer the consequences of political race suicide. This is a plain appeal to race prejudice. It is an effort to brighten and stampede the colored voters. It tells them bluntly that if the Republican party finds out it can win without the colored vote, there will be no more plums for the colored workers.

He added:

In a day and age when racial prejudice, religious animosities, personal strife, and class hatred are threatening the free institutions of America, the leaders of the Republican party in Indiana should realize their responsibilities to good citizenship in this state. Instead of encouraging these destructive sentiments they should do everything in their power to build up harmony and good feeling among citizens. For the sake of expediency, for the price of a few thousand votes, they are willing to add fuel to a fire that already is dangerously bright.

The Klan ran well throughout Indiana in 1924, capturing the governor's office with Ed Jackson. But the seeds of its own self-destruction were also being laid, by Grand Dragon D. C. Stephenson. As Jackson was taking over the state government, Stephenson and some of his friends raped a young girl, Madge Oberholtzer, in March 1925, and she died as a result.

Despite the widening Stephenson scandal, the Klan swept the municipal races all over Indiana in 1925, including the election of John Duvall as mayor of Indianapolis. Lebanon was an exception. Erastus Dayton Wright, with the backing of the Klan, won the Democratic primary, but he lost the election to the candidate backed by the *Reporter*'s favorite, Republican Paul Tauer, who denounced the Klan.

The Klan's success forced Pulliam to question the primary system: it seemed to allow demagogues to get into power. But part of the problem was fear.

"The history of the advance of civilization has been the history of man's conquest of fears," he wrote in an optimistic editorial after the 1925 election.

Every human progress has left behind a fear exposed as ridiculous after being unquestioned for centuries. The number of humanity's fears was once beyond reckoning. There was fear of darkness, fear of nature's elements, fear of all manner of evil spirits, fear of wizards and ghosts, fear of the racially different opinion—the list is without end.

One by one these old fears have been exposed to the pitiless and devastating light of reason. As man's intelligence increases, his fears of the unseen and the inexplicable decrease. The uncivilized and illiterate giant quakes in superstitious fear under circumstances which appear matter-of-fact to the civilized and literate man of much less physical strength.

This generation laughs at the absurdity of some of the things its ancestors shuddered at. The great body of civilized humanity no longer believes in ghosts, witches, spirits, omens, "bad luck," signs, and in other phases of witchcraft and superstition. Posterity will probably ridicule some of the fears of the present generation, among which is man's last fear—the fear of death.

The Klan's fear campaign was bad enough, he thought. But the Klan also brought back the patronage and political spoils that the Bull Moosers vainly sought to abolish. The Klan partly destroyed itself by greed. Indianapolis mayor Duvall was convicted for corruption, and Pulliam wrote:

> The conviction of Mayor Duvall was the first objective in a campaign that should continue until the rotten political conditions brought about in this state as a result of Klan leadership are cleaned up. Scandal, dirt and corruption have marked the administration of office wherever Stephenson and his political gangsters were able to seize control. Duvall offers a typical example. It was men of his type that Stephenson picked up and through the power of the Klan elected to office.
>
> The law, civic righteousness, the properties and responsibilities of citizenship, all were sacrificed on the altar of personal greed and graft. There was no thought of consideration given to the rights or welfare of the public.
>
> Of course such a machine could not last. It is a disgrace to this state that it was able to ride roughshod into the highest offices of public trust. But it had to smash sooner or later.
>
> And now with an awakened citizenship aroused to action the machine is going on the rocks. Duvall's conviction is the first blow. Cleanup has started. The decent citizenship of this state should not allow it to lag until the men responsible for this political debauchery have been driven from public offices and from places of party power and influence.

In elections the Klan began to lose sway. The 1926 primary was a clean one, Pulliam wrote afterwards, without the usual Klan-inspired "secret agreements, block trades and bipartisan manipulation" that characterized previous elections.

> Our people have probably discovered that they were allowing prejudices to influence their estimate of neighbors and acquaintances. They have learned that all of us are pretty much the same sort of folks and that it is possible to live together in a spirit of give-and-take neighborliness when there is an honest effort to understand each other.

While he stood firm against racial hatred and had close

friendships with blacks, Pulliam never seemed to have any special sympathy for blacks as a race.

He was never a crusader for black causes, believing, partly from his 1920s experience with the Klan, that crusading only served to stir up more white hatred. To the extent he had sympathy, he rarely showed it. Without fanfare he supported school desegregation moves in Indianapolis and Phoenix in the late 1940s, but not with the kind of crusading spirit he reserved for attacks on big government. He praised Herman Wells, who had worked for him at the *Reporter,* for his efforts to combat the prejudice at Indiana University, writing in the *Indianapolis Star* that Wells "has made Indiana University a bright spot on the patchwork of tolerance, and intolerance, brotherhood and bigotry." But he did not believe in wearing his charity on his sleeve, and later in life, he thought liberals who bragged about their sympathy for the poor were often, as he called them, "phony hypocrites."

9

Lebanon Life

LEBANON WAS GENE Pulliam's home base for almost fifteen years after he bought the *Reporter* and moved there in 1923. He now had a new wife, Martha. She came from a Franklin family, went to library school in Albany, New York, and returned to Franklin, where she met Pulliam. Gene, Sr., and Gene, Jr., courted her together, according to Martha's sister. On one visit, Junior, as he was called then, took a present from his father and put it in Martha's lap and asked: "Now will you marry us?" They were married in 1919. In Lebanon, two daughters were born, Corinne in 1922 and Suzanne in 1925.

Apart from his disputes with the Klan, Pulliam's approach to Lebanon was similar to his in Franklin. He still hammered away at the theme of taking partisan politics and greed out of government. He called for a city manager chosen by commissioners to replace the politically oriented council-mayor form of government. He praised the nonpartisan municipal ownership of the Lebanon waterworks. He proposed a pool, zoning, a city plan, wider streets, a public park for the poor section of town, and community recreation areas. He wanted lower gas rates, and wrote that there were still too many one-room schoolhouses in Boone County. But his tone was moderate, not the crusading spirit he had displayed in Atchison.

He thought, for example, that municipal ownership of the light and power plant might work, but might also stray into partisan politics. The goal was lower rates, but he was no longer sure that any one method would guarantee it. Seldom did he revert to his style in Atchison, a table-thumping sort of front-page editorial.

He let loose, though, at the local Gas Company and State Public Service Commission, when the company threatened to increase rates further if Lebanon objected to a smaller increase. Under the title: "Destroy This Power!" he wrote:

> If state regulation of utilities is so completely in the hands of utility officials that communities cannot object to high gas rates without being penalized with higher rates, we have traveled far toward a big business autocracy in state government.
>
> This threat of the higher rates in retaliation for objection to present rates should be accepted by the Chamber of Commerce as a challenge. Let's find out once and for all whether the public service commission of this state is organized for the private benefit of the utility interests, or for safeguarding the rights of the people who have consented to utility monopolies on the understanding that regulation is to be administered impartially on behalf of all parties concerned.
>
> We're inclined to believe that this threat of the gas company is a bluff, but it ought to be called regardless of whether or not the company is in position to exercise the power which its threat intimates. If it has such menacing power then this fight should be continued without quarter until that power is destroyed.

But this sort of outburst was rare in the 1920s and 1930s. His emphasis was on local responsibility, a conviction that would lay the groundwork for his later opposition to more powerful federal and state government. Businessmen were responsible for improving living conditions of the community, not merely opposing socialism. Old-fashioned individualism, which was strong in small midwestern towns, had to give away to a new sense of cooperation and community spirit.

> In years gone by the popular notion of a good citizen in a small town was the man who attended to his own business, kept out of debt and didn't break any laws. . . . But a community's development cannot be promoted in these times on such a limited basis. For instance, Lebanon, a modern county seat town, would go on the rocks if a majority of our people had this spirit. It requires a communitywide cooperation to develop communitywide progress.

He practiced it on a personal level. If someone were arrested in Lebanon without any money, Pulliam would often bail him out, writing a sympathetic article on his situation. If he knew of a family without food, he would go to his home, and then his sister's, take all the food he could find and deliver it to the family. "One time he ran into our house and took food for a woman with a seventh child. He cleared the shelves. He can't stand to see utter poverty," said his younger sister, Helen Swank.

He helped Henry Ulen, whose engineering firm had projects as far away as Greece, develop a unique scheme for a small town, an entire new addition to Lebanon, similar to the kind of city planning that William Rockhill Nelson had promoted in Kansas City when Pulliam was working for him. The Ulen addition had its own park and planned layout, with wide streets. Pulliam moved his family into one of the new homes.

He was still identifying himself as a progressive or a liberal in the 1920s. He was critical of the wealthy, the upper class. He didn't like the idea of fashions and styles in clothing which poor girls could not hope to adopt. And he was wary of the growing amount of wealth among a few people.

The tendency toward endowed financial dynasties in America is a growing menace to the development of a happy democratic state.

He attacked the Race Betterment Conference for its complaint that the upper classes were not reproducing quickly enough. He liked to argue that many of the best people had been poor boys who worked their way out of poverty. "When Providence needs a great man for a great work he usually trains him in the hard school of poverty, where he learns the virtues of courage, common sense, and industry," he wrote. His memories of his own rough-and-tumble childhood on the Kansas prairie made him wonder about what was happening to the more sheltered children in Lebanon. On one occasion he praised a little boy for jumping out of his second-story window as part of a game. Mothers were irate, worried about what advice the crazy publisher would give the kids next. But he thought they were coddling the poor little boys—he had survived all sorts of fights in his own childhood and he believed they had contributed to his character growth.

As was expected, several and sundry Lebanon mothers were quite shocked by our salute to little Johnny who jumped from the second-

story window of his home as the climax of an indoor Wild West show.
One mother refused to let her children read the *Reporter* Wednesday
night for fear our comment would put "wild thoughts in their dear
young minds." All the same and despite which, we still are strong for
Johnny. He will be worth a dozen other youngsters who are protected
and sheltered and "sissied" by their coddling mammas. And by the way,
we wonder if these protesting Lebanon mothers read the story of the
little Ohio boy whose mother refused to let him play Wild West or go to
a Wild West movie or even have a wooden gun. That little boy became
fed up with so much solicitude on his behalf and ran away, got onto a
cake of floating ice in Lake Erie, and was drowned. He would be alive
today if his mother had not tried to make a little Lord Fauntleroy out of
him. A live American boy with red blood in his veins has to have an
outlet for his energy and his imagination—or else. And the "or else"
usually results in some sort of tragedy. So again we salute our friend
Johnny and hope his leg isn't hurting too much.

He complained that people with a lot of capital were able to
evade taxes. Still he was satisfied that business had broadened its
base, that more people had a piece of the action in the 1920s,
compared to the late 1800s.

Strikes, he argued, were caused by bad working conditions, not
by radicals out to disrupt the social order.

Child labor, bad housing, and similar social ills are the basic causes of
strikes and social disorder, yet government is giving little heed to the
solution of these problems.

He had been pleased when socialist Eugene Debs, from Terre
Haute, Indiana, visited the Masonic Home in Franklin, in January
1923. Debs liked Franklin, telling the *Evening Star:* "It is in towns
like this that children have their best chance and our social problems
are most easily solved." Three years later Pulliam wanted to see Debs
in the Hall of Fame, as he was "the nation's greatest socialist leader,
as the only man to direct his own presidential campaign from a
prison wall."

Pulliam opposed capital punishment—"the crime against
nature which is committed every time the death penalty is inflicted."

He defined himself as a liberal, and a moderate, somewhere in-
between the extreme poles of conservatism and radicalism. He said
he was not a radical like Senator Robert LaFollette, the Progressive

party candidate for president in 1924. Nor did he cast himself as a conservative like President Warren G. Harding or Indiana Republican Senator James Watson.

> A conservative travels in a rut. The radical jumps out of the rut and skids. The only man who really make safe progress is the one who gets out of the rut but stays in the road.

He said restless discontent was essential for progress:

> The men and women who are discontented with themselves, their business, their environment, their station in life, are the men and women who are accomplishing the things worthwhile.

He knew his discontent wouldn't make him popular. "The so called popular fellows seldom accomplish anything of definite benefit for their home communities." And he still had a temper that got him into trouble, and into his first physical fight since he tangled with Gene Howe in Atchison.

> I once paid a $10 fine for assault and battery for dragging Dr. Kirtley out of the *Reporter* office and into the street. Kirtley had spread a rumor that I was having an affair with Esther Aikens, the daughter of W. W. Aikens in Franklin. She had taken care of Gene Jr. in Franklin some. I had a worse temper then. Kirtley hated the *Reporter*—perhaps over some item about one of the business deals. We wouldn't retract the story. I threw him in the street. "Oh, I'll get you for this," he sputtered.

In the 1924 presidential race, he preferred Coolidge over the Democratic nominee, James Davis, a New York lawyer who got the nomination after Al Smith deadlocked in the convention with William McAdoo. But he was hardly excited by either candidate. The problem the Democrats faced, he observed after the election, was to shake off the control of the city machines and the South and find a broader base. They would have to "attract progressive support on grounds of modern, liberal, constructive policy divorced from the past, from sectionalism, and from the professional operation for profit of commercialized municipal machines." Ironically it would be Franklin Roosevelt who would accomplish at least some of these recommendations, although he never gave up on the machines, or the South, using them instead to his own political benefit.

In 1928, Pulliam liked both presidential candidates, Republican Herbert Hoover, and Democrat Al Smith. Hoover he thought was a lot like Coolidge, very competent in ability, yet lacking the charisma and articulate ability to lead that Teddy Roosevelt had displayed. Hoover was an orphan from Iowa who had worked his way through Stanford University, and Pulliam could identify with that sort of background. He called him "the most competent living American" when the Republicans nominated him.

> His work has given a great worldwide perspective, and his freedom from the party prejudices and personal pulls of partisan politics will make it possible for him to act in the interest of the nation rather than in behalf of political factions and groups.

Alfred E. Smith, the New York City Catholic, was satisfactory also, though not quite as good as Hoover. He had met Smith in 1928 at the annual Beefsteak Dinner in Lebanon, where prominent political figures were invited each year.

> Alfred Smith's record as governor of New York is without parallel in that state. He is a splendid executive and if elected will make a great president.

Ultimately he voted for Smith to protest the anti-Catholic bigotry that ran wild during the campaign. "I voted for Al Smith because I hated the Klan," he later remarked. He complained in editorials during the campaign that religion should not be the issue between Hoover and Smith.

> Every good American knows it is contrary to the spirit and tradition of American liberty to take into account a man's personal religion when considering him as a candidate for office. Yet today the burning issue of the presidential campaign is not prohibition, not farm relief, not foreign relations. It is Governor Smith's personal religion....
> How absurd and yet tragic that these age-old hates and prejudices— all of them rooted in ignorance and fear—should suddenly burst into flames in our national life. It is all very much un-American. It is a shameful indictment of our much boasted American democracy. It has no proper place in political discussions or considerations.

10

Buying

GENE PULLIAM HAD gone to Franklin a defeated entrepreneur, a business failure in Atchison. He had lost most of his savings and his newspaper. All he had was some land in Colorado. But he bounced back. In Franklin, he and Aikens started buying some weekly newspapers in Johnson County. After Myrta's death in 1917, Aikens was apparently worried about losing Pulliam and sold him half of the *Evening Star* for $17,000. Pulliam made the purchase with notes he gradually repaid. Aikens later sold another part of his stock to Ray Sellers, and according to Pulliam's story, Sellers and Aikens tried to edge him out of the picture in 1922 because he was becoming too controversial.

He was controversial. He stepped on toes, attacked the established interests, and was an outsider in a small town, unlike Aikens and Sellers who had grown up in Franklin. But they miscalculated Pulliam's resources. They exercised a buy-or-sell option clause, forcing him either to sell his part of the stock or to buy them out for $20,000. To their surprise, he was able to borrow the money from a local banker and he bought them out.

It was a major break for Pulliam. He had come to town defeated and he now had a base to work from. He later had setbacks on the road to becoming a major newspaper publisher, but never again would he lose everything as he had in Atchison. He was on his way.

Perhaps his desire to own newspapers hampered his growth as a a writer. He had shown talent at a young age, a flair that got him the first reporting job at the *Chanute Sun*, that landed him a position at the prestigious *Kansas City Star*. In Franklin, one of his stories on a county fair was reprinted in the *Literary Digest*.

If you would know how old you have grown; if you would brush the cobwebs from a rusting viewpoint; if you would see life at its most alluring appeal; if you would sidestep the routine ruts of the blasé and the sophisticated, take a trip with some wide-awake boy or girl. Go traveling with Youth. . . . Kansas City with its myriad hills and millions of dancing lights was a fantasy of exquisite delight. The magnificent union station there was another palace of wonder. The Kansas prairies, the muddy Missouri River, the chaos of Chicago's teeming industrialism, the modern miracles revealed in a marvelous toy shop at Marshall Field's, the vantage ground afforded by traveling on the observation platform of a Monon parlor car, contributed only their everyday scenes, but through Youth's eyes they were transformed into living realities that challenged the very depths of imagination's resources.

He wrote editorials all of his life. One, on the death of his mother in 1932, drew tributes throughout the country. A similar one on his father's death in 1946 was nominated for a Pulitzer Prize. But he never put all of his energies into writing. If he had, he might have emerged more as a William Allen White, a small-town country editor whose words captured the essence of thought and life in the Midwest at key times in American history. White was twenty-one years older than Pulliam and other young reporters at the *Kansas City Star*. He had been an editorial writer for Nelson at the *Star* before be bought his own newspaper, the *Emporia Gazette* in eastern Kansas. Pulliam leaned on White for advice during his years there. When White's classic autobiography came out after World War II, Pulliam declared that, next to the Bible, it was the most inspiring book he had ever read.

But Pulliam had a restless streak. He wanted to be a William Rockhill Nelson, a Roy Howard, an E. W. Scripps, an owner of big-city newspapers. In 1934, preparing a speech to aspiring Indiana University journalists, he wrote letters to a number of publishers asking them how they had worked their way up in the newspaper business, and received answers from several: Adolph Ochs of the *New York Times,* Frank Knox of the *Chicago Daily News,* Kent Cooper, general manager of the Associated Press, and Roy Howard, then president of Scripps-Howard newspapers.

"A survey of the success achieved by America's leading living journalists shows that with few exceptions the men now at the top began at the bottom," he told the students, adding that they might not want to join the newspaper field:

The beginner's life is a hard row, but in the game, as in all worthwhile endeavor, he gains the prize who most endures. It isn't an easy game, but it's a glorious game. It isn't for weaklings, but it thrills the heart of strong-minded and big-visioned men. Its rewards are small in terms of the gold standard, but abundant in terms of useful living. And so in closing I warn you against even considering this game. I seriously counsel you to direct your energies to other fields. Out of a long experience I observe that not one in ten who enter the game ever gets to first base.

He couldn't join the ranks of Howard, Nelson, Knox and the others by spending the rest of this life writing about county fairs in Franklin, Indiana. "He had too big a mind to stay in a small town," commented one of this *Lebanon Reporter* employees, Lucille Slagle.

He knew he was not well liked in Franklin, and Aikens was no longer with him to smooth over the feathers he ruffled. So when he had an opportunty to buy the *Lebanon Reporter* for $38,000, he sold the *Evening Star* back to Aikens and Sellers for $57,000 in September 1923.

With the profit from the sale of the *Evening Star* and several weeklies, Pulliam was ready to branch out. "From then on, I began to look for papers wherever I could," he recalled.

It was a good time to buy newspapers. They had sprung up all over the country in Pulliam's lifetime. In 1880 there were 850 daily newspapers in America. By 1900, there were 2,600. A young man could still buy a newspaper in the 1920s and 1930s if he could gather up $25,000 or $50,000, or get some credit with bonds or loans. He wouldn't need the millions that were necessary after World War II.

It was a time of consolidation. From 1910 to 1930, 1,399 newspapers were suspended, 362 were merged into others but 1,495 more were started. Pulliam noted the trend in an editorial in the *Evening Star,* pointing to its benefits:

But the interests of the public have been abundantly served by the consolidation plan. Fewer newspapers mean better sevice for both the reader and the advertiser. A newspaper is published primarily from the standpoint of the reader or subscriber. By consolidation, newspapers have been able to furnish news service and feature material which were out of the question under the cut-throat competition days. The advertiser, obviously, is greatly benefited by consolidation. A large circulation is grouped in one newspaper and the advertiser is able to reach practically as many people through one advertisement at about one-half the cost entailed when he advertised in two papers under the old system. Whenever the plan is proposed merchants and other businessmen are encouraging newspaper consolidation as a step toward sensible business economy.

He and Martha had been traveling to Florida for vacations. He always wanted to own a newspaper where he vacationed, and he had his chance in Daytona Beach in the fall of 1926. He bought the *Morning Journal* by assuming its debts of $92,500, in September. The *News* was obtained the next year with $50,000 in bonds, to be paid off over a ten-year period. He merged them, coming up with a combined circulation of 7,328. Daytona Beach, whose winter population was 25,000, became his family home for a couple of winters.

But Pulliam was still looking for the big opportunity. He was studying Commerce Department reports for North Carolina, Oklahoma, and the state of Washington. He wanted to get some newspapers in a place that was going to grow and boom. He bought the *Washington Daily News* in eastern North Carolina. In 1927 he considered buying the *Hattiesburg American* in Mississippi for $37,500, but he decided against it. He turned down an offer to buy the *Mishawakawa Daily Enterprise* in northern Indiana for $27,000. In Lebanon, he bought the weekly Democratic newspaper, the *Lebanon Pioneer,* and turned it over to a local Democrat, E. C. Gullian. He was looking to western Oklahoma at the same time—he thought that section of the state was due to prosper in the 1920s' boom.

He needed capital to go into Oklahoma. He had a chance to sell the Daytona Beach newspaper for $112,000 in 1928 to Herbert and Julius Davidson, winding up with a $40,000 profit. The Davidsons sued for fraud after the sale, charging in court that Pulliam had misled them and sold at too high a price. But they lost the case after Pulliam was aided by the testimony of Florida and Indiana newspaper owner Paul Poynter, who said that that property was worth $200,000.

Pulliam had already established a reputation in Florida when some representatives of a Florida railroad and utility offered to buy him a Tampa and a Jacksonville newspaper. He was to be the general manager and they would have an editorial veto. He turned it down. He knew from Nelson, from his Atchison days, that he had to remain independent or he would never have what he wanted. He needed to be able to attack the railroads and utilities in his editorials. He didn't want to be a "kept" newspaper, the kind he had denounced in the *Champion*. The offer, and there were other similar ones, was tempting. When he finally put together an independent empire after World War II, he remarked to friends occasionally: "If I had made deals with the people who had wanted to make deals with me, I could have had this a long time ago."

11

Oklahoma

Much of western Oklahoma was only beginning to be developed in 1929. A bare forty years before, the area west of Oklahoma City had been opened up to white settlers. Oklahoma had become a state only twenty-two years earlier. Few roads were paved. West of Oklahoma City, it was dirt and gravel all the way, except for a stretch of U.S. 66, the main highway. The territory was dry, dusty, with a few rolling hills and very few trees, similar to the part of western Kansas where Eugene Pulliam had been born. It was the last of the frontier country. His wife Martha didn't like it.

Pulliam had worked in more established towns and cities, Kansas City, Atchison, Franklin, Lebanon, and in some ways he did not get along too well. He was too blunt about his aims, he offended the customs, the established procedures, too often and too easily. He was more effective in unbroken, uncivilized territory, where the customs, if any, were less rigid.

Oklahoma was raw and unsettled. The Ku Klux Klan had dominated politics earlier, in the 1920s. Governor Jack Walton had been impeached for declaring martial law because of the Klan. Another governor, Henry F. Johnston, was impeached later in the decade for incompetence. Impeachment was something of a habit for the opposition in the state legislature. The legislature also tried unsuccessfully to impeach the first depression governor, the popular William "Alfalfa Bill" Murray.

Oil booms allowed a few pioneers to become millionaires overnight. But the boom-and-bust tendencies of the early oil days also led to some ghost towns.

Stories about agriculture and oil dominated the newspapers. "Old Cripple," a wild wolf, was newsworthy enough to be the subject of an editorial in what had become a Pulliam newspaper, the *Clinton Daily News.*

Old Cripple, the red wolf who has for years roamed the range in northern Carter county, is dead. A predatory killer, Old Cripple has destroyed thousands of dollars' worth of livestock and poultry during his career in which he has many times eluded the traps and guns of many men.

Pulliam was looking for the right place, the best territory, the big opportunity. He continued studying the patterns of economic growth in North Carolina, western Texas, the Pacific Northwest states, and Oklahoma. He noticed that the towns had grown faster than the newspapers in western Oklahoma. He had seen the pattern before. He knew how to build up a newspaper, modernize the typography and layout to make it more attractive, build up the news coverage, attract new advertising and circulation. He liked to buy a poorly managed newspaper and turn it around. "I never had a paper that did not practically double its net earnings under my management," he wrote his Lebanon friend, Henry Ulen. He had a way of coming into a small town and attracting attention, favorable or other.

In Oklahoma he hoped to find gold. He wrote letters to several of the newspaper owners in western Oklahoma, offering to buy. Receiving only one reply, he headed out to see what he could do in person. He had the capital now. The *Reporter* was valued at $150,000, and he had collected $145,000 in cash from previous sales and profits. With real estate as collateral, he borrowed more cash from friends, particularly Henry Ulen. Then, with references from Ulen and other Indiana friends, he got the Exchange National Bank in Tulsa to underwrite $25,000 worth of bonds, so he could reimburse his friends and then pay off the bonds from the newspaper profits he expected to reap in Oklahoma. With plenty of cash in the spring of 1929 he could buy newspapers in seven towns. The population ranged from 5,000 to 10,000; circulation was usually much lower than it should have been, 2,000 to 3,000. It was still frontier country.

"When my father came here [in 1929], it was a rough area," recalled Larry Wade, the current *Elk City Daily News* publisher, whose father joined the Pulliam chain in Mangum in 1929. "It was not uncommon for someone to beat up the mayor. One city councilman chased the mayor around, carrying a knife. The people were in armed camps. All these groups despised each other. You couldn't do anything progressive together."

For $175,000 Pulliam bought papers in Alva, Elk City, Hobart, and Mangum. In Alva he bought the *Alva Review-Courier;* in Elk City the weekly *News-Democrat,* converting it into a daily; in Hobart the *Democrat-Chief* and a weekly, the *Kiowa County Review;* in Mangum he bought and merged two weeklies, the *Mangum Star* and *Greer County News,* converting them into a daily.

Mangum was an old cowtown. In one of the newspaper offices, Pulliam found a longhorn steer's head with seventy bullet holes in it. And in a nearby saloon and restaurant he saw a sign:

> If the steak is too tough for you, get the hell out. This is no place for weaklings.

The publishers in western Oklahoma were wary of potential buyers, including Pulliam, until he started making offers. In Hobart, he walked into the *Democrat-Chief* office, asking for Everette Pate, the publisher. Pate insisted the paper was just not up for sale. Pulliam argued. Pate repeatedly stressed it was not for sale. Finally, Pulliam said, "Would you take $75,000?"

"You just bought the newspaper," Pate replied.

Next he picked up the *Altus Times-Democrat* and the *Clinton Daily News* for $70,000 each, along with a nearby weekly, the *Harmon County Democrat.* In El Reno, he bought the *El Reno Democrat* for $64,000 and the *People's Press* for $20,000, merging them to create the *El Reno Tribune.* The immediate impact of the purchases, within a six-month period, was suddenly to shoot up the value of all Oklahoma newspapers. He started a small boom by paying such prices.

Within a few months, with new managers, increased advertising and circulation and a new optimism in western Oklahoma, his papers were worth nearly $1 million. All of a sudden he was at the top of the newspaper world. He was being written up as a major publisher. *Editor and Publisher,* the leading trade magazine for the newspaper industry, featured him in a prominent story, under a regular feature, "Romances of American Journalism."

> There may be many stories of unusual success and rare achievement in the field of American journalism, but one of the most colorful and romantic is the story of Eugene Pulliam as a newspaper and business man who at the age of forty owns a string of newspapers valued at nearly $1 million.

And the *Daily Oklahoman,* the state's major newspaper, wrote:

> Horatio Alger stories are pikers compared with the inky romance of Eugene C. Pulliam's career as a newspaper man and business man—and it is evident that the climax of this modern tale of success has not been reached.

Off on the horizons, the skies were dark. Pulliam couldn't see that far. The Wall Street crash came October 29, 1929. Like many others, Pulliam did not think much of it at first. As the days went by and the economy got worse, he assumed he could wait it out with some perseverance and guts. He had a chance to bail out, but that wasn't his style, nor did it seem wise at the time. "I have my work cut out for me and I am going to stick to the job until all these papers are rolling along like the *Reporter,*" he vowed to Henry Ulen in early December. But he did face immediate problems, decisions that would establish commitments and direction for the next few years. Suddenly the Tulsa Exchange Bank was not interested in handling the sale of preferred stock for Pulliam Publishing Company, which included the seven Oklahoma papers, the *Lebanon Reporter* and the *Linton Citizen,* which he also bought in Indiana in 1929. The bank had underwritten his bonds and was working on arrangements for the preferred stock. He wrote to Henry Ulen:

> The bank simply got caught in the market collapse and has had to retrench on new loans until they see what the local market situation is going to be.

Ulen was the man he could turn to in a crisis. Henry Ulen had made his fortune with his contracting and engineering company. It had worked in thirty states and all over the world, with projects including the Marathon Dam in Greece and the Bolivian Railways in the Andes Mountains in South America. His company headquarters were eventually established in New York City, as the firm expanded. But Ulen preferred life in a small town. He moved some of the central offices back to Lebanon in 1929, and he wound up spending the rest of his life there. "He was one of those rare individuals who wore the mantle of success with deep humility. He never lost the common touch. He never forgot a friend," *Lebanon Reporter* staff writer Al Wynkoop wrote after Ulen's death.

For Pulliam, Ulen always remained the man who had helped him the most along the way to success and fortune in the newspaper business.

> As to friends, I would say that Henry Ulen of Lebanon did more for me than any other one friend I ever had. His knowledge of corporate procedures, bonds, etc., gave me the information and inspiration I needed to finance all the newspapers I ever bought except the first one.

When Ulen died, he called him "one of God's noblest men. I have never had a friend to whom I owed so much and who demanded so little."

Pulliam spilled out his problems to Ulen in a long letter. He needed the money he planned to get from a preferred stock sale to pay off a loan to Ulen and meet a $15,000 payment on January 1 for the El Reno purchase.

> If I had four months in which to conduct a campaign we could sell this issue of preferred in our own towns in lots of $500 to $10,000 and not have to be hooked up to political complications. To sell it quickly— now—I will have to play with one of two political groups and we should not do this if we expect to make an outstanding success of these papers. It would only be postponing the grief.

With hindsight, perhaps he should have bailed out. A Kansas newspaperman offered to go into the Oklahoma chain with him if Pulliam would relinquish control of management and policy, keeping only the Lebanon and Linton papers for himself, as well as 25 percent of the Oklahoma stock:

Under ordinary circumstances this would be a good profit on a quick turnover. I don't like to take it now after we have been through the hard work of putting these papers on their feet. They are all doing splendidly and I would be passing up the big profit I could make by carrying on. None of our papers will make less than $12,000 net and Altus will make at least $25,000 this year. Clinton and El Reno will be making $20,000 within another year.

Few ever questioned Pulliam's financial ability as it applied to buying and selling newspapers. "He could read a balance sheet faster than anyone I ever saw," summed up Paul Porter who worked for him in Oklahoma and later went on to various New Deal jobs before becoming chairman of the Federal Communications Commission after World War II. But in his analysis in 1929, Pulliam left out the impact of the massive depression. Oklahoma was especially hard hit, as drought and dust storms set the state's economy even further back. If he had known what was coming in the next ten years, he probably would have sold to the Kansas man.

This Kansas offer would enable me to meet all my obligations, keep clear my record for clean-cut non-political management and leave me with Lebanon and Linton. But it would rob me of the long profit which is mine if I can ride out the present market situation.

His alternative was to let the politicians in on the operation, bringing their money but spoiling Pulliam's clean record. He gave in to the temptation. He turned to one of the politicians. It never led to the profits he expected, and it put him in a compromising alliance with a political figure. Although he was a proud man and never inclined flatly to acknowledge he had erred, he must have always regretted the move. Late in life he recalled it as "the only time I ever let a politician outtalk me."

He sold $150,000 worth of stock to Frank Buttram of Oklahoma City in January 1930. Under the agreement, Buttram controlled the dividends, and Pulliam was in control of policy and management, a precarious arrangement that lasted only a few years.

Buttram appealed to Pulliam. He did not have a political background when they met. He decided to run for governor in 1930, his first try for political office. Born in a log cabin in Indian Territory in 1886, he had been a poor boy who became a millionaire as one of the oil pioneers in Oklahoma. He threw himself into civic affairs in Oklahoma and led the kind of fight Pulliam would have approved of, in favor of the nonpartisan city-manager form of government in Oklahoma City.

But 1930 was the wrong time for a wealthy man to run for governor, no matter how many newspapers he had. The depression was hitting the state hard. A drought came in the summer of 1930, when the two key Democratic primaries were held. William "Alfalfa Bill" Murray was the man for the times. Murray, Buttram, A.S.U. Shaw of Altus and others were running in the Democrat primary. Murray was an old-fashioned populist and dreamer, the odd combination that touched the needs of the average man hit by a depression and a drought.

Murray had an intriguing background. He had been chairman of the Oklahoma constitutional convention in 1907. He went on to try to set up a utopian colony in Bolivia, but it didn't work out; he lost his money and returned to Oklahoma in 1929, just before the debacle. He ran the kind of campaign that endeared him to the man in the street, the unemployed who had lost their jobs in the crash.

He borrowed $40, let his beard grow, wore shoes with holes, and ate cheese and cracker meals outdoors. He made himself look like a tramp. He had personal sympathy for those who suffered from the depression. A populist in style, in much of his substance he was a conservative. He was opposed to federal relief measures, both Hoover's and Roosevelt's. He was against woman's suffrage and favored the Prussian tax system—no vote for those with no property. He was far more appealing than Buttram and won the first race with 134,243 votes to Buttram's second place 69,506. Murray clobbered Buttram in the runoff, 196,966 to 113,122, and went on to win the race in the fall.

Pulliam's alliance with Buttram was the one time he compromised his principles. One could argue that it was the depression, and it was. Times were hard and he needed the money. One could argue that he would have supported Buttram anyway in the race for governor. And one could argue that politics and newspapers were closely tied anyway in Oklahoma. One of his managers worked for one candidate, Shaw, and another worked for Buttram. But the financial involvement of Buttram gave the appearance of a wheeling-and-dealing financial alliance with a candidate for governor.

The other side, though, is that, if Buttram was trying to buy the news and editorial support of the Pulliam papers, he did not get his money's worth. Only one of the seven Pulliam papers ran a front-page editorial in favor of Buttram, and that was the *Altus Times-Democrat*. An occasional "special" story would appear in some of the papers, a kind of puff for Buttram's campaign, but most of the papers ran balanced United Press stories on the front page, during the first primary and runoff campaigns. If Buttram was trying to buy news coverage, he didn't get it.

Some of the newspapers ran endorsements on the editorial page, or attacks on Murray. But others did not. And the *Alva Review-Courier* endorsed a Republican candidate for governor instead of Buttram. The *Hobart Democrat-Chief* was favorable to Murray. The Hobart paper's only front-page editorial blast was a demand that everyone back the winner of the runoff and not indulge in the kind of impeachment proceedings that were popular in the state government in the 1920s. "Be loyal, support the nominee," the newspaper advised at a time when it was clear that Murray would win the primary. The only editorial that ran in all the newspapers was "Test the Candidates," which simply told the voters:

> Voters should not allow propaganda, gossip and whispered rumors to becloud their judgment. Neither should they be influenced by visionary promises and impossible pledges.

Whatever Buttram got out of the Pulliam papers, Pulliam had stumbled and violated his own standards. The alliance called into question the claim made by his *Clinton Daily News.*

> We are for Buttram solely because we think he is the better of the two men—the man with the most qualifications and more able to fill the governor's chair.

12

Texas Partner

THE DEPRESSION ROLLED on. The money from Buttram was not going to be enough. Gene Pulliam had to meet dozens of payments on bonds and payrolls at nine newspapers. Advertisers were going out of business right and left. People could no longer afford to pay for their daily newspaper delivery in some of the small towns.

Then Pulliam met Charles Marsh. Marsh had been a crusading editor in Austin, Texas, pushing through a council-manager form of city government to replace the aldermanic spoils system of city government. Marsh attained financial success more quickly than Pulliam—the Texan was a millionaire at the age of thirty-one.

He was two years older than Pulliam, had started as a reporter and then gone on to build up a chain of newspapers in Texas. Both men helped countless individuals, sometimes with money, sometimes with advice and encouragement and always with little fanfare or publicity. Both liked to wheel and deal in politics. Marsh later grew intimate with and encouraged a young Texan named Lyndon Johnson early in his political career.

In other ways Marsh and Pulliam were very different. Marsh had a wider range of business interests and investments than Pulliam, who only wanted to buy and run newspapers. Marsh invested in banking, oil, and real estate ventures, and had less interest than Pulliam in the editorial side of newspapers.

Pulliam thought newspapers should remain free of all entangling alliances with politicians, banks, utilities, and other businesses, and would stick with that principle for the rest of his life. Marsh and Pulliam parted company partly over this issue, but in

1930 they joined hands. "Both were strong, individualistic, dominating types; I was surprised they could work together," observed newspaper broker Vincent Manno, who worked with both men at different times.

The partnership lasted only four years. But their chemistry clicked, and together they did more newspaper purchasing in that short span than most in their trade accomplished in a lifetime. Like Pulliam, Marsh thought the depression was going to end quickly. And Marsh was a dreamer; Pulliam began to share his dream of a giant newspaper empire.

Another man who knew Pulliam and Marsh thought about joining them during the 1930s. Oscar Stauffer, who had worked with Pulliam at the *Kansas City Star*, was building his own smaller chain in Kansas and surrounding states but decided against teaming up with Pulliam and Marsh.

Their formal partnership began August 1, 1930. Pulliam brought in his Oklahoma newspapers, Linton, Lebanon, and the *Huntington Herald-Press*, which he was in the process of buying in northern Indiana. Marsh brought in some stock from his Texas newspapers. Together they established General Newspapers, Inc., and headed off on a frantic spree which climaxed in the final months of 1930. Pulliam recalled their techniques.

> Marsh and I would usually travel together. He was a smooth talker, and I was ardent, so we'd make deals wherever we could through bond financing.

They roamed all over the country, sometimes in a car, sometimes by train, looking for newspapers to buy. Pulliam's home was back in Lebanon, since his family had not liked Oklahoma City. His home was a car or a hotel for a couple of frantic, wild years.

In late August 1930, they bought the *Paducah Sun-Democrat* in Kentucky, and were looking for other newspapers to buy in the state. In September, Pulliam completed the purchase he had already been working on in Vincennes, Indiana, buying the *Sun* for $112,500 and the *Commercial*, paying $50,000 and assuming a $60,000 debt. He did it all with paper, bonds, and preferred stock in General Newspapers, Inc. This merger of the Vincennes newspapers, the *Vincennes Sun-Commercial*, was the only newspaper that remained in Pulliam's organization from the prewar years until his death in 1975.

A few days after closing the Vincennes deal, he and Marsh met in Anderson, South Carolina, and bought the *Anderson Daily Mail* for $86,000. From South Carolina they made their way up the East coast, to Quincy, Massachusetts, to buy the *Quincy News* for $100,000, again with bonds and General stock. By the end of the year Pulliam had picked up the *Bicknell Daily News* in southern Indiana for $25,000. Back in New Jersey they completed a deal for North Jersey Publishing Company, which owned the *North Jersey Courier* in Orange. Pulliam drove into Georgia in early December to put the final touches on purchases in LaGrange, Americus, and Dublin. Out in Kansas, he was also trying to buy a newspaper in Chanute, where he got his first newspaper job, but he never could work it out. Between August and December 9, he had traveled 42,000 miles, mainly by car. Sometimes, if the price was right, he and Marsh would sell quickly to make a profit. The Paducah newspaper, for example, was unloaded within a few months, for an $8,000 profit.

In January 1931, they ranged down into Florida. Within a year they had bought the *Orlando Morning Sentinel* and the *Orlando Evening Reporter Star* and merged the newspapers, paying $37,500 and assuming nearly $100,000 in debt. (In 1965 Martin Anderson, who had worked for Marsh and Pulliam in Orlando, sold the newspapers for just under $30 million to the *Chicago Tribune.*)

In the summer of 1931 Pulliam wrote Will Hays in New York telling him that General had expanded to twenty-three newspapers in seven states in one year and was looking for potential investors. He wrote about their interest in buying nineteen Texas dailies, as well as eight possibilities in Kansas and Nebraska. They had opened an office in New York City. But the depression rolled on. They never attracted any other investors.

Somewhere along the way Pulliam began to wonder about it all. He was driving 10,000 miles a month, but what for? He was shaken early the next year when, driving back from Florida with Martha in the rain, he ran into a man. Lonnie Casey was killed as he was thrown into a nearby bridge after Pulliam's car struck him. Pulliam was exonerated legally, but perhaps the death made him wonder why he went on with all the hurry and travel.

Yet he continued for a time. He and Marsh made a quick

$75,000 profit in Lansing, Michigan, in the summer of 1932, buying the *Lansing Capital News* from Bernard MacFadden for $50,000 and selling it quickly. In September they worked out a consolidation of two newspapers in Uniontown, Pennsylvania, the *Morning Herald* and the *Evening Standard.*

In 1933 he was still busy, trying to work out a consolidation in Bartlesville, Oklahoma, negotiating for the *Danville Commercial News* in Illinois. Some businessmen in Oklahoma City asked him to buy the local Scripps-Howard newspaper, the *Oklahoma City News,* so he could challenge E. K. Gaylord's more dominant *Oklahoman.*

He continued, however, to doubt the wisdom of his course. He owned part of a major newspaper empire, General Newspapers, ranging from Massachusetts to Florida, out to Oklahoma and up to Indiana. In a sense he had achieved his dream. But in another sense, what did he really have? An entangling, embarrassing alliance with an Oklahoma oil man who had run for governor; and a partnership in a corporation with opportunities to buy newspapers the way most people buy bargains at a sale. He was not adhering to the principles he had set forth in the first editorial he ran in his seven Oklahoma newspapers when he bought them in 1929, the same one he would rewrite only slightly when he bought the *Indianapolis Star* in 1944. It was a magnificent statement of what newspapers ought to be and what he really wanted to do.

> A newspaper is a human institution and as such is subject to all the ills and fortunes that man is heir to. It is not like other business chattels that can be bought and sold in cold barter. It is peculiarly human. It takes heart-hold and a spiritual grip on the men and women who produce it day by day. It becomes a part of their very existence. Through it they find themselves giving expression to their highest ideals. It reveals their deepest life interests. The opportunity it affords for satisfying service keeps them in the game when other fields offer more lucrative compensation.
>
> The basic policy of the *Democrat-Chief* under the new management will be to give Hobart and Kiowa County the very best community newspaper that our fine family of splendid employees can produce. The first duty of citizenship is useful service to one's local community, and the *Democrat-Chief* wants to be a good citizen. We want to render every possible assistance in the progress of community development (which is everywhere so apparent to the newcomer in Hobart and Kiowa County).

We cherish the ambition to be known as the strongest booster and most ardent backer of Kiowa County's agricultural interests.

We expect to be counted on when there is worthy work of any sort to be done. We offer friendly and definite cooperation to the churches, the schools, the Chamber of Commerce, the civic organizations, fraternal bodies, and community institutions. These columns will be open for discussion of civic, political, social and economic questions in signed contributions. Established policies of the retiring management will be preserved. The newspaper will not indulge in personal criticism of citizens of the community. Smut, scandal and gossip will find no place in our columns. We will strive to be clean, broadminded, progressive, fair, helpful and, above all, truthful and accurate.

This is the creed of the *Democrat-Chief*. On this policy we solicit the support, confidence and good will of the citizens of Hobart and Kiowa County.

But how could he carry out that policy with twenty-five newspapers to think about and dozens of bond payments to meet? In Oklahoma he had brought in managers to carry out his ideals. But he couldn't do it all over the country. He began to work his way out of a complicated mess. He started to refinance the Oklahoma newspapers, which were a subsidiary of General. He resold all but $15,000 of his bonds, started to buy out Buttram and then borrowed another $15,000 from Lou Wentz, another oil man, newspaper owner and chairman of the State Highway Commission. His bondholders went along with the refinancing because he had not defaulted, even though bankruptcy would have had financial advantages for him.

His partnership with Marsh was shaky. Buying newspapers was fun for a time, but Marsh was interested in taking General into other ventures, oil and real estate. Pulliam was interested in newspapers only. They formally started parting company in the spring of 1934, trading stock over a two-year period. Pulliam kept the Oklahoma and Indiana newspapers and Marsh took the rest. Pulliam labeled it the "best deal of my life."

With the Oklahoma daily newspapers *(El Reno Tribune, Hobart Democrat-Chief, Elk City Daily News, Mangum Daily Star, Clinton Daily News, Altus Times-Democrat, Alva Review-Courier)* and some weeklies, and Indiana papers *(Lebanon Reporter, Linton Citizen, Vincennes Sun-Commercial, Huntington Herald-Press)*, he formed Central Newspapers. Financially he didn't get what he had hoped for during those years. Central profits in 1934 were only $54,977. The depression had defeated him, temporarily. However, he learned to practice what he had preached in editorials; not to chase frantically after every chance to buy a newspaper, every opportunity to expand.

He slowed down a little, but his slower pace was still a brisk clip. He was traveling, inquiring, negotiating, buying where he could. But he took the time to start writing a daily column in the *Reporter*, from December 1933 until March 1936, a remarkably perceptive series of columns for a small-town newspaper. He took the first steps toward selling most of his Oklahoma and Indiana newspapers to his managers. He was still looking for the big opportunity. He didn't see it now in Oklahoma and he wanted to give his young managers what he had, an opportunity to own a newspaper at a young age. He sold them as he had bought them, with bonds, giving his managers ten years to pay them off.

He traveled to New Mexico, negotiating for various papers that he never bought. He tried unsuccessfully to buy the *Wichita Beacon* in Kansas. And despite several efforts, he never got another newspaper in Kansas after the *Atchison Champion*.

The pace was taking its toll on him, as he wrote his son, Eugene, then working for United Press:

> Am just coming out of one of my terrific headaches this afternoon so am not quite as definite in my thinking and direction as usual. You could buy me out lock, stock and typewriter, also my bank book, for 10 cents on installment payments. But tomorrow it will cost you the regular price.

The traveling, the hours, the frantic buying and selling, the hectic pace, were damaging his health during the depression. Because of his boundless energy, he always had trouble relaxing. This nervous energy brought on various stomach difficulties, requiring two operations in his earlier years. He learned to take daily naps to relax and to curb tendencies toward exhaustion. His Elk City manager, Paul Wade, once mentioned his own exhaustion problems a few years later during World War II, as he was buying one of Pulliam's newspapers. Pulliam liked to play doctor to his employees, and wrote his own prescription for the problem he had lived with:

Watch this nerve exhaustion thing—it can certainly get you down. The best thing to do for the next six months is to try to take thirty minutes out sometime during the middle of the day and force yourself to go to sleep. If you will just close your eyes and refuse to think about anything or see anything—particularly refuse to think in terms of words—you will drop off to sleep and thirty minutes rest in the middle of the day will knock the daylights out of that nervous condition.

He developed back trouble, blaming it on the driving, 50,000 to 100,000 miles a year in the early depression years, on bumpy and sometimes unpaved roads. He was hospitalized several times and eventually had to have a painful spinal fusion operation in 1941.

He tried to buy the Hearst newspapers in Omaha, Nebraska, the *Bee-News* and *World Herald,* offering $700,000. Hearst tried to get him to work for his organization, but Pulliam balked. He wanted to be the boss of his own newspaper empire.

Your question about Hearst: I'd been trying to see Hearst for two years, and finally got Tom White, general manager of Hearst, and Harry Bitner, who was business manager of the whole organization, to make an appointment for me to see Hearst at his apartment up on Riverside Drive in New York.

As I recall, this was some time in 1934 or 1935, but the time is of no importance. He came down the stairs and the first thing he asked me was, "Young man, would you like to go to Rochester and run my paper there?" I said, "Mr. Hearst, I don't want to work for you. I have several papers of my own. All I'm interested in is in buying the papers in Omaha. I know how much you paid for them, and I'm prepared to bail you out so you won't lose any money on the whole transaction."

He said, "Well, I never sell anything, young man. How about going to Syracuse? Syracuse is a good town and I think you would fit in there. Tom White and Harry Bitner tell me you are pretty energetic and I'd like to see you come into our organization."

I said, "Mr. Hearst, I wouldn't work for you for $100,000 a year, but I do want to buy the Omaha papers. You are losing money, but I think I could make another *Kansas City Star* out of them." And I told him I had started my work on the *Kansas City Star.*

He said, "Well, I told you I never sell anything. Are you sure you don't want to go to Rochester?" I said, "No." "You don't want to go to Syracuse?" I said, "No, I just want to buy the Omaha papers."

"Well," he said, "let's have a drink and have lunch." So we had a drink and had lunch and he wouldn't answer a question. I couldn't get another word out of him and I never did. Two years later those papers folded and he got $86,000 out of the whole mess, where he could have gotten $700,000 if he had made the deal with me.

You asked if I knew Hearst. I only knew him by correspondence and the one meeting I had with him. He really had great confidence in himself, and in his early days he had a great vision as a newspaperman. But my opinion of him was that egotism ruined a great man. He really thought he was going to be the Czar of America.

Pulliam's memory on the figures was confused, or he was exaggerating. Hearst sold the Omaha papers in 1937 for $750,000.

13

Leaving Oklahoma

THE DEPRESSION CONTINUED for five years, with no clear end in sight. It hit western Oklahoma especially hard. Banks and businesses closed, drying up credit and the flow of money. Droughts dried up water supplies. Dust storms swept through constantly, ruining the farm crops, which were bringing in very little income anyway. The Oklahoma newspapers were not going to be the big opportunity Gene Pulliam had been seeking.

In the beginning, he and his managers had to overcome the resentment of rival newspapers and old-timers. Small towns in states like Oklahoma seldom welcomed newcomers, and Pulliam brought new managers, mostly from Indiana, for nearly every town. One rival newspaper in Elk City started calling the Pulliam opposition the "Indiana chain gang." The Pulliam newspapers represented the biggest chain ever put together in the state up to 1929. But the resentment faded rather quickly, especially in newspaper circles, as Pulliam's managers showed what they could do with their newspapers, for their communities and for the quality of journalism in western Oklahoma. The prices Pulliam paid for the newspapers caused a minor boom, bringing up the value of all newspapers in Oklahoma. Newspaper owners had not realized the value of their property until Pulliam came in; nor had they kept up with the economic growth of their own communities.

Pulliam's managers found all kinds of new advertising that previous owners had not bothered to go after. Getting ads was like "shooting fish in a barrel," recalled Dave Vandivier, Pulliam's first manager in Mangum, where they converted two weeklies into a daily. Circulation shot up in every town, despite the depression, sometimes nearly doubling.

Scrip, issued by the newspapers as a form of credit when money was scarce, helped overcome the early resentment against outsiders. Most of the managers joined in some sort of community work, remembering Pulliam's lectures to them about its importance. Paul Porter recalled giving out food and water in Mangum during a dry spell. The quality of the newspapers improved, as Pulliam's managers brought in modernized equipment, changed layout techniques, added new content and features. In some of the towns, Pulliam started the first daily, for example in Elk City. He had bought the weekly *Elk City News-Democrat* and gambled that a daily could attract the necessary circulation and advertising. His managers took on the United Press, putting it in the window of the office so that for the first time everyone in town could walk by and see news from around the world coming into Elk City by telegraph.

In 1933 the Pulliam papers swept the awards at the annual state newspaper contest. "It had an impact on the state," recalled H. Merle Woods, then the editor of the *El Reno American* and a competitor of Pulliam's *El Reno Tribune*. "Getting young, vigorous, talented managers eliminated some of the old-timers who were not actually good journalists. A lot of them never had much training. Newspapers had been looked down on; they were owned by banks or were political organs. He helped Oklahoma newspapers by putting these young guys in charge—it seemed to be the push the state needed. It put newspapers on a better financial basis; these seven had never realized what their value was." Or, as one of his own managers, Ray Dyer, put it, "Those who were really interested in newspapers knew that Gene increased the value of small-town papers 100 percent by buying them. And he gave a number of young newspapermen a chance to own their own newspapers."

Pulliam had been a kind of father figure or big brother to a number of high school and college students in Franklin, and later in Lebanon. Many of them were preachers' kids who went to DePauw, the Methodist school where they could get a break on tuition. They were "his boys," as he sometimes called them, a phrase that indicated a family-like concern for his employees. It also revealed his unwillingness to have an equal or to condone a challenge to his authority.

Yet he wanted to be one of them. He had a friendly familiar way about him that could mask his power and authority and his willingness to assert it. "He never acted like a big wheel," recalled Harry Schroeder, then and now the office and circulation manager of the *El Reno Tribune*. Or, as he wrote in a characteristic note to Lucille Slagle, a *Reporter* employee, "Don't be so damn formal." He would fish, play bridge, bowl with employees. He was always ready to help and he knew what it was like from childhood to need money desperately.

In his frantic travels , he heard about one employee who needed money and a top coat. At the next town he wired: "Good work. Expect raise. Plus top coat. Buy now."

Yandell Cline joined the organization as manager in Elk City, taking his wife and son down to Oklahoma from their home in Indiana. His son, Allen, caught tubercular meningitis. Pulliam arranged for transportation back to Indiana and took care of Allen at night while the Clines slept. "We never felt we could repay him for that kind of gesture," Cline's ex-wife recalled.

But he could also be insensitive when he was trying to keep costs down during the depression. In 1933 he wired Vandivier, by then general manager of his Oklahoma newspapers, and told him to cut salaries in half. Vandivier replied that he would quit rather than follow the order in the middle of hard times. Pulliam backed down.

Some of his boys stayed in the newspaper business, often buying one of Pulliam's newspapers at a low price, with easy long-term payments. Others moved on, some to high positions. Paul Porter, from Kentucky and freshly out of law school, joined Pulliam in 1929, working in Mangum, then LaGrange, Georgia, before moving on to various jobs in the Roosevelt administration. Eventually he became chairman of the Federal Communications Commission and practiced law with Abe Fortas, a Supreme Court justice and adviser to Lyndon Johnson. Porter, a New Deal Democrat, always remembered Pulliam fondly and never developed the hostility that liberal Democrats would later feel toward him. Porter, who died a few months after Pulliam in 1975, appreciated the complexity of Pulliam's political views as they shifted before and after World War II. He wrote:

You have set a formidable task for yourself in an effort to identify Gene's political philosophy. None of the labels such as liberal, conservative, populist and certainly not radical is appropriate. I would say that he is what we lawyers would describe as *sui generis*.

My recollection is that he was a great admirer and devotee of William Allen White of Kansas. Although not always agreeing with the policy or programs of this great editor, he had an enduring admiration of White's fierce independence and his writing skills. Gene is of course, as you say, a realist, approaching most political and economic problems in a pragmatic sense. He was tolerant of dissent and encouraged autonomy and independence of the young editors in his organization. I suspect, however, that his most identifiable characteristic was his detestation of power. He was suspicious of power in government and overconcentration of industrial or economic power and had an almost religious faith in individualism. His later polemics against bureaucracy gave me great pleasure because I believe, as I wrote him, there was still fire in his belly and his great capacity for indignation against what he thought were excesses in the use of power remained undiminished with the passage of time.

Another Oklahoma manager for Pulliam, Harry Wimberly, bought the *Altus Times-Democrat* from him. Later Wimberly became chairman of the Federal Power Commission.

Bill Bridges, who worked at Franklin, became a writer for the *New York Sun*, the Bronx Zoo, and the *Reader's Digest*. Herman Wells, who worked for him at the *Lebanon Reporter*, later became president of Indiana University. Wayne Coy, after working for him in Franklin, went into politics as secretary of Indiana governor Paul McNutt and later ran the FTC in the Roosevelt administration. Vandivier, who had worked in Franklin and Frankfort for Pulliam, became vice president and general manager of the Oklahoma newspapers in the early 1930s, when Pulliam was traveling and buying so frantically with Marsh. Later he bought half of the *Chickasha Daily Express*, sold his stock in 1956, and worked for the Treasury Department in Oklahoma City.

Pulliam loved to brag about his "boys," how he had given them their first jobs and taught them the ways of the real world. A more publicized case was Roger Branigin, later governor of Indiana, who, according to popular stories, had delivered the *Evening Star* for Pulliam in Franklin. It was a nice, romantic story because they became close friends after World War II. But the story about the newspaper route was apocryphal. Branigin never told Pulliam that, in fact, he had delivered an opposition newspaper.

After these early successes in 1929 and 1930, the depression caught up with Pulliam's properties. He was deeply in debt. Bankruptcy would have been the easy way out, saving him thousands of dollars. But bankruptcy also would have hurt his future chances to finance larger purchases. He stuck it out. It was a moral issue, according to Porter, who said that he first was confused by Pulliam's unwillingness to take bankruptcy. Later he wrote: "The tenaciousness which I sometimes equated to excessive stubbornness now I realize was a kind of moral issue with him."

> Thereafter came the massive depression, a disaster . . . . However, I think it is to Gene's lasting credit that in this period of financial crisis, there was never any default on these bonds. Interest requirements were deferred on several occasions and maturities were extended. But I believe that ultimately these bonds were redeemed at or about par—an unusual record for that time.

As most of the other ventures financed by the Tulsa bank in 1929 did take bankruptcy, the bank was surprised at Pulliam's staying power. At one point it demanded proof that he had no debts except for his bonds, making him drive all around western Oklahoma for three days getting the appropriate statements from county clerks.

> I didn't expect the depression, and it almost broke me. I had to go to court for the banks. I didn't default. The politicians appointed receivers for everything, and assumed we were broke too, since seventy-eight companies had been financed by the bank; all but us were broke. We had to get statements from all the county clerks that we weren't broke.

Somehow he pulled through. It was a great triumph for him and later laid the groundwork for larger purchases.

His managers could see the difficulties in buying the Oklahoma papers, but some decided to take the risk. It gave Pulliam an opportunity to unload his Oklahoma chain. In Indiana he also wanted to give some of his boys a chance. He started in 1934 by selling the *Bicknell Daily News* to his manager, William D. Murray, for $9,500 and Central stock that Pulliam usually gave the executives who ran his newspapers. George Carey, his *Lebanon Reporter* advertising manager, wanted his own newspaper also, but not the one in Altus, Oklahoma, that Pulliam had offered him. Carey heard about a possible newspaper sale of the *Clintonian* in southern Indiana, near Vincennes, and told Pulliam about it.

"Go down to Clinton and see if you can make a deal," he told me. "Don't close anything but see if you can come to a tentative agreement. If you can I'll go down with you and close the deal for you." Mrs. Harriet Pierce, trying to carry on the business her late husband started, was only too glad to make a deal. Gene came down, wrote the contract and I had an almost-broke newspaper.

But he went farther than that. I had assumed a heavy burden of indebtedness as the *Clintonian* owed several banks. He went to the banks with me, explained that I had virtually no working capital and the *Clintonian* was technically broke. If they pushed me, it would put me out of business.

"Give him a break," he told the bankers, "and I am sure he can make it. I'll give you this further assurance: If he doesn't pay you, I will." Fortunately he never had to.

That was the Gene Pulliam I knew...as fine a friend as any man could have. He gave me a break and a chance. He never owned a dime's worth of the *Clintonian* and he left a hole in his organization, for I think I made him a pretty good employee. Do you wonder that I held him in such high esteem?

In Oklahoma, Ray Dyer bought the *El Reno Tribune,* paying $90,000 over a five and a half year period. He worked for Pulliam a short time later in Phoenix after World War II but returned to El Reno to run the *Tribune.* Wimberly agreed to buy the *Altus Times-Democrat* for $100,000. After a stint as chairman of the Federal Power Commission in Washington, he returned to Oklahoma, buying the *Duncan Banner.*

To Mangum, Pulliam sent Paul Wade, who had planned to go to Harvard Business School in 1929 after graduating from DePauw. Instead, he went to Oklahoma for Pulliam. He started in Mangum, worked later in El Reno and eventually became manager in Elk City. He bought the paper from Pulliam for $40,000 over a ten-year period, starting in 1934.

Pulliam's managers in the four other towns spent several years trying to buy their papers but couldn't keep up payments and eventually gave up. Pulliam sold all four to Nance-McBride newspapers, another Oklahoma chain started by one of Pulliam's

Oklahoma boys, Joel McBride, who began as manager in Elk City. But Buff Burtis, his manager in Clinton, was bitter about Pulliam's terms, which he thought were too harsh. Wimberly, though, said, "I knew you couldn't pay dividends and retire bonds so Gene and I got along. Buff didn't."

Pulliam was glad to get out of Oklahoma. He had poured about $400,000 into the purchases in 1929 and his sales brought back about $450,000 with delayed payments. He was preparing for another major move. He was looking at the *Wichita Beacon* in 1936, after he had worked out the details of selling the Oklahoma papers. He wrote his son:

> Have just returned from Oklahoma where disposed of the five smallest papers for $305,000, which puts me on ice—or on fire—just as you look at it. Stopped at Wichita on the way back and offered $1.6 million for the *Wichita Beacon* and almost bought it. I didn't have the half-million cash in my purse that afternoon for the down payment so had to stall along a bit but I can get the half-million all right if they decide to take up offer.

He was still BSC Pulliam, Buy, Sell, Consolidate, a nickname he detested, but appropriate at the time.

14

The New Deal

PULLIAM WAS NOT active in the 1932 presidential race. He kept most of his newspapers neutral, as had been his custom since 1912, although he allowed a couple of his traditional Democratic newspapers to endorse Roosevelt. His mother was sick much of the year, and died shortly before the election, on October 22. Her death brought forth one of his best literary efforts.

> During the middle nineties, when another real depression was causing nationwide suffering, tramps were numerous. Our front fence had signs put there by tramps to indicate the place was "friendly" to indigent wayfarers of the road. Throughout those bitter winter months Mother never turned a single tramp away hungry. She made each do some little job for his meal. It didn't occur to her to be afraid. She fed literally scores of them but did not have even one unpleasant experience with a tramp.

The editorial drew letters from all over the country, including William Allen White and Arthur Capper in Kansas and from one of his former boys, Paul Porter, who said:

> You have done many things for me and taught me many things. But the greatest of these, I believe, comes from the inspiration that reading what you have written from the heart gives.

Pulliam was dissatisfied with Herbert Hoover as the Republican nominee; he preferred Chicago banker Charles Dawes, who had been vice president under Calvin Coolidge, because he thought Hoover would lose anyway. After the election of Roosevelt, he looked on the early New Deal favorably. It sounded so good,

something like the Bull Moose program, like Methodism applied to
politics. In a speech at the time, he declared:

> This is the biggest benefit of the New Deal. The more fortunate people
> have accepted their responsibility to the less fortunate....We are our
> brother's keeper from now on.

If the depression didn't do anything else good, he reasoned, at
least it firmly established this fundamental principle. He defended
Roosevelt in columns and editorials, even in a long, rather rare
front-page editorial after an FDR speech. He went so far as to
suggest that Roosevelt was providing a timely reinterpretation of
the message of Jesus Christ.

> The most significant statement made by Franklin D. Roosevelt since he
> became president was contained in his address before the Federal
> Council of Churches at Washington last night. Heretofore in his public
> addresses the president had dealt largely with political, economic and
> governmental factors involved in his aggressive program for national
> business recovery. Last night he discussed the fundamental problem not
> only of this generation, but of the ages. He gave expression to his
> philosophy of the "More Abundant Life" and appealed to all thinking
> Americans to take their stand patriotically on the side of Social Justice
> vs. Human Greed. Acceptance of this philosophy by a majority of
> Americans would afford prompt solution of our economic problems
> and lead the other nations out of the worldwide morass of despair into
> which they have been plunged by the accumulated greed of many
> generations. It is too much to expect but a tremendously significant step
> has been taken by the president. For the first time in history the head of a
> great nation has frankly declared that government must be operated on
> the premise that civilization's progress is measured in terms of spiritual
> rather than material values.
>
> The philosophy of the "More Abundant Life" says that greed has
> been responsible for most of mankind's troubles. It has caused all the
> wars and misunderstandings that have developed between nations. It
> has even been the motive force in the quarrels and strife among
> individuals. For ages and ages it has blocked the way to a more abundant
> life for all the peoples of all nations. Now the president of this country
> with great courage and greater vision proposes that thinking Americans
> of all creeds join with government in a collective war on greed in behalf
> of social justice.
>
> It is possible that Franklin D. Roosevelt in his effort to solve the
> nation's economic problems also has given a timely reinterpretation to
> the philosophy of the Man of Galilee. "I am my brother's keeper," said

the Man of Galilee. That is the essence of Roosevelt's philosophy, "the kingdom of heaven is within you." That is what the president meant last night when he declared that in this new era church and state are demanding the same objective—a more abundant life for every man and woman and child in this country. In effect he appealed to the churches to leave off their discussion and dissensions regarding theories of the life that now is more abundant for every human being. The real message of the Man of Galilee was that of brotherly love; his mission was to make life more abundant. After two thousand years the attention of the world's greatest nation is dramatically focused on that simple philosophy, which is at once the salvation and preservation of the race.

Pulliam was convinced that something had to be done in such a drastic emergency and defended the New Deal as a better-than-nothing sort of proposition.

The price of our present "spending spree," high though it may be, is exceedingly low when you consider the cost of further inaction would have been complete collapse of the nation's financial and industrial structure....And that collapse probably would have involved our social and political foundations. We are actually on the road back to recovery now.... Had Roosevelt not acted, the American social order as we know it would have been on the way out.

Yet there were lurking doubts that would grow greater as the decade went on. He soon realized that the New Deal idea of massive government intervention in the economy was not a temporary but a permanent innovation. But in 1934, he was unable to pinpoint the problem.

But somehow we feel convinced that the spirit of American individualism on which this country was built and developed has been dealt a tragic blow in the economic upheaval of the last four years.

Despite his doubts, he defended Roosevelt against many of the charges that came from conservatives, for example that the president was a "Red."

As a matter of truth, Mr. Roosevelt is by inheritance and at heart a conservative with liberal impulses. His is a typical American leadership of the highest order and while he is the leader, this country will not "go" fascist or communistic. We don't agree with a lot of the Roosevelt experiments, but we vigorously resent the implications that he wants to wave a red flag or wear a black shirt.

He let fly at a Republican critic of government welfare in his front-page column, which he was calling the Uncongressional Record in 1934.

In opposing President Roosevelt's program for drought and unemployment relief Congressman Taber, a silk-stocking Republican from New York, declared that the government is now supporting more than five million families. "We must stop this wholesale relief and present a program for the revival of business," Taber shouted on the floor of the house, In the meantime, while business is being revived, what about the five million families? Does the smug Mr. Taber believe the country would be better off simply to allow these five million families to starve and thus solve the unemployment problem? Fortunately for the future progress of organized society we are permanently committed in this nation to the principle that human rights are above private rights. Unfortunate people are not going to starve while it is humanly possible for government to afford them subsistence even though taxes may be doubled or trebled, Mr. Taber and all his conservative cohorts to the contrary notwithstanding.

He was also finding the Republicans in Indiana too negative during the New Deal era. The state platform in 1934, for example, had the same weakness he discovered in the national party.

The Republican attack on the various alphabetical relief agencies calls pertinent attention to the terrific cost of federal relief but suggests no other way of caring for the millions of unemployed.

In Indianapolis, a Democrat, Governor Paul McNutt, was willing to take the sort of emergency measures Pulliam wanted to see. Elected in 1932, McNutt's key adviser was Logansport lawyer Frank McHale, who later became Pulliam's closest friend in Indiana politics. With McHale at his side and an overwhelming majority in the state legislature, McNutt started a massive reorganization of the state government, introduced new relief and old-age pension measures, and obtained approval for the state's first gross income tax. He built a powerful political machine for himself, with the "two percent club" requiring state employees to contribute to the party, and a beer-liquor distribution scheme that Pulliam would challenge after World War II when the Republicans took over the state government. Out of step with Republican editorial writers in the rest of Indiana, Pulliam praised McNutt in editorials and letters. He was pleased with McNutt's choice for the 1934 U.S. Senate race, Sherman Minton, calling him a "splendid choice" in the *Reporter*.

Our sincere and heartfelt congratulations to Governor Paul McNutt. If there was any doubt as to who was the boss of the Democratic party in Indiana the state convention removed it. The nomination of Sherman Minton for United States senator was not only a fine tribute to the very excellent gentleman from Albany but it was a convincing vote of confidence in the leadership of Governor McNutt. Pleas Greenlee, the governor's man Farley, organized and piloted the Minton campaign. That Minton was able to win so easily significantly shows how completely the McNutt forces dominated the convention. As a result of this convention the governor's national star is shining with new brightness.

Minton went on to lead Roosevelt's unsuccessful effort to pack the U.S. Supreme Court with his own appointees in 1937 and was later named to the Supreme Court by Truman.

McNutt continued to dominate state politics in 1936; his choice to succeed him, Clifford Townsend, won the Democratic nomination and the election in the fall.

McNutt, who could serve only one term as governor, was appointed high commissioner of the Philippines by Roosevelt. Some McNutt supporters thought it was an attempt to get him out of the country should FDR decide to run for a third term in 1940. At any rate, he resigned and started testing the waters for a presidential run in 1938, aided by McHale and fundraiser Frank McKinney. Pulliam helped the campaign with his contacts in various states, including Florida, Georgia, and Oklahoma, but Roosevelt went for his third term. The decision kept another Hoosier out of the White House in the fall election, Republican Wendell Willkie. It was a bad year for Indiana. Pulliam later recalled:

I knew Paul McNutt very well. He was not a New Dealer and he didn't believe in Roosevelt's policies, except he almost had to politically. He was a very ambitious man. He had the nomination for vice president

sewed up, and if he had had the personal courage he would have been
president when Truman was, but Roosevelt called him and told him he
wanted Henry Wallace as his running mate again and wanted McNutt
to be the first secretary of Health, Education, and Welfare. Later he sent
him to the Philippines, but it was really the end of Paul's career.

He was elected governor overwhelmingly, but the disappointment
about the presidency did something peculiar to him mentally. He was
never the same man again. . . . But he was really a good governor and a
very able man. He was dean of the Indiana Law School and was one of
the most interesting men I've ever known in Indiana. We were good
friends except for a few things about which we didn't agree. But I wish
we had a lot more like him in public life today. Of course you know that
Franklin Roosevelt could get any politician to do anything he wanted
him to do—that is, practically anything. That was Paul's undoing.

He was now developing greater doubts about Roosevelt's New
Deal. Like many Bull Moosers, he went back and forth on the New
Deal. The New Deal program in some respects was consistent with
an extension of some of the Bull Moose principles, but Roosevelt's
style was distasteful to him, with the emphasis on patronage and the
big-city machines. The spending seemed to be getting out of hand.

On the whole the New Deal has been a blessing and a benefit to the
nation, but the reckless, wasteful expenditure of federal funds is
beginning to defeat the New Deal.

Was the New Deal just a series of emergency measures, or was it a
whole new concept, permanent planning by the central
government? Roosevelt himself was not a consistent enough thinker
to settle that issue. But Pulliam did not like the trend. The National
Recovery Act, he thought, was no longer needed and had outlived its
usefulness by 1935.

The people have come to the conclusion that after all government
officials don't know very much about business, and the more they
interfere with business the worse off it is.

The bureaucracy often did not work, regardless of good
intentions. He wrote about giving a ride to a poor boy and, hearing
his sad story, trying to get him into a state Civilian Conservation
Corps program. But because both parents were dead, Pulliam
learned, the boy wasn't allowed into the program.

Of course the CCC officer could not break the rules, but if that boy turns out to be a gangster, the cockeyed regulations of the relief program will be largely to blame.

Pulliam did not know where to turn. He wrote of his uncertainty about Roosevelt in his column.

The inspiring quality of President Roosevelt's golden voice was never more strikingly manifest than in his Green Bay radio speech. No American ever has shown such ability to reach the hearts of American citizens. The president sells himself personally even to persons who do not approve of the New Deal. There is almost unanimous confidence in his sincerity and honesty of purpose. The last paragraph of his Green Bay speech was a clarion call of almost utopian idealism. To a dreamer his speech is milk and honey, even thrilling. To a practical mind it seems he doesn't realize America, with all its benevolent liberalism, is not prepared for the leveling processes of his program. He may be a great prophet, living years ahead of his times. Who knows?

When Republicans were looking for leadership, the name of Ogden Mills, Hoover's secretary of the treasury, was suggested, and Pulliam stated his opposition:

Ogden Mills typifies the arrogance of the conservative East that has ridden the Republican saddle for so many years. . . . In their minds the might of money gives them the right to rule.

He had no place to turn. In 1936 he could not get enthusiastic about Alf Landon, despite his Kansas background, and it was clear Landon wasn't going to win anyway. He was becoming fed up with Roosevelt, though. He wrote his father:

With thirteen million unemployed people in the country, I am wondering just how Mr. Roosevelt looks at Hoover as he thinks back over the days gone by. . . . I realize that Roosevelt would like to be God, but he just isn't, that's all, and never will be. He never made a dollar in his life; he doesn't know the relation between earned dollars and success; he has a spoiled rich man's attitude toward people who do succeed; and he's petulant besides. At heart I know he would like to help the underdog and the underprivileged, but he has experimented with everything under the sun and now he's mad at business and is pouting and will not give business a chance to go to bar and bring the country out of the doldrums. . . . Conditions really are far worse than they were during Hoover's regime. There are more unemployed and less confidence in government and in the stability of things generally than there were at any time during Hoover's time. This country would be on the road to unusual prosperity within six months if Roosevelt would simply definitely and firmly say that he is going to quit harassing business every time it made a foot of progress. I am not against his taxation program; I am not against his idea of taking care of underprivileged people; I am not against his feeding the starving—although there has never been anybody starved in this country—but when it comes to punitive legislation and dictatorial powers which he wants vested in himself so that he can spank people that he doesn't like, then I am off of him and I am sure that the American people are getting off of him rapidly.

In 1940 a new figure arrived on the Republican scene. Wendell Willkie was a poor boy who became a successful businessman. He understood the problems of business, Pulliam thought, in contrast to Roosevelt. Willkie had vision. He was not just against every idea that the Democrats proposed—the trouble with so many Republicans. Willkie was an amateur, not one of the professional politicians like Roosevelt, who seemed to seek his own benefit first in politics.

Pulliam helped Willkie's preconvention campaign, advising him about the Indiana, Oklahoma, Arkansas delegations and holding a luncheon in May in Indianapolis for him. Excited by Willkie's dramatic nomination at the Republican convention, he telegraphed him to say:

> It is too marvelous to believe and the most significant American incident since Lincoln's nomination.... Regret I had to leave Philadelphia before offering personal congratulations. Now for heaven's sake keep your amateur standing and don't let them make a professional candidate out of you as they did Hughes and Landon.

Willkie gave Roosevelt the biggest challenge Roosevelt had faced, but he could not beat him. Willkie remained Pulliam's new hope for liberal or moderate Republicanism until his untimely death in 1944.

15

Radio

IN THE 1930s a new field was opening up. Radio broadcasting had developed slowly in the 1920s, and Pulliam noted its potential, especially as a news medium. Newspapers were his first love, but if radio was the wave of the future, he wanted to be in on it. He was unloading his newspapers in Oklahoma, and had always been interested in Indianapolis. In 1936 a small radio station, WIRE, was going up for sale, and he saw his chance to get a foot in the door in Indianapolis.

WIRE was the smallest station in Indianapolis, behind WFBM, owned by the Indianapolis Power & Light Company. He bought it from a Chicago man, W.E. Vogelback, for $340,000, using the capital from the sale of the Oklahoma newspapers and their outstanding bonds, and borrowing money. He started on expansion soon after he bought the station, putting $80,000 into a new radio transmitter and plant in 1938. He poured $75,000 more into studios in 1940. Messages of congratulations poured in for the special opening ceremonies, from President Roosevelt, Herbert Hoover, Vice President Henry Wallace and Republican presidential candidate Wendell Willkie. He quickly made WIRE into the biggest station in Indiana and one of the leading stations in the Midwest. The *Indianapolis News*, which Pulliam bought eight years later, offered tribute to WIRE's success.

> The countrywide attention which is being given today to the opening of WIRE's new home is well deserved. Under the leadership of Eugene C. Pulliam, president of Indianapolis Broadcasting, Inc., which owns the station, WIRE has become a community institution and added greatly to the prestige of the state.

The station's national standing is demonstrated by the coming to Indianapolis for the opening ceremonies of some of the most prominent men in radio. They have shown a growing interest in WIRE as its sphere of influence and range of service have been expanded.

His son, Gene, Jr., left a United Press career to beef up WIRE's news program. He had been a history major at DePauw, president of the Sigma Delta Chi chapter, editor of the school yearbook and had joined the United Press bureau in Chicago after his graduation in 1935. He had considered heading to the Far East, in hopes of landing a position as a foreign correspondent. It was an idea that his father suggested could be interesting but not as romantic as it might appear:

Your suggestion about the Far East and other interesting ports is alluring, but it takes a real constitution to stand the food and the climate in the Orient. Also I doubt if you could get a job—just like that—because there are usually more Journalists of Fortune in such places as there are jobs—I may be mistaken. My advice would be, being a conservative, to write about a dozen foreign papers in the East [Orient] applying for a job before you try the trip. Find out in advance what the chances are, then if you want to shoot at the moon, go ahead. Just remember though that any phenomenally fast jump upward involves the danger of a headlong plunge downward.

Gene, Jr. stayed with the UP in Detroit, Buffalo, and Rochester before joining his father at WIRE. They would form an effective team. The elder Pulliam led the way, buying newspapers, barging into Indiana Republican politics after World War II, stirring up controversy wherever he went with his blunt, outspoken manner. The younger Pulliam was more like his mother, Myrta, steady, consistent, not given to emotional outbursts or hasty decisions like his father. The son would smooth over some of his father's rough edges in the community and among employees.

When Pulliam bought WIRE, it had 1,000 watts of day power, 500 at night. By 1940, he had increased the power to 5,000, day and night. He affiliated with the NBC Red Network and Blue Network, as well as Mutual Broadcasting System, at a time when a station could have more than one affiliate. He liked to fight with the networks, cancel a program if another network had a better show. By 1941 he had become president of Network Affiliates Inc., representing independent stations.

Pulliam rarely did anything halfheartedly. Radio was no exception. He started another station in Vincennes, WAOV, where he already owned the *Sun-Commercial*. He bought a partial interest in a Richmond, Indiana, station, and bought part of another station in Phoenix, Arizona, where he liked to vacation.

In the meantime, his family life had fallen apart. There had been long periods of separation from "Mattie," as he called his wife, Martha, during the depression, when he spent so much time traveling, buying and selling newspapers. She and the three children, Gene, Jr., Corinne, and Suzanne, had moved to Oklahoma City with him in 1929 for a few months, but they returned the next year. While he traveled with Marsh and tried to build a newspaper empire, she cared for his family back in Lebanon, including his aging father, their children, and his wide range of relatives who had moved from Kansas.

He had a secretary, Nina Mason, the daughter of a Monroe County naturalist. She came from a talented, literary family that included three sisters: Miriam E. Mason, who wrote children's books; Rachel Peden, who later wrote a popular daily column on farm life for the *Indianapolis Star;* and Josephine Mason, who would be editor of the *Arizona Republic* Sunday magazine. After college, Nina worked for *Farm Life* magazine and then came to Lebanon as Pulliam's secretary. She became a tremendous asset to his work, a shrewd businesswoman and a key partner in the Oklahoma and General newspaper purchases.

To Pulliam, life was business. When he wrapped his life up in business during the depression, he lost touch with his family. He could be thoughtless when he wanted something—and now he wanted to marry Nina.

He divorced Martha in 1941 and married Nina. "Mattie," or "Nana," to her grandchildren, became the matriarch of his family after World War II, as their three children, Gene, Jr., Corinne, and Suzanne, started giving them grandchildren. The family came to Lebanon for Thanksgiving each year and she took care of the grandchildren during the summers. Nana would be the stable one his ten grandchildren turned to for advice and help, especially during some of their turbulent and confusing teenage years. She also became publisher of the *Lebanon Reporter* after the war, buying it from Pulliam over a period of years.

Nina was already one of the top figures in the Pulliam organization. She was to be his traveling companion around the world after the war, author of a book on Australia, the head of his organization after he died, and one of the leading newspaperwomen in the United States. She was also the first woman to be admitted to Sigma Delta Chi, the organization he had helped start at DePauw. He liked to tell how she had run the organization when he had a spinal fusion in 1941.

> As a matter of fact, one time when I was in the hospital for eight months with a spinal fusion she ran the radio station and our newspapers and we made more money than we ever did before.
>
> I thought I should have remained incapacitated.

Ultimately, she was his principal helpmate.

> The most important person in my life of course has been Nina. She has really been a tower of strength in a business capacity. As Jim Rogan [Indianapolis bank executive] once said, "Nina Pulliam is the best businessman in Indianapolis."

16

World War II

GENE PULLIAM HAD never joined in the isolationist cries between the wars. He wrote few editorials and columns on international affairs, though in 1936 he did travel to Hawaii and predicted that Japan would attack the United States. He wrote critically of the isolationists who kept the United States out of the League of Nations but at times sounded like a naive idealist on the subject of international affairs. Writing about Hitler and Germany's growing air power, he noted:

> How absurd it is that man with his unbelievable opportunities for making life happy and rich should devote his major energies to devising ways and means of killing off the race. If all the effort that is expended on war were directed toward peace and plenty the millennium would be so close you could smell the fragrance of it by tomorrow morning.

In the late 1930s, however, he could see that war was coming. In 1941 he started putting together the Indiana Defense Savings Committee, and had it in operation a month before Pearl Harbor. He made good use of his experience in World War I under Will H. Hays, later president of Motion Pictures Producers and Distributors of America, who had run the Indiana Liberty Loan drive.

After Pearl Harbor, Pulliam quickly set up the nation's first statewide defense bond rally, January 15, 1942, raising $2 million in bonds, drawing 6,000 to Indianapolis and putting the state far ahead of others in raising money. Tragedy came out of the first rally. He had arranged for Hollywood star Carole Lombard, a native of Fort Wayne, Indiana, to come to the rally and she died in a plane crash on the return flight.

Within a year, Treasury Secretary Henry Morgenthau wanted to unify the bankers and others who were selling war bonds. Pulliam met Morgenthau in June 1943 with the head of the Indiana Bankers' Victory Fund Committee, Dwight Peterson. Pulliam emerged as chairman of the new War Finance Committee, and Peterson was named vice chairman, handling the financing staff. Pulliam was the promoter, traveling over the state, making two or three speeches some days, recruiting old friends from newspaper work to organize local committees. "He was a great salesman," Peterson said. "He knew someone everywhere." Indiana was constantly exceeding its quota in each drive, ranging up to 193 percent above the quota during the eighth drive.

He would tell Republican audiences:

> You people know that I am a Republican, but I want to say to you here tonight that there is only one commander-in-chief in this country and he is Franklin Delano Roosevelt...This is our war. This is our America. Indiana has never failed.

But because of his combative side, he wound up in several controversies.

A CBS reporter, Cecil Brown, came to Indiana in May 1942 and broadcast internationally that

> Everyone I've talked to here says the people of Indiana don't know there is a war going on.

CBS "World Today" was not broadcast in Indianapolis, but Will Hays heard it in New York City and called Pulliam, who quickly let loose at Brown:

> What is patriotism? Shouting in the streets? Or buying bonds, volunteering and producing war materials twenty-four hours a day? I don't know to whom Mr. Brown could've been talking to here, unless he was talking to himself in a hotel room.

Another time three Treasury Department officials came from Washington, investigating the background of Willis Connor, his deputy, who had a fight in high school with the principal. Pulliam could not restrain himself—a war was on.

I had some reputation in the state. At least I was no crook. So I told them off. They said we've got a job to do. So I said you've got the job of getting the hell out of here and onto the next train or I'm going to have you arrested.

"What for?"

"For impeding justice and interfering with the war work."

I called Morgenthau and said, "Three of your stooges are out here making life miserable for this guy."

Morgenthau ordered them to leave. I threatened to quit if it happened again. I was in an independent position, backed by the banks. They had lent guys to us. We were setting records and developed a payroll savings plan.

This instinct for a good fight, his bluntness, made him realize he could never make it in public service. He had job offers from the Treasury Department after the war, from Fred Vinson, who later became chief justice of the Supreme Court. He turned them down, later noting that,

I wouldn't have lasted thirty days. I'd tell all the bankers to go to hell. They wouldn't take a two percent cut on war bonds.

He was not writing a column anymore. He and Nina lived in Indianapolis, in a home in a north side suburban area. His net worth in 1939 was $403,000. He still had WIRE and a few newspapers in Indiana, Vincennes, Lebanon, Huntington. He was also checking periodically on a possible purchase of the *Indianapolis Star.*

The founders of Sigma Delta Chi
journalism fraternity. Left to right,
Leroy H. Millikan, Eugene Pulliam,
Lawrence H. Sloan, and Paul M.
Reddick. Taken at a DePauw
alumni meeting in 1934.

Gene Pulliam, probably 1929.

Gene Pulliam with Carole Lombard,
January 1942, shortly before her
death.

Gene Pulliam in 1943. Blackstone
Studios portrait.

Gene Pulliam in 1945, with Ann
Sheridan and Will Hays, right, who
came to Indianapolis to promote war
bonds.

Pulliam was executive chairman of
Indiana's Defense Savings staff. At
left is Charles E. Hoover; at right is
Wray E. Fleming. 1942 photo.

A 1948 *Indianapolis Star* party.
Left is *Star* managing editor
Robert Early.

Republican politics in 1945. From
left, Indiana Governor Ralph F.
Gates, National GOP Chairman
Herbert Brownell, radio executive
Joseph Bryant, and Gene Pulliam.

The publisher meets the presidential
hopeful in 1949 in Indianapolis.

Gene and Nina Pulliam, off to the Korean front in 1951, in an Air Force C-54 that was forced to turn back.

A rare plunge into politics for
publisher Gene Pulliam in 1952.

A Pan Am publicity photo. The
Pulliams were lining up a Latin
American trip in 1950.

Pulliam with William Glenn, a
Sigma Delta Chi founder, in 1959.

The publisher at his spotless desk
in 1950.

Attending Sigma Delta Chi's fiftieth
anniversary at DePauw University
in 1959. Left to right, Bernard
Kilgore, president of the *Wall Street
Journal*; Gene Pulliam; Laurence P.
Scott, publisher of the *Manchester
Guardian*.

Pulliam greets Vice President
Richard Nixon, who attended the
SDX fiftieth anniversary in 1959.

Pulliam conversing with Senator
Barry Goldwater, 1960.

Pulliam with Senator Lyndon
Johnson, May, 1960.

Senator Barry Goldwater and Gene
Pulliam share a moment on a platform in 1962.

President Johnson and a bemused
publisher, 1966.

**Gene Pulliam with Vice President
Hubert Humphrey and Indiana
Governor Roger Branigin in 1967.**

Lunch at the Indianapolis Athletic
Club with former Prime Minister
Harold Macmillan, left, and *Chicago
Tribune* editor Donald Maxwell,
right. Macmillan had made a major
address at DePauw the previous
evening. 1968 photo.

Patriarch Gene Pulliam with Joan
Young, daughter of a *News*
photographer, at annual staff
picnic, 1970.

1972 portrait.

Eugene C. Pulliam 1889-1975

Part II

The Publisher

17

Buying the Star

THE *INDIANAPOLIS STAR* was the only morning newspaper in Indianapolis, a sure moneymaker except during the depression. It belonged to John Shaffer, who owned a number of other newspapers, the *Chicago Evening Post*, the *Louisville Herald*, the *Denver Times* and the *Denver Republican*. Shaffer died during World War II, and potential buyers quickly started talking to the trustees of his estate, which included the *Muncie Star* and the *Indianapolis Star*.

The Fairbanks family, which already owned the bigger and better afternoon *Indianapolis News*, was interested. George Ball, the Muncie industrialist and jarmaker, already had preferred stock in the *Star* and started checking into buying a controlling interest. The heavyweights in the newspaper industry wanted it badly. Roy Howard, head of the Scripps-Howard newspaper chain, already owned the afternoon *Indianapolis Times*, and a morning-evening combination with the *Star* would save money and put the chain in a stronger position to challenge the *News*. Howard also had a sentimental interest in the *Star*. He had been its first sports editor. Samuel I. Newhouse, who already had a chain of newspapers, was interested, as was Marshall Field, the department store heir who already owned the *Chicago Daily News*. Colonel Robert McCormick, publisher of the *Chicago Tribune*, thought he might extend his conservative influence down into Indiana by buying the *Star*. And the Cowles brothers, who already had *Look* magazine and newspapers in Des Moines, Iowa, and Minneapolis, Minnesota, were potential buyers as well.

Pulliam had never faced this sort of competition, but he had learned some lessons. He did his homework better than the competition. And he was willing to gamble.

The *Star* was nearly $1 million in debt, including outstanding bonds from the depression years. The trustees of the Shaffer estate were demanding that any prospective owner assume the debts, and the Ball family, with the preferred stock, would take the first five percent of the profits. A war was still on, with no guarantee that prosperity would follow. Newsprint was scarce, and an invasion and conquest of Japan might take several years.

Pulliam was willing to gamble again. A morning paper in a large city was his dream—the fact that it was named the *Star* added to the appeal. It reminded him of his hero, W.R. Nelson, and his *Kansas City Star*.

He borrowed $1 million from the Jefferson Standard Life Insurance Company in North Carolina. His Oklahoma record of paying off bonds when no one else did helped him get the loan from the company, which specialized in newspaper financing. The price of the *Star* ultimately came to $2.35 million, including $715,490 worth of outstanding bonds.

Overnight, he had become a major publisher. *Time* magazine called him the "Hoosier Dark Horse," because he had been overshadowed by the other big names in the newspaper industry in the competition. Buying the *Star* was risky. "He had steel guts," commented Charles Brownson, later an Indianapolis congressman. "There were a lot of wolves waiting for him to stub his toe."

The *Star* was the number three newspaper in town, behind the *News* and the *Times*, both afternoon newspapers. The *News* was still considered the best paper, although it was beginning to slip. It had a glorious history, a Pulitzer Prize in 1932, and a reputation as one of the leading newspapers in the Midwest. In 1944 its circulation was well ahead of the *Star*, 156,000 to 130,000.

Pulliam was eager to compete with the Fairbanks family and the *News*. Mark Ferree, then the advertising manager of the *Indianapolis Times*, thought he resented the Fairbanks because of their differences in social background.

> The Fairbanks, they were an old-line family, aristocratic, and he resented them. Warren [Fairbanks—*News* publisher in the 1930s] wouldn't give Gene the time of day; he was above him, aloof and removed, stuffy.

The *Times* was also considered a better newspaper than the *Star* and ran ahead of the morning paper in circulation within Marion County, despite competition from the *News* in the afternoon.

All that changed in four short years after Pulliam bought the *Star*. "He made the town a hell of a lot livelier," said Fremont Power, then a reporter for the *News*. "Before that the policy of both papers seemed to be, don't make anybody mad about anything." The *Star* had been primarily a businessman's newspaper. Pulliam started women's pages, challenging the theory that women would only read afternoon newspapers. He started a magazine in the Sunday newspaper, beefed up the sports section, added columns on the editorial pages, and brought in more national and international news.

His personal style was a contrast to Shaffer's. "Shaffer had owned several papers, but he was primarily a utilities operator and not too interested in the paper except for money," recalled a *Star* reporter at the time, Lowell Parker, who later went to Pulliam's *Arizona Republic*. "Gene changed that, he livened it up and allowed more money to be spent. We started covering stories around the state." Pulliam made himself the editor as well as the publisher, and, for the first time since the 1920s, started spending a great deal of time on one newspaper. "You could bring up complaints with him, go to his house in the evening. He seemed accessible," recalled Al McCord, who was covering City Hall for the *Star* when Pulliam bought the paper. "I'll run a newspaper, not be a damned art collector," he would tell the staff at meetings, in reference to Shaffer's interest in art.

He eliminated Shaffer's list of people and institutions that could not be criticized in the newspaper. "We felt freer. We found there weren't any sacred cows," McCord said. He recalled a story he was writing, before Pulliam bought the paper, that Mayor Robert Tyndall did not like. "Tyndall called someone at the Chamber of Commerce, who called Ben Lawrence, *Star* publisher, and the story was killed." The *Star* now became an exciting place to work. Charles Griffo, then a reporter and later an assistant managing editor, was surprised at the personal interchanges the staff had with Pulliam:

> He'd have a lot of contact with us then. He'd call guys on bylines, chew them out. He'd have dinner meetings for the staff at his house, ask about

problems. He was great with tips on stories. He was an unusual publisher—instead of being a figurehead or being at the country club, he was involved.

He also boosted staff morale with a series of measures that would not become common in the industry for years. He set up a pension plan, medical insurance, life insurance, a Christmas bonus—and began planning an employee recreation area.

Pulliam played an active day-to-day role in the news coverage in his first few years with the *Star*. He wrote editorials, taking on a wide range of opponents—the state Republican party, the briefly reborn Ku Klux Klan, the Columbians. "They were very gutsy about printing stories," said Fremont Power, who was at the *News*. "For the first time in Indianapolis in my memory, people were being challenged. The *Times* would go through the motions of doing this, but they weren't strong enough to really put it off. And they got intimidated by advertisers."

The Klan controversy started with *Star* stories on its revival in sixty of Indiana's ninety-two counties. State Republican officials, who would balk at Pulliam's efforts to reform their own affairs, were quick to jump on his side on the Klan issue, which had hurt the Republicans so badly after the 1920s.

The *Star*'s front-page editorial mocked the Klan revival:

> The "King Kleagle" of the Indiana Ku Klux Klan, a division of the "Association of Georgia Klans, Invisible Empire, Knights of the Ku Klux Klan," had already made up his sucker list. Are you on it? He's offering 121,000 secret nightshirts at $10 apiece. That's $1.21 million of easy money—if you give it to him.
>
> Is it really possible that there are still some Hoosiers left who are gullible enough to fall for the mumbo-jumbo of this brazen membership racket? Can there still be intelligent Indiana citizens who will believe the appeals to prejudice, the "white supremacy" nonsense, or the fantastic claim that men in hooded nightshirts burning fiery crosses are needed to "protect" our people from the dangers of Catholics, Jews, and Negroes? If there are really 121,000 Hoosiers silly enough to contribute $10 for a "Klecktokon," or membership in this Georgia-spawned monstrosity, there are a lot of people who have forgotten the experiences of a generation ago.
>
> This is the same old Klan. The "King Kleagle" says he's been a member for twenty-four years. He and the "secret five" are trying to dress up the old hag in a "streamlined" nightshirt. But look at their program.

It's the same old stuff—threats of fear and appeals to hate and ignorance. They've got the same ridiculous titles, the same discredited Georgia leadership, and best of all, friends, the same membership fee—$10.

The Klan stories and editorials, which also ran in Pulliam's recently acquired *Muncie Star,* brought an odd accusation from the *X-Ray,* a taxpayers' newspaper in Muncie, which said the Klan stories appeared in a "Red CIO" newspaper and were part of a "Red Democrat New Deal" plot.

Pulliam's treatment of the Klan was gentle compared to the way he took out after the Republican party in Indiana. He was a surprise to the Republicans because the *Star,* along with the *News,* had always been a Republican newspaper. Neither newspaper had seriously criticized the Republican party in years. Top executives at the *News* were friendly advisers to Republican governor Ralph Gates. Suddenly a major Republican newspaper was castigating the Republican party, in some of the harshest language Pulliam had used since his days in Atchison. The attack on the Republicans started within a few weeks of his purchase of the *Star.* Robert Lyons, a former Klansman, was elected Republican National Committeeman at a state convention in June 1944. Pulliam demanded his resignation in a front-page editorial. Lyons stepped down a few days later under pressure from the *Star* and the *South Bend Tribune.*

Pulliam was bent on reforming the Republican party in Indianapolis and Indiana. It was an uphill battle all the way, one he never fully won. What looked like sin of the worst sort to him was just normal business to Indiana politicians. Pulliam believed in separating political spoils and governmental administration and regulation. In Indiana, however, with no sense of shame, Republicans and Democrats thought they deserved special rewards for getting in office, rewards like liquor licenses to give their friends and loyal supporters.

By 1945, Pulliam had launched the *Star* upon a massive editorial campaign to take liquor licensing out of the political process, an arrangement that went back to the depression. At that time he had criticized Governor Paul McNutt for setting up the liquor licensing on a political basis, but he was writing only in the *Lebanon Reporter.* Now he was editor and publisher of the state's major morning newspaper. Blasting away with front-page editorials, he was shocking the party regulars and changing the political scene in Indiana. His front-page editorials had the same Methodist revival fervor of his campaigns in Atchison:

> If this racket isn't stopped the Republican party will face scandals far worse than anything that harassed it during the days of Jackson and McCray [governors during the 1920s]. All of it was avoidable. All of it is indefensible. All of it is due to the stupid greedy exploitation of a political racket that contaminates everyone who touches it.

The politicians hated it. Newspapers in Indianapolis had not challenged the political structure so brashly since the early years of the depression, when the *Times* won a Pulitzer Prize for a Klan exposé in 1929 and the *News* series on state government waste won its Pulitzer in 1932.

The *Star* became the newspaper to read. Pulliam gambled rather boldly in attacking the established political powers. But he was also helping the circulation of his newspaper, dramatically bringing it up to and ultimately ahead of the *News*. By the end of 1946 *Star* circulation was 168,000, nearly even with the *News* at 171,000. By the end of the next year, the *Star* had gone past the *News*, 177,392 to 171,000. There had been an unwritten agreement that the *Star* would not challenge the *News* in circulation if the *News* would not start a Sunday newspaper, leaving the Sunday field to the *Star*. With Pulliam, all the old agreements were off. He would be happy to see the *News* start a Sunday newspaper, he said, and liked to tell how he tricked Dick Fairbanks into staying out of the Sunday field.

> I offered Dick Fairbanks, who was the present and last publisher representing the Fairbanks family, of the *News*, $100,000 if he would start a Sunday paper. He didn't believe me. I had Emil Woempner go and get a certified check for $100,000 and offered it to him telling him that it was worth $100,000 to have the *News* start a Sunday paper because six days against six they had the *Star* badly beaten, but seven days against seven with the bulge we had on our Sunday paper, we would be the number one paper in Indianapolis. That was a slight exaggeration, but it worried Dick enough that he never started a Sunday paper.

Pulliam could challenge the *News* partly because the afternoon newspaper was resting on past laurels. It had been the greatest paper in Indianapolis. Started in 1869 by twenty-three-year-old John

Holliday, the *News* had found a place in journalism history by reprinting a *New York World* series on the United States purchase of the Panama Canal, drawing an unsuccessful libel suit from President Theodore Roosevelt.

The *News* had been owned by the family of Vice President Charles Warren Fairbanks, whose three sons were the publishers from 1921 to 1944. By the end of World War II the Fairbanks heirs could no longer unite around a single approach to the newspaper. The division in the family and the desire for dividends without regard to the quality of the newspaper made the *News* vulnerable to a challenge from an independent morning newspaper. The *News* lost a valuable newsprint contract, and with uncertain management, could not cope with the aggressive editorial stance of the *Star*. Wendell Phillippi, who later became managing editor of the *News*, recalled:

> The Fairbanks weren't interested in the paper. They just wanted money for trips. They had pitiful pay scales. Inertia had set in. The *Star* went after Gates, but [managing editor C. Walter] McCarty was a friend of Gates and Tyndall was mayor—McCarty was friendly with him. We couldn't use bad stories on either administration. The old *News* was just standing still.

Before long it was for sale.

The *News* was an attractive property, an afternoon newspaper with a good reputation and a strong tradition. The Cowles family was interested. So was Samuel I. Newhouse. John Knight, who built up Knight newspapers into a major chain, was interested. Roy Howard and Gene Pulliam were too.

As serious negotiations started in 1948, it became Howard against Pulliam. The others were from out of town. Howard had been born in Indianapolis, carried an *Indianapolis Times* route, was the first sports editor of the *Star*, had been a high school correspondent for the *News*, and still kept an interest in the city through the *Times*. Pulliam had lived in Indianapolis since he bought WIRE ten years before, and he had lived in the state since 1915. Pulliam and Howard were the last of a special breed of newspaper publisher that soon passed away, the self-made man who worked his way out of poverty and managed to start or buy his own newspapers.

With the *News*, Howard could merge the *Indianapolis Times*, a weaker afternoon newspaper with a circulation of only about 95,000. Pulliam, however, could merge the *Star* and *News* to set up a dominant morning-evening combination.

Howard wanted more than he could get, and Pulliam walked away with the prize. Howard wanted all of the *News*, but the Fairbanks wanted to keep a financial interest. Pulliam's lawyer, Kurt Pantzer, worked out long-term bonds that were attractive to the Fairbanks family, giving Pulliam the edge he needed in the negotiations. "It was the most brilliant deal I've ever done," Pantzer said, a Harvard Law School graduate and senior partner in one of the most prestigious Indianapolis law firms, Barnes, Hickam, Pantzer and Boyd.

Pulliam kept Pantzer as his newspaper lawyer, occasionally getting complaints from his staff that Pantzer was at times abrasive and arrogant. "I didn't hire him for his personality," Pulliam liked to explain.

Pantzer knew Pulliam could also be abrasive. "Gene could fight with anyone," he recalled. "When he became angry with a person, he'd call him a son of a bitch, which I must confess the person usually was."

The sale, which was technically a merger, cost Pulliam $4 million. The Fairbanks kept one-third of the stock of Indianapolis Newspapers, Inc., the product of the merger, as well as the long-term bonds.

Pulliam's empire was established. Two years earlier he had bought the *Arizona Republic* and *Phoenix Gazette,* and in Indiana the *Muncie Evening Press.* From earlier years, he had the *Huntington Herald-Press,* and the *Vincennes Sun-Commercial.* Now he had the *Indianapolis News.* It was the fifty-first and last newspaper he ever bought.

18

Postwar Politics

GENE PULLIAM WAS a man without a comfortable political home during and after World War II. He didn't like Roosevelt's Democratic party and its commitment to a permanent New Deal. The Democrats appeared to be on the road to bigger and bigger government. In the Indiana Republican party, Pulliam was out of step with the isolationists who dominated the party, and who had opposed American involvement in World War II until Pearl Harbor. After the war, the isolationists were still opposed to heavy American commitments overseas, as demonstrated by one of their slogans, "America First." The internationalists, on the other hand, argued that the United States had grown into a major power and had to be involved in world affairs. There was the Marshall Plan to rebuild Europe, the United Nations, the new threat of communism. The internationalists carried the day, through the postwar bipartisan foreign policy that emerged with Truman, and Republicans like Senator Arthur Vandenberg of Michigan.

Pulliam concluded that only the Republicans could halt the trend toward big government and socialism. But the Republicans needed a positive program as an alternative to the New Deal. He thought the conservative Republicans like Ohio's Robert Taft were too negative.

Wendell Willkie had fulfilled Pulliam's expectations in 1940, but he had not been able to beat Roosevelt. Willkie tried again in 1944, but he was still out of favor with the party regulars, lost the Wisconsin primary and never got near the nomination.

Despite Willkie's poor showing in 1944, Pulliam still looked to him as the man who could lead the Republicans out of the wilderness. Willkie was toying with the idea of a third, liberal party, perhaps in some sort of coalition with liberal Democrats. Pulliam urged Willkie to stay in the Republican party, bide his time and wait for 1948. "You may be ahead of your time," he wrote Willkie after the 1944 primaries. "You are the outstanding liberal leader of America." He urged him to endorse the Republican nominee, Thomas Dewey, and keep his standing in the party. Pulliam had been young and idealistic once and he had seen third-party movements before, and it had not worked in 1912. He wrote Willkie shortly after they met in New York, trying to help him plot his political future, but within the Republican party.

> Since our breakfast chat at your home the other morning I've been thinking a great deal about your situation and your opportunity in the present campaign. I am more convinced than ever that you have a decision to make which should be made promptly and decisively. There are several things you should take into serious account as you give consideration to your decision.
>
> One. You are the outstanding liberal leader of America, and Indiana's most distinguished son. You are destined eventually to lead the liberal element of American citizenship in political action, but you could very easily lose the support of a great segment of this liberal element by remaining on the sidelines during the next sixty days.
>
> Two. You may be ahead of your time now, but you will not be in 1948; therefore, it especially behooves you to keep a firm grip as the leader of liberal thought in America, and for the present it is necessary for you to maintain this leadership within the framework of one of the two parties. The Democratic party is out of the question for you with the Roosevelt domination; therefore, there is one other place for you at the present time, and that is in the Republican party.
>
> Three. Under no circumstance can you afford to let the impression be created that you are a bad loser or that you are sulking. The history of America shows that the American people lose interest and confidence in a man who sulks. I know you are not sulking, but you cannot afford to create that impression anywhere in this country.
>
> Four. By coming out decisively and definitely for Dewey within the next two or three weeks you will force the Republican party to follow your leadership on so many questions which are dear to your heart, and I am sure that you owe it to yourself and to the people who believe in you to do this.

Five. Again I want to urge you to come to Indiana and make the greatest speech you ever made in your life. We will organize a meeting that will be the top political meeting of this nation for you. I can arrange an NBC coast-to-coast broadcast for you, and it is the thing for you to do and to do without too much delay.

When your plans are completed as to your trip to Indiana, won't you either call me or wire me so that I can make definite arrangements to be in the state. I have several pressing matters in connection with this War Bond campaign which may take me to Washington, but I do want to be here when you come out.

Willkie responded:

I cannot tell you how much I appreciate the concern and the kindness with which you have given me your opinion. I hope to be out to Indiana before long.

He never got there. Herbert Brownell, the manager of Dewey's campaign and later attorney general under Eisenhower, said Willkie was ready to do the broadcast suggested by Pulliam, but he suffered a heart attack and died October 7. His secretary, Helen Tucker, wrote Pulliam after Willkie was hospitalized, telling him that Willkie expected to be out of it in two weeks:

In conversation with him this morning, he mentioned that he hoped you had a chance to read his article in the September 16th issue of *Collier's.*

In that article, "Cowardice at Chicago," Willkie had complained about how both parties compromised with "reactionary" elements within the parties, telling the Republican party that its future would depend on whether "it had the courage and wisdom to be a party not of expediency but of principle."

Pulliam was never as enthusiastic about Dewey as he had been about Willkie, or Teddy Roosevelt, or the way he would be for Eisenhower eight years later. Dewey was, however, preferable to FDR, he wrote in the *Indianapolis Star* in the months after he bought it. The New York governor was better qualified, "liberal and cooperative in foreign affairs." Pulliam added that, in contrast to Roosevelt, Dewey "will not play one class against another class."

The problem with Roosevelt was his one-man rule, his failure to let another leader emerge to take his place.

> His personal diplomacy is a threat, rather than a boost, to international good will. He plays favorites and that is a fatal error around the world council table.... His administration, in peacetime, has been the most costly in history.

He had not become a bitter, caustic critic of Roosevelt, in contrast to many of his conservative friends and Republican party allies. He liked some of Roosevelt's appointments and especially admired Treasury Secretary Henry Morgenthau, his war bond boss. As the 1944 election drew near, Dewey attacked Morgenthau for his postwar plan for Germany, prompting a spirited defense of Morgenthau from Pulliam in the *Star,* although the newspaper was supporting Dewey.

Pulliam's enthusiasm was unrestrained when Roosevelt named one of his boys, Paul Porter, to head the Federal Communications Commission, writing that "President Roosevelt batted 1,000 percent for the Democratic party and knocked a home run for public service."

Pulliam still had mixed feelings about Roosevelt. The president's death in 1945 brought forth the mixture of awe and respect Pulliam had for nearly all presidents or people in powerful positions.

> The president is dead. The man who for so many months and years has been the shining star, the guiding light, the energizing hope, recognized as a human deity in all lands, and by all peoples, is gone.
>
> When the name of Franklin Roosevelt has been folded into the annals of time, history will judge Franklin Roosevelt by what he accomplished for America and the world, not by the methods he employed to achieve his aims.
>
> What were his works and what did he achieve? It would take pages and more pages to recount the specific contributions President Roosevelt made to the nation he so brilliantly served. Considering his great physical affliction, it is amazing to remember how hard he worked. Undoubtedly he was the greatest social energy of this century. and dimly do we see him through the clouded glass of national bereavement. What a spirit!

The spirit of the man. That was what endeared him to the millions of Americans who adored him. Spirit and courage and sincere love for people. He loved America too, and democracy. His was the high patriotism of the man who wishes all things well for his own country, no matter how small. He was the intelligent patriot, and truly a citizen of the world. His last great appeal was for an international covenant in which justice shall transcend both power and privilege.

And yet as we write this it just cannot be true that he is gone. He was life itself and leadership to the nation. We who also must die salute this name. God grant that the spirit of his ideals abide forever in American hearts.

As Pulliam grew older, he grew more critical of Roosevelt and the New Deal. Travels around the world would convert him into a dedicated opponent of an ever-expanding federal government, and he began to see Roosevelt as the original source of this trend. He also grew more critical of Roosevelt's individualistic approach to foreign policy:

His egotism in foreign policy was stupid. He wanted to be president of the world and thought he could handle Stalin.

Roosevelt had won in 1944, keeping the Democrats in power for another four years. Willkie had died. It became clear that President Truman would continue with the basic framework Roosevelt had established in the New Deal. Pulliam did not like the trend toward big government. A reflective postwar editorial in the *Star* stated:

For some peculiar psychological reason brought on by confusion of the last few years, we half believe that all these powers and riches came to us by accident, instead of by our own hard work and enterprise under the freest and most flexible economic system that ever existed in the world. . . . In our confusion we are tempted to copy the social systems of a bankrupt Europe or the proletarian dictatorship of repressive communism.

One alternative was the moderate wing of the Republican party, now led by New York governor Thomas Dewey. The Republican National Committee met in Indianapolis in January 1945, and the more conservative isolationists, led by Senators John

Bricker and Robert Taft of Ohio and Colonel Robert McCormick, publisher of the *Chicago Tribune,* tried to take over and oust the Dewey forces. Pulliam and Dewey's manager, Herbert Brownell, who stayed at Pulliam's Indianapolis home, plotted strategy. In a front-page editorial Pulliam called on the Republicans to reaffirm the internationalism of Dewey's 1944 campaign and develop an affirmative approach to domestic politics:

> The Republican party must be realistic in its appraisal of world problems. By the startlingly swift development of communication and transportation, we have been made neighbors of all the peoples of the world, without regard to whether we know them well enough to be prepared to like them. It is time, therefore, with a genuine wish for good-neighborliness, to make an organized beginning toward the establishment of law and order in the world. . . .
>
> It is late; but there is still time for the Republican party to rise above the partisan ambition of any man. Most certainly it must rise above its bitter disapproval of the New Deal administration. The wave of cynicism which has swept across America in the last sixty days has been due almost entirely to lack of leadership on the question of foreign policy. The Republican party has a tremendous obligation in this hour to give leadership to the problems of the peace and to help broaden and crystalize American public opinion of foreign policy. The Republican party must equip itself with a program—not a slingshot. . . .
>
> If we are not to be inexorably propelled into another war twenty years from now, we must act today, as free Americans, for a free world. We must not allow Churchill's imperialism or Stalin's nationalism to make cynics of us. Neither must we permit them to dissipate or dilute the confidence which the injured nations of the world now have in our integrity and our purpose for world peace.

Pulliam was still looking for someone to fill Willkie's shoes, the right kind of Republican. He kept in touch with California governor Earl Warren, who had established a progressive record as governor. He told him, in an apparent reference to Warren's presidential aspirations: "You were my choice then—you are still my choice." He was not ready for Eisenhower in 1948. He thought the military had in any case too much influence after the war.

After Dewey's GOP nomination in 1948, Pulliam could not get excited about the fall election, though he did not like the way Truman was continuing the New Deal and the growth of federal government. Nor did he like Truman's origins in the Pendergast political machine in Missouri, the machine that William Rockhill Nelson had fought with the *Kansas City Star* for so many years. "I could not like Truman because I saw the inside of the machine that made him," he noted in a speech a few years later.

He was happy to see Earl Warren on the Republican ticket, but he was disappointed with Dewey's campaign and his failure to criticize Truman. He liked a fighting candidate and this time the fighter was Harry Truman. Editorially his Indianapolis newspapers favored Dewey and were critical of Truman. But when Truman won a surprise upset, Pulliam had to admire his spunk.

What fired up Pulliam in 1948 more than any of the major candidates was the independent presidential campaign waged by Henry Wallace, former vice president, who bolted the Democratic party but ultimately failed to attract the liberal support he had anticipated. Pulliam thought Wallace had turned into a threat and, in an unusual move, went out and personally campaigned against him. He declared, in a speech to the Arizona House of Representatives, that Wallace was "a great nincompoop rather than a great liberal."

> I have known Henry Wallace for twenty-five years. For fifteen of them he was sincere, though at times misguided. Henry Wallace, my fellow Americans, is a false prophet. He believes we can have peace by shouting for it.

19

The Reformer

INDIANA REPUBLICANS WERE just beginning to taste political power when Gene Pulliam bought the *Indianapolis Star* in 1944. The Republicans had been left out in the wilderness during the depression, when Democrats controlled the governor's office. They retrieved the governor's office in the 1944 election, along with the legislature. Now, hungry after several years out of power, they were set to reap the benefits in patronage and other available political spoils. What they had not counted on, though, was Gene Pulliam.

Pulliam's aim was to reform the Republicans, to save them from the kind of greed and corruption that had ruined the party in the scandals of the 1920s. But to Republicans Gene Pulliam was a puzzle. He did not fit into their ordinary categories. No one could buy him off, nor would he bow to advertising or financial pressure. Stories abounded about his personal ambitions—he wanted to be U.S. senator, national committeeman, governor, ambassador, secretary of treasury. Indiana politicians were not accustomed to an editor and publisher, an apparent Republican, who lectured and admonished his own party on the front pages of a major newspaper. The *Indianapolis News* never did it, nor did the *Times* or the *Star* before Pulliam bought it. Edward Ziegner, a political reporter for the *News*, then and now, explained:

> His sort of editorials were unknown. No other papers did them. They [Republicans] were used to mild treatment from the *Star* and the *News*. They weren't accustomed to his personality. He was kind of an unknown quantity.

To Pulliam, the feeling was mutual—the politicians seemed a little odd, apparently interested in patronage, with no notions about the public interest. "Politics in Marion County was a little strange to him," explained a DePauw classmate, Henry Ostrom, who had risen from business manager of the *DePauw Daily* in 1908 to a key role in the Marion County Republican organization.

The first step in his attack on the Republican party was his assault on former Klansman Robert Lyons, who was elected national committeeman "under a rule not yet adopted." To Pulliam, the Lyons incident was an example of the arrogance of the Republicans, who, back in office after twelve years out of power, intended to do as they pleased.

Pulliam started his campaign to remove the beer and liquor licenses from politics in the 1946 primary, writing front-page editorials and demanding that all candidates take a stand for or against the political control of the liquor licenses. A few candidates flocked to his side, but he provoked regular Republicans into rage. He revived the vehemence and fighting spirit reminiscent of his Bull Moose days at the *Atchison Champion.*

> The citizens of Indiana gave a clear mandate to the Republican party in 1944 to clean out the beer and liquor autocracy set up by the Democrats under Paul McNutt. It had become a bad, smelly mess. The people didn't like it. They voted out the Democrats and voted in the Republicans. And then the Republican leaders broke faith with the people and made the most grievous mistake in party history. They set up the county chairmen as beer and liquor czars. They placed the temptation of easy money in front of them and thereby turned over the administration of beer and liquor to politicians whose sole objectives now are to squeeze more power and more profits out of the racket. Party control is back in the gutter, and its leadership is suffocated by the mire and the stench of bickering over beer. For everybody who has touched the racket has been debauched by it.

He also brought back the revival preaching style he had learned from his father, who died a few months later. "We believe the ministers and church members were in earnest when they called and wrote the *Star*," he wrote after some of the editorials drew support from the ministers.

We believe they will remember the anguish of the old Psalmist when he cried out in the name of the Lord, "Who will rise up for me against the evildoers? Who will stand up for me against the workers of iniquity?" We believe they will recall the old proverb, "A righteous man falling down before the wicked is as a troubled fountain and a corrupt spring." We believe they will stand up for decency and not fall down on their duty as righteous citizens.

He was drawing support from ministers and local-option supporters who wanted to revive a form of prohibition that would permit each county to vote on the legality of liquor sales. But his aim was not a revival of prohibition, as some ministers learned in a meeting with him. The ministers had asked for the meeting in hopes of persuading him to eliminate the *Star*'s retail liquor advertising. It was a short meeting. He listened for a while. Then he told them a few stories about his father, who had never had a drink since his conversion in the 1880s, until a doctor told him to drink a small glass of whiskey each day for his health. Liquor advertising continued.

The *Star* had some success in the May primary. Anti-organization candidates won the races for Marion County sheriff and prosecutor. It was a heavy blow to the organization, showing that the *Star* could mount and win a primary campaign. But the real political powers, Ostrom and James Bradford, remained in power behind the scenes. Unfortunately, Judson Stark, the new prosecutor, turned out to be anything but the reformer Pulliam expected him to be.

The May primary decided only local races. The state convention in June would settle the Republican nomination for the U.S. senate seat held by Republican Raymond Willis. Here, Pulliam pitted himself against the rising star in the Republican party, William Jenner.

Jenner was one of the last great fairground orators, a rough-and-tumble sort from a rural part of southern Indiana. His constant profanity shocked even some of the more profane men in Indiana politics, and his fighting oratory earned him the loyalty of his close friends and admirers. Jenner was a zealous anticommunist who later sided with Senator Joseph McCarthy in congressional battles over communism in the federal government. Pulliam was backing

Evansville congressman Charles LaFollette for the senatorial nomination. Jenner had the backing of Governor Ralph Gates and a strong Republican organization that had tight control of the June convention.

Pulliam and Jenner had known each other for a number of years. Jenner had come to Pulliam for advice during the New Deal, asking whether he should swing over to the liberal approach to politics because it seemed to be the popular trend. Pulliam answered no, keep your conservative convictions, Indiana is basically a conservative state and your time will come.

But after World War II they were on a collision course. Pulliam wanted to reform Indiana politics and gain some influence. Jenner was on the other side, an ambitious rising star in the organization and thus hardly a reformer of liquor and patronage arrangements. Also, they were bound to clash because of their personalities. "The best archangel in heaven couldn't get along with Bill Jenner without a scrap," explained Henry Ostrom. "Jenner was basically a bully," added one-time Republican congressman Charles Brownson. Jenner would shove anyone if he could get away with it, and he usually did. Gene Pulliam he couldn't shove. Pulliam also pushed people as far as he could. Jameson Campaigne, Pulliam's chief editorial writer at the *Star* at the time, explained the conflict that emerged:

> As far as the relationship between your grandfather and Bill Jenner, that is not something that is simply described. Both of them were tough guys. Their general philosophical positions were not very far apart, but Jenner was a very emotional and blunt-spoken guy.
>
> Also, at that time, it seemed to me that your grandfather was trying to become the major influence in the GOP in Indiana and Jenner was not an easy guy to shove around. In addition, there were the beer licenses—I don't recall the exact circumstances involving Governor Gates and the state chairman, but Jenner was involved with them. At that time, however, I was more the instrument of the Boss than his confidant.

Pulliam threw the weight of the *Star* behind Jenner's opponent in the state convention, Congressman LaFollette, who agreed with the *Star*'s position on liquor and politics. Pulliam put his entire newspaper into the fight, writing front-page editorials on beer and liquor and slanting the news coverage in favor of LaFollette and

Jenner's other opponent, the incumbent Raymond Willis. One of LaFollette's attacks on Jenner included an accusation that Jenner had received liquor money for his campaign.

The next day Jenner denied the charge and threatened to sue the *Star* if a retraction were not printed. Pulliam refused, replying on the front page:

> Since the *Star* made no charges against Mr. Jenner and since it offered to print any statement Mr. Jenner desired to make in reply to Mr. LaFollette, there is nothing for the *Star* to retract. . . . The people have a right to know what the candidates for the United States senator are saying in their own behalf and about each other. What they say and what they do is news. The *Star* intends to continue to print the news.

Jenner sued for libel but dropped the suit the next year, after winning the election. In return, Pulliam did not retract the article but praised Jenner on the front page for acting "in a spirit of broadminded public stewardship." He repeated the earlier contention that the *Star* was merely printing the news and added, "From its investigation of the matter, the *Star* is convinced that Mr. Jenner never personally received a dollar of liquor money from Lake County. As a matter of fact the *Star* never said that he did."

Exchanging conciliatory letters, Jenner and Pulliam reached some sort of understanding not to fight openly again. Both had come to stay. Neither could crush the other. They learned to live with each other—they never liked each other—but they learned not to fight. They both learned to compromise a little for the sake of peace, perhaps also for the sake of large conservative goals that they essentially shared. They would clash again and again, but not so much in public and not with the same fury.

Some assumed the battle was still on. After Pulliam bought the *News* in 1948, assistant managing editor Wendell Phillippi asked for Pulliam's advice on how to handle some committee testimony that Jenner drank to excess during World War II. Remembering Pulliam's past feud with Jenner, Phillippi thought Pulliam might be interested in making a story out of it. "Well, hell, Wendell, we all drank during the war," Pulliam told him.

The 1946 Senate race also pitted Pulliam against the rest of the Republican state organization, Governor Ralph Gates, State

Chairman Clark Springer, Gates' supporters in the state legislature, and the Marion County organization. When Springer told the brewery executives to get out of politics and not give either party a campaign contribution, Pulliam came back with another front-page editorial:

> Well, that is a pious and wholesome thing to do. It would be just fine and dandy if Mr. Springer had not missed or evaded completely the point of the beer racket fight. Mr. Springer has been patronage boss of the state administration since the day the Gates administration came into power. Nobody knows better than Mr. Springer that the beer racket was extended, strengthened and has flourished under the Republican setup that made the county chairmen the beer czars in each county. The fight against the beer racket has been directed at the county chairmen and their personally appointed beer distributors who have made a financial field day out of the exclusive right to distribute beer.

Pulliam wound up under indirect attack from the *Indianapolis News*, which was then a key supporter of the Gates administration. Joseph Daniels, an attorney married to one of the Fairbanks heirs, was a close adviser to Gates, along with *News* publisher Mickey McCarty. They tended to go through third parties when they played politics, using their influence in subtle ways. "You never had to go through a third party to know where he [Pulliam] stood," Gates recalled. "The Fairbanks always had someone dealing for them." If Pulliam wanted something done, he picked up the telephone and called the governor, the state chairman, whomever he wanted. He never believed in channels, even on his own newspapers. Or, he would write a front-page editorial about the matter, a frightening and sometimes embarrassing spectacle to political figures, especially as he wrote in such a blunt and vigorous manner.

The *News*, trying to defend the Gates administration in the face of front-page editorials in the *Star*, gently chided Pulliam without naming him:

> Political opportunists, playing both sides of the board, are a menace to a sound solution of a dangerous and difficult situation.

Two days later Pulliam came out banging on the front page. He denied that he had any personal political ambitions and declared that:

The *Star* will continue to oppose any alliance between beer and politics. The *Star* knows there is a group of greedy Democrats who would give their shirts to trade places with the men who run the present beer racket. But if the Democrats should come into power and attempt to revive the racket, the *Star* will expose and oppose them just as vigorously as it has the present setup.

The *Star* has no personal grudges to settle. It has no political axes to grind. It wants nothing except what is good for Indianapolis, for Indiana and for America. It wants to be fair. It tries hard to be first. It insists on its reporters making every effort for truth and accuracy. It believes wholeheartedly in common sense, common honesty and common decency. And on that policy it intends to continue to print the news and to strive earnestly to merit the confidence and the respect of its readers.

Pulliam's campaign did draw support from other newspapers in the state, as well as out of state, such as the *Louisville Courier-Journal* in Kentucky.

Some of the best friends of the Republican party in Indiana have become its severest critics on the point of a flagrant traffic in alcoholic beverage licenses as an item of political loot.

At the June convention, Jenner won the Republican senatorial nomination and defeated his Democratic opponent Clifford Townsend in the fall. The next year Pulliam continued the campaign against the political control of beer and liquor, forcing Gates to push mild reform legislation through a resistant Republican legislature. The demanding front-page editorials continued, day after day, when the legislature balked: "What kind of dunderheads do Republican organization leaders think the people of Indiana are, anyway?" the *Star* asked in one editorial.

In the fall of 1947, he came out in favor of the Republicans in the Indianapolis mayoral election, but only in a front-page editorial criticizing the entire Marion County Republican organization, including Joseph Daniels.

His repeated attacks on Daniels drew a libel suit from the lawyer. Pulliam came charging back with a long editorial on the *Star* front page, claiming he had only been commenting on Daniels' political maneuverings.

Mr. Daniels is an attorney of unquestioned repute. Mr. Daniels is also one of the most active politicians in Indiana. As such, he is a public figure whose conduct, plans, appointments, and leadership are and should be subject to public scrutiny. One of a newspaper's highest responsibilities is to tell the public what politicians are doing and why. Only through the service of a vigilant press has America been kept free and progressive. The *Star* does not always disagree with Mr. Daniels' political leadership. In the past it has frequently supported the candidates he has nominated.

But the *Star* regards it as its duty to comment frankly and vigorously on the conduct of politicians when public service is concerned. When Mr. Daniels or any other politician is right, the *Star* will commend him. When Mr. Daniels or any other politician is wrong, the *Star* will say so, in editorials and in cartoons. Public service is the *Star*'s business and we intend to continue to print news and to comment about politicians whenever in our judgment it will serve the public good.

He retracted a small part of the attack on Daniels five months later, as Daniels withdrew his suit. Pulliam wrote on the front page that he had been wrong about Daniels' influence on the state Public Service Commission, claiming his motives were good.

The *Star*'s editorial comment was based on information which it regarded as entirely reliable, but it since has learned that these statements in the editorial were inaccurate and incorrect. The *Star* regrets that it was misinformed and that the statements were unjust to the individuals mentioned.

A few months later, Daniels helped sell the *News* to Pulliam.

Pulliam emerged from the 1945 and 1947 elections completely at odds with the Republican organization. Stories in Republican newspapers speculated widely about his motives and personal ambitions, accusing him of disloyalty. Party loyalty was an absolute in Indiana politics, even for editors. Pulliam had come out of a different tradition, starting at the *Kansas City Star*. He didn't fit the Indiana pattern. H. Dale Brown, who later rose to head the Marion County organization, noted the surprise Pulliam caused:

He was a surprise after the war, an independent Republican. I don't think any Republican knew Pulliam too well. They weren't used to this strong stuff. A front-page editorial was unheard of. People always thought he was a manipulator in politics. He was just trying to get things done. No politician ever felt close to him, buddy-buddy. He wasn't overly friendly with them. He wanted things changed first, friendship second.

Republican papers made him a frequent target. The *Republican Record* called the *Star* the "mischievous poisoner of Republican hopes." The *Indiana Transcript* ran an entire issue attacking Pulliam and his political maneuvers.

> The Republican party came into being long before Eugene C. Pulliam was born and from all indications will be around long after he is gone. Unfortunately while he sticks around with the power of his press, the *Indianapolis Star* and *News*, he has made a monkey out of the party.

His own comment, in response to charges that he was furthering his own political ambitions, was:

> If the editor of the *Star* wanted to run for office, public or private, he would be playing ball with the politicians, not throwing balls at them.

Pulliam certainly wanted influence and power, if not an office. *Star* editor Jameson Campaigne, who observed him closely but not uncritically, tried to assess his motives:

> In the early days most of the campaigns originated with your grandfather. I don't know all his motives, but generally speaking I always believed he did what he thought was right at the time, though sometimes he was hasty. I don't believe he sided with any faction particularly, but he did trust some politicians, I thought too much, and we sometimes got burned because of it. I never thought the Boss sought personal power for its own sake. And as the years went on he became much more concerned with being fair and more deliberate in attack or defense. He wanted us to praise anyone we had attacked, if he did something good or something the *Star* approved of. Like all of us, he made mistakes of judgment, but I never thought he deliberately carried on personal vendettas.

Whatever his motives, he was then out of step with the Republicans, but he eventually obtained the influence he wanted. Jenner maintained control of much of the state party in the 1950s, but governors, mayors, and candidates began to court Pulliam, to ask for his support, get his advice, seek his favor. Marion County Congressman Charles Brownson, an Eisenhower Republican, summed up the new mood among so many Republicans and political candidates in the 1950s and 1960s. He was asked whether he tended to accept Mr. Pulliam's advice when it was offered.

"I never argue with a man who buys ink by the barrel," he answered.

20

Phoenix

GENE PULLIAM HAD been vacationing in Phoenix, Arizona, since the early 1940s. He was comparing it to Florida, where he visited on vacations, still vaguely looking for newspapers. It was hard for him just to vacation somewhere—he always had to be working. So he bought a minority interest in Phoenix radio station KPHO during World War II, along with Tom Chauncey and actor Gene Autry. He sold his interest in 1944 but kept visiting Phoenix. He always made a point of seeing Charles Stauffer and Wesley Knorpp, who had the morning Phoenix newspaper, the *Arizona Republic*, with the evening *Phoenix Gazette*.

Even before buying those newspapers, Pulliam was boosting Arizona. Stauffer, after playing golf with him one day, decided to order a front-page *Republic* article on Pulliam's vision for the future of the state. It was an ironic interview, for Pulliam set forth the key elements in what would emerge as the civic plan that he promoted in his future newspapers, a plan to attract tourists and develop downtown Phoenix. He was giving a blueprint for the future of Phoenix on the front page of the newspaper that would one day be his.

> I am very bullish on Arizona. You have everything the winter tourist wants except possibly the ocean, and that's not always an asset. You have delightful weather from October to May, and no other American resort section can make that statement. But you need to awaken more acutely to the possibilities of the Salt River valley as mecca for sun-hungry Americans. You know, next to water, air, food, and sex, Americans want sunshine most. They love to live outdoors and they can do it here to their heart's content.

The great majority of winter visitors are people past fifty years of age. Make your city attractive to that class and you won't be able to accommodate the visitors you'll receive. You need a close-in downtown park, not large, but with shuffleboard courts, comfortable benches and facilities for older people to sit in the sun and visit. You need another good golf course. You have horse racing, and it should be developed and refined, for winter visitors love the horses. But you already have what it takes to be the greatest winter resort in America—you've got continuous sunshine.

The newspapers made good money, although they seldom started the kind of controversy Pulliam brought with him wherever he went. Knorpp and Stauffer were impressed with Pulliam's knowledge of Arizona, his apparent interest in its future. Other potential buyers, the Knight brothers, John and Jim, and the Cowles brothers, Mike and John, seldom came to Arizona and were largely ignorant about the state. Sidney Meyers, a top stockholder and executive under Knorpp and Stauffer, recalled:

We talked about whom to sell to and we wanted first to find the right people. We decided to offer it to Gene first, since he'd indicated an interest and had spent fourteen straight years here in the winter.

During the summer of 1946, Pulliam started negotiating for a loan from the Mutual Life Insurance Company of New York, headed by Lewis Douglas, but Douglas changed his terms too many times for Pulliam, and he decided to go elsewhere for the financing. But the group he was heading was intriguing. Pulliam was to be president of the new corporation. Joining him were New York advertising executive Bruce Barton, Arizona Republican leader and author Clarence "Bud" Keeland, and the crusty and feisty *Tuscon Daily Star* publisher, William Mathews. Pulliam was to run the editorial side of the *Republic* and Mathews was to be in charge of the *Gazette*.

The Pulliam-Mathews combination would have been fascinating to watch, if they could have worked together. Both were publishers of the old school, blunt, strong-minded, quick to fight, putting a strong personal stamp on their own newspapers. Later in Arizona politics, Mathews and Pulliam tangled in front-page editorials. Their alliance to buy the Phoenix papers never got on track.

Pulliam went to Jefferson Standard Life Company of North Carolina, instead, borrowed $2.5 million and, with several other investors, paid $4 million for the newspapers. Later he called it "the best buy I ever made." Joining him in the purchase as minority stockholders were newspaper broker Smith Davis, Jefferson Standard Life, Bruce Barton, and Clarence Buddington Kelland. He took charge of the newspapers in late October 1946, and started to put money into the plant, reviving plans for a new plant that Knorpp and Stauffer had set aside.

The first and most important thing he did was modernize the operation. "He always put money back into it," said Lee Hover, then the new classified advertising manager. Advertisers were starting to drift to the new *Arizona Times*, run by President Roosevelt's daughter, Anna, and John Boettiger.

The *Times* was started just as Pulliam bought the *Republic* and *Gazette*. Some felt it might have been a success if the old management had continued at the *Republic* and *Gazette*. Advertisers were attracted to the *Times* partly because Knorpp was an inflexible man, difficult to deal with. Barry Goldwater, an executive in his family business at the time, was considering advertising in the *Times*.

> The advertisers had long wanted to have a change in the *Republic* and *Gazette* management. Knorpp had the monopoly and just did it his way. They had this dictatorial control over the ads, the same ad in each paper, and the rates were too high. But Gene sat down with us and stated his plans.

He added to each news staff and separated it from the editorial page staff. Neither newspaper had a city editor to oversee the local news coverage. To run the news side of the newspapers, he brought in a former Associated Press bureau chief, Harry Montgomery, who recalled his first few months:

> They had no city editor, they had never had one. Neither did the *Gazette*. A slot man just ran it all. There was no state coverage in the papers. I used to go home at night wondering whether they'd even get out a newspaper the next morning.

The editorials began to take sides on issues, in contrast to the past. "If he brought anything, he brought vigor," said Ben Avery, a reporter who had worked under both regimes. Most of Pulliam's early involvement came from a distance, phone calls from Indianapolis, or around the world. He was traveling all over the globe, fighting battles against the Indiana Republicans, buying the *Indianapolis News*, promoting Dwight D. Eisenhower for president. He did not have much time to spare for Arizona in the late 1940s and early 1950s. But Phoenix was the right kind of territory for him.

It resembled an old frontier town when he started visiting in the 1930s, similar to Kansas City when William Rockhill Nelson went there in 1880. It was not unlike some of the smaller towns in Kansas where Pulliam grew up. Before and after World War II, the small town of 75,000 was wide open. Gambling and prostitution flourished without any protest from the town or check from city police. Local politicians routinely received kickbacks on city contracts. "Phoenix had a crummy reputation around the country. It was known as sin city," commented Walter Meek, who later worked for Pulliam at the *Arizona Republic*.

The city had approved a council-manager form of government in 1913, the same year Atchison, Kansas, said no to the plan that Pulliam had promoted so vigorously but in vain. In Phoenix, that kind of government had not worked out the way the original crusaders had planned. Council members split up the city government into little kingdoms, one councilman running the police department, appointing friends and supporters to jobs, while another council member took over another department. The city manager was unable to run anything. One lasted three weeks, another twenty-nine days.

The economic foundation of Phoenix was weak, unbalanced, based on cattle, citrus, cotton, and copper mining, but lacking industry or manufacturing. Services were the main business. "We took in each other's laundry," recalled Robert Jaap, a prominent bank executive in Phoenix. Tourism, a major factor in the 1960s boom in Phoenix, had not yet developed.

It was Gene Pulliam's kind of territory, unsettled, a little raw, with few strongly established customs, procedures, or bosses, ripe for a civic and economic boom. Here Pulliam finally found his opportunity to follow the example of William Rockhill Nelson.

21

Phoenix Growth

A VARIETY OF factors was responsible for the postwar economic boom in Phoenix. The part played by Gene Pulliam, Walter Bimson, Frank Snell, and Sherman Hazeltine was crucial. Nearly everyone who watched the growth of Phoenix would point first to Bimson and Pulliam when asked why Phoenix, not Tucson or Albuquerque, had boomed. It might have been that phone call from Pulliam to the head of a major industry that contemplated coming to Phoenix. Or Bimson's aggressive and risky loan program at the Valley National Bank that eventually put his bank ahead of the others in Arizona. And, too, it was the newspapers' support for charter government, which cleaned up a corrupt political mess that had discouraged businesses from coming to the city.

The first and most important step was charter government. A reform group had been formed during World War II, but it had a hard time winning anything. The reformers needed some help—a boost, a prominent leader.

Barry Goldwater had the name. Eventually in Arizona his name would carry some of the magic that Kennedy and Roosevelt had in other parts of the country. An Air Force veteran of World War II, he had helped on civic projects, and run his family department store. But he was not attracted to politics. He said what was on his mind, going his own way without paying much attention to what other people thought of him. Politics seemed like dirty business to most businessmen in Phoenix. Banker Bob Jaap said that

Barry was the first really respected citizen who got into politics. Before him, Republican and Democratic candidates were really political hacks.

Goldwater was reluctant to run for the city council when the reform group approached him. Pulliam could be very persuasive when he wanted someone to do something. Now he wanted Goldwater to head the charter government ticket and help the reformers take over city government. "He was the one who talked me into it," Goldwater recalled. The charter government group, with Goldwater and other prominent civic figures like Nicholas Udall on the ticket, won its first election in 1949, with Goldwater leading the slate and the reform group sweeping all the council seats. The key was Pulliam's support in the *Republic* and *Gazette*, with investigative stories on corruption in city government, and editorials in a pretelevision era when newspapers could sway elections more easily. "It couldn't have worked without Gene Pulliam," recalled one of the original members of the reform group, Dick Smith.

The new council started to clean up, establishing competitive bidding for city contracts, bringing in a new city manager, Ray Wilson of Kansas City, who refused to allow councilmen to go over his head to city departments. Corruption was all but eliminated; prostitution and gambling were driven underground. The next year, Phoenix won the All-American City Award from the National Municipal League and *Look* magazine.

The charter group kept winning elections for the next twenty-five years. By the time of Gene Pulliam's death in 1975, it was accused of being an undemocratic small group of businessmen running the city for their own financial interests. But in the early years it was the key to the growth of Phoenix, providing an efficient, growth-oriented city administration that could attract industry.

Pulliam's support was crucial. With the newspapers, he could make or break charter government. The charter committee, which nominated the slate, sometimes included an executive from the newspapers. The committee always cleared the slate with Pulliam before announcing it. It was a great deal of power for one man to have, especially for a newspaperman, since he was also supervising his newspapers' effort to inform the community.

Probably he never thought of it in that way. In the smaller towns where he had worked, or even in larger ones like Kansas City, the newspaper editor or publisher was sometimes active politically, running for office, using his newspaper as a platform. Pulliam shied away from a direct role, but as publisher he was sought out for advice, and he liked to give advice. He wanted to see Phoenix grow, and the charter committee provided the opportunity.

Dick Smith, a movie theater operator who also was active in charter campaigns, recalled an incident that illustrated the charter's impact.

> Motorola representatives came out—they were trying to decide on one of four cities. One guy found a ticket on his car and asked how to fix it. The Chamber of Commerce guy said, "No one can fix it." So the Motorola guy said, "That's the kind of town we're looking for."

Gene Pulliam and banker Walter Bimson were never close friends. Bimson was more formal, more refined in his manners. Some thought he was stuffy; others only that he was a fine gentleman. Although Pulliam and Bimson were never close, they were both behind almost every civic cause. Businessmen would go to them for help, money, and publicity. "I'd go to Pulliam first for money on any cause," said broadcaster Tom Chauncey. "He acts blunt and cantankerous, but that's a façade. He's really a softie underneath. He's the opposite of what you'd think he'd be like. You can get to Gene Pulliam pretty quick if you're talking about helping kids."

More important, he was a leading influence in the way the city expanded, annexed, and zoned to promote the growth of business— growth that converted Phoenix from a small town of 75,000 to a major urban area of more than a million people. Annexation of major sections of Maricopa County in the 1950s prevented the suburbs of Phoenix from strangling the urban area, taking money and a strong property tax base outside the city, a problem at the root of the urban decay in other parts of the United States. "We kept it from being a one-horse town," was the way Pulliam summarized it.

Initially, annexation developed out of a meeting between Pulliam and the mayor of Phoenix, Jack Williams, later the governor. Williams was a shy, humble man, almost out of place in politics. He had come to Phoenix before World War II to work for a radio station owned by Brig Butler. Butler was the unquestioned boss of his radio station, authoritarian in manner, a commanding figure. When Williams came to know Pulliam before the war, he noticed the resemblance. "He had a lot of machismo then, self-confidence, authority, dependability—you were drawn to him, he could move the world," said Williams. Williams came to think of Pulliam as the last of the great newspapermen, the kind who had made it on his own, crawled up the ladder of American success, running his business with an iron hand. "He's the last of a breed. You'll never find them anymore," Williams noted.

> Hearst, Copley, Butler, the greats of that era are no longer possible in our society.... They were the boss. Today you have to have committees and debate everything.

Williams was one of the prominent businessmen drawn into city politics by the charter government group. He did not like being involved, but the charter people were persuasive and told him it was his civic duty. By 1956, he was their candidate for mayor, which was becoming an important and powerful office. He was elected, along with the rest of the charter slate. He went to talk to Pulliam.

> I didn't know what to do as mayor. I had no plan. So I went to Gene Pulliam and told him. I asked him, what's the biggest problem of Phoenix? He said: satellite towns—start an annexation program.

Williams then checked with Bimson, who agreed with Pulliam's recommendation. A $70 million bond issue was drawn up, and a growth committee was established.

By 1975, with 750,000 people in the city limits, Phoenix was sixty miles larger than Chicago, and only fifty square miles smaller than all of New York City with its eight million people. There were more bond issues, for parks, water, sewers, streets, libraries, and other city services, some of them crucial for city growth. "The papers never failed to support strongly a city bond issue," commented a top *Republic* reporter in the 1960s, Walter Meek, adding, "They supported them even when it required extra taxes." Newspaper support was the key. "City Hall wouldn't consider it [a bond issue] seriously for one hour if the papers didn't support it."

22

World Travels

AFTER WORLD WAR II, Gene Pulliam decided to go back to reporting. This time his story was a reporter's dream—the whole world. His interest had been sparked by his father, who had written about international affairs in the 1920s and 1930s, and by Henry Ulen, who would come home and tell him about overseas trips when the Ulen company had projects all over the world. Pulliam knew the United States was going to be involved in world affairs in one way or another, and he wanted to be on top of the story now that he was a major publisher.

He and Nina started a series of foreign trips, the first one in 1947. He tried to go with an open mind. Setting off in July 1947, he told a *New York Herald Tribune* reporter:

> I don't know any more about this story than I used to when I was sent out as a police reporter in Kansas City. I'll wait till I get there and see what it's all about.

They traveled the way Gene Pulliam did nearly everything—almost frantically. The first trip, from July to October in 1947, took them to England, Scotland, France, Belgium, Holland, Denmark, Sweden, Norway, Germany, Austria, Italy, Switzerland, Greece, Palestine, Egypt, Algeria, Spain, and Portugal. Back for a month in October, Pulliam took a quick dive into the Indianapolis mayoralty election. He wrote a long editorial endorsing the Republican candidate William Wemmer, but blasted away at the entire Marion County Republican machine. Democrat Al Feeney won the race.

Then he and Nina were off to the Far East in November and early December, including stops in Japan and the Philippines. In late January of the following year, they went down into Central America, Mexico, the Canal Zone, Guatemala, and Panama. In May they headed back to Europe, retracing some of their previous steps.

The travels had a deep impact on Pulliam. They shaped his postwar political views, led him to his 1952 presidential candidate, turned him into an implacable anticommunist and established his major goal for the rest of his life—the preservation of freedom by checking the growth of federal government in his native land.

This was an exciting time in his life—Hawaii was the farthest he had been from the United States before the war. Both he and Nina could write vividly and they brought a freshness that was hard for regular foreign correspondents to provide. From Berlin, Pulliam wrote a moving story on the impact of nazism.

What price dictatorships? That is the question that gnaws at your soul as you ride through this mass of ruins that once was one of the world's great and prosperous cities.

You walk in and out of the demolished Reichstag building. You gaze stupefied on the charred and broken walls of the Reich's chancellery where Hitler ruled in the strutting elegance of nazi glory. Then down into the now musty, damp and begrimmed wetness of the bunker that Der Fuehrer built as his final retreat from the avenging justice of freedom on the march, and where he died like the ordinary hunted criminal that he was.

Rows and rows of magnificent state buildings all in stark ruin—street after street without a single roofed house, only great jagged piles of brick and concrete that once were the homes of industrious people. You know there are still hundreds, probably thousands, of bodies lying beneath all the rubble and you gasp, "In God's name, what price dictatorships?"

Does man ever learn anything from the past? Is arrogant egotism so dominant in the minds of the military leaders that they cannot see the lesson of Berlin and Frankfurt and Munich and Vienna? Down through the ages of civilized man, the same thing has happened to dictators with the penalty increasing as free men increased their willingness to fight and die that other men could also be free.

Have the Russians studied the lesson of these devastated cities or, in their blind hatred for democratic nations and intoxicated by their fanatical zeal for Soviet domination, do they believe we are not good enough to stop them as we did the nazis? Do they think that, because of our regard for human life and our reluctance to face the reality of a new and more powerful aggressor, we will refuse to throw the weight of all

our resources, including the atomic bomb, against their plan of world
conquest?

Don't they ever read history? Don't they know that man is determined
to be free of all dictatorial tyranny? Don't they realize that if this be the
Armageddon between reaction and freedom that America will be there
fighting with all her might on the side of mercy and justice and freedom?

These are the questions that trouble your soul and make you sick at
heart as you walk through the desolation and decay that war brought to
Germany.

In England, which they visited several times, they were
disappointed with the Labour party's socialism and its failures. He
concluded that the socialists had made promises and couldn't fulfill
them, cruelly disillusioning the masses. From London he wrote:

After spending ten days in England, I am at a complete loss to
understand how an intelligent American could advocate the adoption of
any part of the British system of socialist government for use in America.

The contrast in living conditions, in personal freedom and in
opportunity is so sharp that every comparison is in America's favor.
America is Utopia compared to England today. It is a common mistake
of almost all people to believe that the pastures are greener on the other
side of the fence. English pastures are definitely not greener, when
surveyed by an American. They are drab and grim.

Elsewhere in Europe, they thought they discovered an alternative to England's socialized medicine program.

In Denmark and Norway, the government makes sure that every family
with an income of less than $2,000 is covered and that the fees are
reasonable. But it keeps its hands off the administration of the plan. It
makes no effort to dictate to either patient or doctor. In England the
government runs the whole show and it is shot full of red tape,
bungling, abuses and high-handed dictation. Both patients and doctors
are under the thumb of the government.

He praised Catholic relief efforts in Europe, drawing the
attention of Francis Cardinal Spellman in New York, who had some
of their stories reprinted in Catholic newspapers. "They are writing
and working for peace in the world," wrote Spellman, in a letter of
introduction. He arranged for them to meet Pope Pius XII in Rome.

In Athens, they inspected the Marathon Dam and water system
built by Lebanon friend Henry Ulen and his company back in 1927.

According to Greek businessmen with whom I have talked it is the only public works project ever built in modern Athens without graft or the usual payoff to Greek politicians.

Henry Ulen's name is still a symbol of honesty and integrity here. The water system, although designed only for a city of 500,000, was so expertly built that it is providing pure, clear water for 1.4 million people in the refugee-congested city that Athens is today.

By far the dominant subject of his articles was the Soviet Union and the impact of communism, the fears in Western Europe of a Russian takeover similar to that of Eastern Europe during and after World War II. From Stockholm, Sweden, he wrote:

The Russian menace to peace in Europe is far more acute today than was the German threat ten short years ago.

Politically, Western Europe is in the same state of apprehensive turmoil it was in 1937. But economically it is in far worse shape.

In every country in Western Europe, as well as in these Scandinavian countries of the North, the whispered question is, "Will the Americans save us from Russia?"

Already Russia dominates by economic pressures and controls by sheer force of her own armed troops two-thirds of the wheat-producing lands of the continent. Soviet secret police are organized and effective in all the Russian satellite states. And in every country the Communist party is serving as a front for Soviet propaganda dealing in hate and ridicule for Americans....

Russia will win or lose in Europe largely on the turn of events in Germany. If America moves fast enough the Iron Curtain will be frozen on its present line. If we falter or back out entirely, Russia will overrun and control Europe within two years.

The communists, they observed, were both impressive and dismaying, with their dedication and ability and drive. He thought the communists were doing what the capitalists ought to have been doing. The capitalists, the pro-Americans, were too soft, too out of touch with the common people. In France, he complained:

All too often the American story is told only at elaborate cocktail parties to people already sold on America, while communists reach the French working class at rest periods in plants and later in sidewalk gatherings or neighborhood meetings. We have by all odds the best story and the money to get it across but we are doing a lousy job of reaching the people who ought to hear it.

In Italy, he heard the communist leader, Palmiro Togliatti, speak a number of times, calling him "the smartest man, I think, in Europe today."

> He's the most eloquent man in the world today, I think—and I've heard all of them since William Jennings Bryan. I heard Togliatti address 16,000 or 17,000 people. I didn't understand a word he said, and yet he stirred me just with the magnetism of his voice.

He watched the communist propaganda system at work. He thought it was a sham, but he could see why it was effective with the average working man.

> He knows he is hungry. He knows his children want clothing. He knows the cost of living is up and so he listens to anybody, especially the communist rabble-rousers who tell him Uncle Sam's imperialist bankers and the pope's slick politicians are starving him to death.

Nina added a poignant element to the reporting, writing:

> I remember a woman in Italy who was exceptionally kind and helpful to me. I remember the stricken look in her eyes when she told me that her family, to keep from starving, had finally eaten their pet cats. I saw hunger which approached starvation all over Italy—even in the heart of downtown Rome as I stood in the shadow of Mussolini's silly, pompous little balcony...and the war in Europe is more than three years behind us.

They wanted to see the Soviet Union and had obtained visas in Washington, but they were turned down in Stockholm. They felt the looming presence of Russia in their travels in Europe. In France, Belgium, and Germany, they saw signs that equated a hammer and a sickle with a swastika.

> The people, the common people of Europe, are alert to the fact that Stalin has taken Hitler's place in their lives and is casting a dark and heavy shadow of armed dictatorship over their future.

They did visit the communist countries in Eastern Europe— Yugoslavia, Hungary, Austria, Czechoslovakia—and their fears about communism were confirmed. From Belgrade Pulliam wrote:

Life behind the Iron Curtain goes on with a varied degree of acceptance by the people who, willingly or otherwise, are regimented to the rule of a police state.

For the young leaders, it is the great adventure of creating a new peoples' world. For the top bosses, it is the fulfillment of a lifelong ambition to destroy the bourgeoisie. For the working classes, it is a time of wonderment, hope and fear—their new "blessings" are so mixed with high prices and high taxes. For the middle and upper classes, who have not embraced communism with convincing enthusiasm, it is an hour-to-hour existence of waiting, eternally waiting, to know what will happen to them next. Most of them have been dispossessed of their property; thousands have been arrested. They look forward to only one of two things: Either death or the miraculous day that they can flee from the country. Meantime their life is a routine of despair.

He didn't think the United States should oppose all forms of communism in Europe. He was an early advocate of the later U.S. strategy of playing one communist country against another, a pragmatic sort of view that would put him at odds with Eisenhower's choice for secretary of state, John Foster Dulles. He suggested that the U.S. back Tito's Yugoslavia or any other communist country that appeared to be breaking away from Soviet domination.

Tito is getting away with it and if we give him just enough help to keep him alive economically, let him build up small industry without war potentials, he will be able to thumb his nose at Stalin. If Tito gets away with it every little dictator in the satellite countries will be following suit.

Earlier in the year he had visited Yugoslavia, concluding in one of his stories that:

After living for five days behind the Iron Curtain, I am convinced that only the assassination of Marshal Tito will prevent Yugoslavia from standing up to Russia and making her independence stick. The break between Tito and Stalin is complete and irretrievable. And this is the greatest opportunity the United States has had in its drive for world peace since Russia wrecked the United States with its veto on peace plans.

The communist strength confirmed his internationalist leanings, particularly when the internationalist-isolationist debate was raging in the Republican party in 1948.

We can't be naive and say that if we build up America, the rest of the world can go hang. We are the greatest world power today. Russia has an ideology and a program and a plan which absolutely will never succeed until America is busted flat and conquered.

In Spain Pulliam was attracted to Franco's anticommunism, while acknowledging that Franco was a dictator. He drew Communist party pickets in a Phoenix speech to the American Legion, as he defended Franco and Spain. Party leaflets said Pulliam's speech was part of the "Wall Street plot to whip up hysteria to lead us into a needless and devastating atomic war." Pulliam knew he had come to an unpopular position, particularly with the Left, but he said he didn't care.

Had the communists won in Spain, Russia would now be in control of Europe. So while I have no brief for Franco, he did save Europe from Russia. . . . Everybody who has tried to tell the two sides has been blasted as a fascist—well, hell, I don't care.

In South America where they traveled in 1950 and 1951, they saw some of the bitter anti-American spirit that was emerging. In Mexico, Pulliam wrote that he could understand how communist leader Lombardo Toledano took advantage of anti-American sentiment.

Take the case of Raymond Beteta, Mexican minister of finance. Beteta came from a good Mexican family. He entered Texas University at Austin and made a splendid record as an outstanding student. But because he was a Mexican he was shunned socially, especially by the college fraternities. Despite all this Beteta completed his university work and later married an American girl. However, he has never forgotton the treatment accorded him at Texas University nor has he forgiven the Americans for their discrimination against him and other Mexicans. Today Beteta holds a position in the Mexican government second only to President Alemán. He doesn't go around shouting "Death to Yankee imperialism." Actually he is trying to persuade American capital to come back to Mexico, but basically he distrusts Americans and in his heart he hates us. Beteta is a patriotic Mexican who believes in the future of his country. He has a sound understanding of economics. He is for private enterprise and against communism, but he doesn't intend ever to forget that they called him "greaser" on the Texas campus. And who can blame him? This is only one instance of how discrimination bobs up to plague and harass our good neighbor program.

When bitter anti-American sentiment born of discrimination permeates the whole social structure from top to bottom it is easy to understand why the communists get an audience when they shout, "Down with the Yankees."

Farther south in little Uruguay, they found a "miracle," a country where the free enterprise system semed to be working the way it was supposed to work. It was the only country where they found the kind of freedom they knew in the United States. After thousands of words from places like Belgrade, Mexico City, London, Paris and a depressing analysis of the postwar world, now he could finally write a happy story on an upbeat optimistic note:

Miracle of miracles. Here in Uruguay I have found an amazing little country without income taxes, and more remarkable still, a country that doesn't need and doesn't want a loan or other financial help from the United States.

The answer to the communist threat, he concluded, was right here in Uruguay:

I am leaving Montevideo with the definite conviction that if it were possible to transplant the economy and the democratic policies of free enterprise of this wonderful little country into the other small nations of the world we would have a complete answer to communism. Where there is freedom of opportunity and incentive for private enterprise, communism doesn't stand a chance.

Later in the same year they headed back to the Middle and Far East, interviewing Prime Minister Jawaharlal Nehru in India. Pulliam was baffled by the man, an apparent mixture of pragmatism and idealism. Nehru told them he wanted to steer an independent, middle course in the growing ideological competition between the United States and the Soviet Union. After their first meeting, Pulliam wrote about Nehru sympathetically:

On handling government affairs, Nehru is practical, sometimes devious, sometimes quite ruthless; but he convinces you that at heart he is a sincere idealist who earnestly tries to walk faithfully in the footsteps of his beloved Mahatma.

But the more he pondered the Indian, the less he was impressed. Speaking to a Muncie Rotary Club a few months later, he concluded:

> He's a very strange mixture. He ought to be the professor of philosophy in some university and has no business at the head of government.

In Japan they met MacArthur and were impressed by his work in rebuilding a war-torn country. Pulliam suggested that MacArthur next be assigned to administer the Marshall Plan in Europe. A few months after MacArthur was fired from his command in the Korean War, they visited Tokyo and were pleased with the way General Matthew Ridgway followed in MacArthur's footsteps.

> Without fanfare, without pomp, but with a rare understanding of his grave responsibilities General Ridgway assumed command. There was no break in the supply line to Korea. There was no time out for setting up a new palace guard. General Ridgway went to work to get the job done and it has been a magnificent performance.

Later in the year he went to see MacArthur in New York City, when the general was toying with the thought of running for president in 1952. MacArthur asked Pulliam for his support. But Pulliam said no, he already had another candidate, another general he had met in his world travels.

23

Foreign Travels, New Ideas

SEVERAL TRIPS AROUND the world had a deep impact on Eugene Pulliam's political views. He now had more experience in the ways of the world. He had seen the free enterprise system at work. Most of all, he had seen socialism and communism and they didn't seem to be working at all. His travels strengthened his political views. For the rest of his life, whenever he was writing or speaking about freedom and socialism and communism and big government, there was always a certainty, a conviction he had lacked during the depression. Now he was sure he was right. He became an evangelist for the cause of freedom from the federal government, freedom from a meddlesome, intervening bureaucracy.

He started accepting speaking engagements everywhere, alone, or with Nina, and sometimes Nina would receive the invitation. His pace was hectic in the 1940s and 1950s. In the first six months of 1959, for example, he spoke at the California-Nevada Associated Press meeting in San Francisco in February; the Chicago Headline Club and the Arizona State University Foundation in April; the Sons of Indiana dinner in New York, followed the next day by a speech to the New York Deadline Club in May; and the Franklin Rotary Club he had started forty years before, then the Plainfield, Indiana, Rotary Club in June. Later that summer he was slowed down by an operation—the blood flow from his heart was hampered by an aneurysm, ballooning blood vessels. He had what was then a complex operation in Houston, Texas, in August.

By October he had recovered sufficiently enough to jump into a fight with Scottsdale superintendent of schools John Ashe, who declared that Pulliam's newspapers opposed a school bond issue because Pulliam was a Roman Catholic and sent his son to a Catholic school. Pulliam charged back with an angry front-page editorial in the *Republic*:

> One telephone call to anybody at the *Republic* could have given Superintendent Ashe the facts, but he was so eager to smear the *Republic* and the *Gazette* that he stooped to the age-old technique of religious bigotry to make it appear that the editorial policy of the Phoenix newspapers is influenced by religion. . . .
>
> The insinuation that these newspapers are opposed to public schools is just as false as the statement Superintendent Ashe made to the parent-teacher meeting. We did oppose one bond issue because it was a blank check bond issue. The taxpayers have a right to know how tax money is to be spent and have a right to decide whether they want it to be spent that way. That bond issue was beaten four to one, but it is the only bond issue which these newspapers have opposed.
>
> We are not against the schools. We are for the schools. We have supported the teachers, we support merit salary increases for teachers, we support a policy which will give us better school rooms, more facilities for school children and better-educated graduates. We have opposed overlapping administration. We have opposed the puddle-headed ideas and programs of men such as Superintendent Ashe, who, if he is as careless with the truth in talking to pupils as he is when talking to teachers and parents, certainly is not qualified for the position he holds.

By November he was back speaking for freedom, at Baker University in Kansas. In nearly every speech, he spoke about the blessings of freedom and the curses of socialism. His remarks to the 1954 graduating class at the University of Arizona carried the essential message:

> All over the world the twentieth-century version of socialism—no matter what hi-falutin name it takes—has planted its vision in the bloodstream of the human race, leaving us wishy-washy, weakened and groggy—spiritually, morally and financially. The soft soap promises of easy living and the power-mad politicians and the hybrid socialists—whether they call themselves nazis, fascists, or communists—they have sold the common people of nearly every country on earth down the river.
>
> Socialism is as old as the hills. It has been tried for thousands of years and it has been found utterly wanting as far as the needs of mankind are concerned. It is the essence of retrogression, utterly threadbare of virtue.

It deprives the individual of his hard-won freedom and stops his slow but thrilling march toward real civilization. It is a flagrant fraud which masquerades as a democracy come to save the common man, but in reality it is nothing but the tyranny of an organized and greedy minority which eventually saddles onto its supine victims the stultifying shackles of admitted dictatorship.

He also emerged from worldwide travels as a severe critic of the U.S. State Department. Many of the ambassadors he met were "lameduck nincompoops," he declared. Department personnel were pompous, highbrow, arrogant, and stuffy.

At the White House, he complained to Eisenhower about the quality of the State Department personnel in overseas embassies. In one of the meetings, Eisenhower apparently decided to needle John Foster Dulles through Pulliam. Dulles was defending his overseas staff, until Pulliam asked how many embassies he had visited. After the answer, Pulliam replied: "Well, I've been in eighty, and I wouldn't pay but three of your men more than $35 a week."

He also became a critic of foreign aid—it didn't seem to win friends for the United States or stop communism. In Guatemala he had encountered several people, including a newspaperman, who explained why foreign aid would not win friends for the U.S., particularly when it was tied to paternalistic attitudes. One businessman told him:

You cannot buy a friend with a dollar. You must trust him, he must trust you. There must be mutuality. Your country lends money to these little countries and looks down its nose at them. We are weak, but we are not necessarily inferior. We have made great progress considering that all of these Latin American countries have large Indian populations which must be assimilated or at least fed. You killed off your Indians and you had no such problem in your pioneer days.

A Guatemala newspaperman listed a long string of grievances, including:

Your government has helped keep in power the most ruthless sort of dictators in Central America because those dictators were playing ball with your businessmen.

At the same time, Pulliam was favorably impressed with Senator Joseph McCarthy because of his vigorous anticommunism. They exchanged a few letters in 1951. Pulliam offered to make speeches for him in his 1952 primary campaign when he was threatened with challenges in his own party in Wisconsin. "I think it would be a rotten shame if the left-wingers of both parties ganged up on you in the primary," he wrote McCarthy. He also had no particular quarrel with Indiana senator William Jenner's anti-communism in the Senate.

But McCarthy's moves and behavior in the next couple of years began to change Pulliam's mind. He had agreed with McCarthy's basic objectives, to clear former communists and communist sympathizers out of the federal government, but McCarthy's erratic behavior turned Pulliam against him.

McCarthy's committee questioned *New York Post* editor James Wechsler in 1953. Wechsler, after testifying to his own association with the Communist party and answering the committee's questions, appealed to the American Society of Newspaper Editors and its Freedom of Information Committee to take a stand on the congressional investigation. At first Pulliam feared that Wechsler was trying to use ASNE to get back at McCarthy. He advised his son, a committee member: "Both Wechsler and McCarthy in many respects are bad actors."

> Wechsler was trying to use ASNE to crack McCarthy over the head, and if there is any intimidation of the press by McCarthy, I'm damned if I can see it—and anyway he is too smart to try to get away with it.

But the final ASNE report was a broader argument, contending that a free press would not survive the harassment of "unlimited inquiring into the conduct of newspapers" by Congress. Pulliam suggested to his son, Gene, Jr., that he go ahead and sign it, noting:

> Without regard to McCarthy's motives, I think Wiggins and Brucker made an excellent point. We can't allow the forces of investigation to become law in this country. It certainly is impingement on freedom of the press and under certain demagogues the press wouldn't be any more free here than it is in Argentina. This report of theirs is not an indictment of McCarthy; it simply is a defense of the free press, and if I were on the committee I would sign them both.

Only four, including Gene, Jr., signed the report, out of eleven committee members, and the votes were viewed as an attack on McCarthy. From then on, Gene, Jr., noticed that any correspondence he had with McCarthy was answered and signed by one of the senator's staff, in contrast to former personal letters from McCarthy.

The next year CBS's Edward R. Murrow and Fred Friendly went after McCarthy on their "See It Now" show, a few weeks before the Army-McCarthy hearings that sealed McCarthy's demise. "You are 100 percent right on McCarthy. Stand by you guns," Pulliam wired CBS president William S. Paley when McCarthy and conservative columnists like Westbrook Pegler attacked the program and the network.

A few months later he was quoting McCarthy's comment, "If the newspapers cannot control and regulate themselves, the United States Senate may have to do it for them," and suggested that:

> This points out the thing we must never forget—that while we may not have actual suppression, there is always with us a tendency toward suppression.

His travels had given him a love for American freedoms, its free enterprise system, and most especially its freedom of the press. He developed a stronger appreciation for the freedom he had in his newspapers after meeting with the editors in other countries. For the rest of his life he would view an attack on freedom of the press as the first step toward dictatorship and totalitarianism.

During this period he changed the motto of his newspapers. The motto of the *Star* had been "Fair and First." Now it was to be, along with all his other newspapers, "Where the Spirit of the Lord Is, There Is Liberty," from Paul's second letter to the Corinthians in the New Testament. An editorial explained the new motto:

> Today the motto of the *Indianapolis Star* has been changed from "Fair and First" to "Where the Spirit of the Lord Is, There Is Liberty." There are compelling reasons for this change, reasons that go to the heart of the purpose of this newspaper.
>
> The new motto is a quotation from II Corinthians, 3:17. These are the words of the apostle Paul, who spread the word of God and the faith of Christ to every corner of the known world. We believe in these words are capsuled the whole spirit of Christian living, the whole meaning of human freedom, the whole reason for the existence of man on earth.

For it is the Christian doctrine of all Christian churches that there can be no liberty without God. No nation of free men has ever existed for long unless the idea of God existed, and lived in the hearts of its citizens. The men who founded the Unites States of America based their entire hope, their fervid faith in the future of this free nation on these words in the Declaration of Independence: "We hold these truths to be self-evident, that all men are created equal, that they are endowed by their Creator with certain inalienable rights, that among these are life, liberty, and the pursuit of happiness. That to secure these rights, governments are instituted among men, deriving their just powers from the consent of the governed."

We the people derive our rights and our liberties from God. Governments derive their rights from us. There is no law of man above the law of God. It is in this faith that free America was born. It is in this faith that America will live in freedom.

Eugene Pulliam would hold these convictions to the end of his life, telling people in speeches, in editorials, and on a statue of himself in his newspaper plants:

If you forget everything else I say, remember this: America is great because America is free.

In Paris, October 1951, he and Nina stopped in to see one of the heroes of World War II, Dwight D. Eisenhower, now the commander of NATO forces in Europe. A fellow Kansan, Eisenhower swept Pulliam off his feet. They talked about freedom, the need to stop communism. Pulliam was captivated. He wrote to Kansas Republican Harry Darby, who was trying to plot a campaign, but without a declared candidate:

I don't know when I have been so inspired by a man's conception of freedom as I was by Eisenhower's—and I am still something of a cynical newspaper reporter.

Eisenhower breathed a sense of command, an aura of authority. Yet he was anything but stuffy and proper. Eisenhower was a boost to their spirits—world travels had been exciting, but also depressing, as Nina indicated in her description of Eisenhower:

His blue eyes turned bluer when he laughed, went gray with occasional solemnity . . . and always the deeply spiritual nature of the man looked out through clear mirrors of his conscience . . . there is not the slightest suggestion of vanity about him..he does not look in the least tired...his devotion to his job is utter. . . .

I came away with the secret thought, the personal conviction that Dwight D. Eisenhower as president of this country would give to its economic and political forces the moral rejuvenation they so desperately need in order to stop the crawling poison of communism from becoming a world-engulfing torrent, bent on destroying men's souls. This long journey around the world has taken us into many places and has shown us many things which lead us only to a feeling of futility and heartache and despair . . . but I left General Eisenhower with a new lease of hope . . . a reestablished belief . . . an assurance that the impossible is not impossible . . . my mood of last midnight had been completely dispelled.

Eisenhower seemed to have everything Pulliam was looking for in a presidential candidate. On domestic issues, he could talk about the need for freedom, the problems of bureaucracy. In foreign affairs, Eisenhower was an internationalist, not an isolationist, and he knew all the world leaders. Pulliam called Eisenhower's postwar effort with NATO "probably the greatest organizing job in history."

General Eisenhower has proved that the integration and unification of Western Europe can be achieved because under his direction it is being achieved every day in the building of defense equipment and material. What couldn't be done, General Eisenhower did by the sheer force of his personality.

Eisenhower was also an amateur in politics, a contrast to Truman with his roots in the Pendergast political machine. The party professionals, for the most part, were wary of Eisenhower or hostile, especially in Indiana, where they were closing ranks behind Senator Robert A. Taft. Indiana Republican senator Homer Capehart, for example, told Republicans to oppose Eisenhower— "We can't win with an amateur in politics." The Kansas remnant of the old Bull Moose movement was looking to Eisenhower—Roy Roberts, by then the editor of the *Kansas City Star*, and Ben Hibbs, a Kansas native and former Bull Mooser, now editor of the *Saturday Evening Post*.

But the final and most important key that put Pulliam behind Eisenhower was his belief that Eisenhower, and not Taft, could win in the fall of 1952 and end twenty years of Democratic rule. He was a shrewd pragmatist. Principles were no good, he reasoned, if they were always going down the drain on the losing side. Taft was soiled by his battles with the New Deal, whereas Eisenhower had a fresh image.

Pulliam came back from Paris ready to join the Eisenhower crusade. He joined it with the same sort of enthusiasm he had poured into the Bull Moose movement in 1912, enthusiasm he never displayed for any other presidential candidate except for Teddy Roosevelt. But his crusade for Eisenhower was to be very bumpy in Indiana. His old friend and foe, William Jenner, stood in his way.

24

1952

Dwight Eisenhower's lack of liberal or conservative identity didn't bother Eugene Pulliam, even though he shared with Taft Republicans, such as Senator William Jenner, a common opposition to an expanding federal government. Pulliam and Jenner also had more in common in their views on foreign policy than their rhetoric suggested.

But Pulliam was far from a regular Republican in spirit or personality—he was an insurgent by nature. He called Taft a "stand-patter," the same term the Bull Moosers used for Taft's father in 1912. Pulliam had no strong factional party ties. His only major ally for "Ike" was Congressman Charles Halleck, who had nominated Wendell Willkie at the 1940 convention. Halleck had shifted to the internationalist position on foreign policy after World War II, backing the Marshall Plan and costing himself support among more conservative Republicans back home in Indiana. Out of favor with much of the rest of the Indiana Republic party, particularly Jenner, Halleck found a sympathetic supporter in Pulliam. "The Jenner people, they argued I was a wild-eyed liberal," Halleck recalled. "Gene Pulliam was a conservative, but he had some sense too. Well hell, you know, you're not gonna repeal the social security act. Some of these things became a part of the fabric of society. Gene, he didn't suit some of these extreme right-wing people."

Eisenhower seemed to fit in well with Pulliam's own conservative political preferences. The general was neither conservative nor liberal in domestic affairs. He spoke inspirationally about freedom, and that satisfied Pulliam. Eisenhower was also an insurgent, a challenger of the Republican political powers, an amateur who was naively ignorant of the sordid details of the political process. It all appealed to Pulliam. He dove into the campaign with enthusiasm. He tried to invoke the divine blessing on Eisenhower, claiming God had raised up the general to save freedom in America and the world at a crucial time in history.

Pulliam concentrated his efforts in Indiana, rather than Arizona, which was much smaller and less important politically, and surprised his conservative followers. He frequently answered letters from people who asked how he could be for Eisenhower rather than Taft. An Indianapolis businessman, W. H. Bacon, wrote:

> Why did Mr. Eisenhower have the support of Dewey, Brownell, Lodge, Stassen, and others that we associate with the Republican New Deal?

Pulliam answered:

> I can't agree with you that Herb Brownell belongs in a class with Lodge, Dewey and Stassen. However, Senator Carlson of Kansas, Roy Roberts of the *Kansas City Star* and a few others of us were responsible largely in persuading Eisenhower to become a candidate. Lodge jumped into the picture to help himself in Massachusetts and Dewey already had announced himself for Eisenhower, but Brownell ran the show in Chicago. He and Wes Roberts of Kansas and Harry Darby were the real men behind the scene, and you can be assured that Lodge and Dewey are not going to run Eisenhower's administration if he is elected president.
>
> I agree with you that the public has to be informed on Eisenhower's views of socialism, bureaucracy and foreign policy. I think as this campaign progresses you will see that he is an outstanding candidate. If anything he is to the right of Taft. He is a natural conservative. He believes in everything that is fundamentally America. Otherwise, I couldn't possibly be for him, and I had to know definitely from him, himself—which I did—before ever I agreed to support him.

Taft was the hero of conservatives in the Midwest. Colonel Robert McCormick, a potent political influence in Midwest Republican affairs with his *Chicago Tribune*, was supporting Taft. Pulliam tried to counter his influence with Republican congressmen. He spoke for Eisenhower at a GOP congressional breakfast arranged by Indianapolis congressman Charles Brownson, one of the few Eisenhower supporters in Indiana. Eisenhower also had some support from Indianapolis businessmen

Fred Tucker, Warren Atkinson, and Gene Hibbs, but the Republican party in Indiana was under the tight control of Bill Jenner. He and U.S. Senator Homer Capehart wanted Taft. They did not even know if Eisenhower would run, but they feared he was a liberal, or at least not conservative enough. "Unless we nominate Taft, the New Deal is going to take over the Republican party," Capehart complained in an open letter to Indiana Republicans. Jenner did not like Eisenhower—Ike had gotten his job from George Marshall, whom Jenner called "a front man for traitors" in a famous Senate speech two years earlier.

Pulliam and Jenner had fought before. They were the two most powerful men in Indiana politics at the time, and two of the most strong-willed men in the state. But they were shrewd also. They decided not to make the Eisenhower-Taft contest a personal dispute between themselves. Instead Pulliam fought the Taft campaign primarily against Republican state chairman Cale Holder, a Jenner protégé whose later reward was a federal judgeship. Jenner made a minor concession to Pulliam—he decided to let him be a delegate for Eisenhower.

Even before delegate selection began, some Republicans were asking Pulliam to run for Jenner's U.S. Senate seat. There were two possibilities. The first was for Pulliam to challenge Jenner for the nomination in the state convention, although his chances of winning would have been very poor. The other choice was for Jenner to step aside from the Senate race and go for what had always been his real goal, the governor's office, which he had sought in 1948. Then Pulliam, with Jenner's support, would seek the Senate nomination. Pulliam was apparently tempted. He tried it out on his top executives at the *Indianapolis Star* and *News*. The then editor of the *Star*, Jameson Campaigne, recalled a meeting with the executives:

> Your grandfather asked, beginning with the business and advertising people, what they would think about his running for the Senate. He said that Eisenhower had asked him to do so, that Jenner was in agreement and that Bill would then run for governor, and that Ike had said it was his duty to run as a patriot.
>
> The question went around the table, and until it got to me, maybe four or five had said it was a great idea. I raised the question as to what would happen to the newspapers if he were nominated and elected to the

Senate. I asked what he would do, if a party question arose, that required him to take a position different from what his newspapers had taken in the past. It appeared to me, I said, that we who ran the newspapers in his absence would no longer be free to take positions on principle, but rather would have to wait upon his political accommodations with the party faithful.

I do not remember how many of us were opposed to the Boss becoming a senator. All I do remember is that when I opposed it, I felt that I was the only one who did. But that is probably not the case. Anyway, I was certain that if he ran for the Senate and won it would be very bad for the newspapers, regardless of other advantages that might accrue. I was certain that if he was in the Senate, I, as editor of the editorial page, would be no longer free to call them as I had been calling them.

The upshot of this meeting was, however, that the Boss (the Majority of One, as we called him) said he was astonished that anybody would have thought he would go into politics and run for the Senate. He said the most important thing to him was the integrity of his newspapers, and that he knew if he became a party politician, they would no longer be free to call them as they saw them. All of which was a relief to me.

I do not believe, even though it may have come up, that your grandfather ever seriously considered running for public office in 1952 or 1958, though I am sure he was tempted, as all people would be.

Although he decided against the Senate race, he was determined to do something for Eisenhower. He wanted to be a delegate to the national convention, to get in the thick of the fight himself.

The problem he faced, though, was that Jenner and the other Taft supporters wanted a delegation 100 percent bound to Taft. He and Jenner had one of their stormy meetings. Pulliam finally said: "Now, I want to be a delegate. Now, do you want to fight or are you going to let me be a delegate?" Jenner finally agreed. Why have a fight with the state's most powerful newspaper publisher? Taft supporters could remember what he did to other Republicans in the past. "We decided it'd be better to make him a delegate than have him hounding us all the time," explained the chairman of the Taft campaign in Indiana, Lisle Wallace.

He hounded them anyway. And they still tried to force him to vote for Taft. It was a strange arrangement, uncomfortable for both sides. Indiana had thirty-two delegates, twenty-two of them to be named in the eleven congressional district meetings. A May primary, although not binding at the district meetings, had provided an Eisenhower victory in the Eleventh (Indianapolis) District. So the party forces decided to give them two delegates: Pulliam, and, to court labor support, William "Big Bill" Hutcheson, the former president of the United Brotherhood of Carpenters and Joiners. Hutcheson, a veteran of internal labor disputes, was a rough-and-tumble type—he had engaged coal miners' union leader John L. Lewis in a fist fight in 1935 at an American Federation of Labor meeting.

The stories vary on what happened at the Eleventh District meeting. Dale Brown, a leader of the Eisenhower forces in Marion County, recalled that the Taft forces, having made a deal with Pulliam, were trying to divide the Eisenhower supporters by pitting Pulliam and Hutcheson against Brown and another Eisenhower delegate candidate, George Diener. Brown and Diener pulled out when they learned that Pulliam and Hutcheson had the support of the Taft forces, Brown said, adding:

> I pulled George aside and said let's don't file. Harriet Stout and Gene Fife were nominated from the floor to challenge Pulliam and Hutcheson. They were mad because they'd already selected us as delegates the night before the meeting. I had to calm her down. We went into caucus and they thought our names would be put into nomination. I took the mike and said to the Ike people, we're satisfied with Pulliam, don't play into the hands of the Taft people. Harriet finally agreed not to contest it.

Indianapolis Times columnist Irving Leibowitz, who was helping the Taft people and liked to mock "Publisher-Politician" Pulliam, saw the meeting from a different perspective. He wrote that the Bradford-Ostrom Taft machine, denounced for years by Pulliam in the *Star*, had made a deal with the publisher and steamrolled the arrangement over the protests of the Eisenhower supporters. It was a stormy proceeding. Perhaps the most accurate summary of the situation came from State Representative Thomas Hasbrook, a Republican, who complained:

> I do not favor the way Pulliam and Hutcheson were elected. The smoke-filled room apparently has given way to the ink-filled room.

The next day, June 7, was the state convention, when the ten other delegates-at-large were to be selected. The Taft forces, in tight control of the convention, approved a resolution pledging the entire delegation to support Taft. Pulliam, who was in Chicago, hit the ceiling, threatening to sue. Speaking for himself and Hutcheson, he told the *New York Times*:

> We will vote as we damn please. The convention cannot gag us and make us vote to suit them.

A day later, the controversy continued to gain national attention because the delegate race between Eisenhower and Taft was so close. Pulliam told United Press International:

> I was not elected by the state convention. If they think they can bind me, they have a horse on their hands.... He'll [Holder] do it over a lot of dead bodies.

The *Indianapolis Times* blasted him in an editorial, criticizing him for making the deal with the Taft forces in the first place.

The *Times* and the *Star* had battled earlier in the year when the *Times* hinted that Pulliam and Democratic national committeeman Frank McHale, a close friend of Pulliam, were working together in a bipartisan alliance to control both political parties in Indiana. Several abrasive front-page editorials in the *Star* and the *Times* heated up the controversy, which was reported in *Newsweek* magazine under the headline: "Indiana Warfare." *Times* columnist Irving Leibowitz dug up a story on how McHale's law firm, ten years earlier, had represented a Chicago brewery linked to the Al Capone gang during prohibition.

At the same time, Pulliam was using the *Star* in behalf of the Eisenhower effort. "Taft Steamroller Gains," declared one *Star* headline, and a few days later it was, "Ike's Bandwagon Starts." A page-one story on the state convention nomination of the pro-Eisenhower candidate for governor, George Craig, showed which side the *Star* was taking:

George N. Craig, former national commander of the American Legion, won the Republican nomination for governor last night from a rebellious state convention that repudiated dictatorial rule.

Party bosses were unable to stop Craig after losing control of the delegates at the convention held at the Indiana State Fairgrounds Coliseum.

Craig's victory on the third ballot was a revolt against the bossism tactics of state chairman Cale J. Holder and United States Senator Homer E. Capehart.

Holder got so tired of the *Star* coverage that he ordered subscriptions to the pro-Taft *Chicago Tribune* for a number of Taft supporters during the month before the national convention. Getting Eisenhower nominated was a do-or-die position for Pulliam. He threw the *Star* and everything else he had into the battle. The next step was the national convention in Chicago.

25

Crusade

I NEVER SAW him enjoy himself so much," commented Edward Ziegner, a political reporter for the *Indianapolis News,* who observed Gene Pulliam as a delegate at the Republican National Convention in Chicago in 1952. "He was really having a ball. He enjoyed all the fighting on the floor." Pulliam's main effort was to get the rest of the Indiana delegation to switch to Eisenhower. Congresswoman Cecil Harden was one of his prime targets, but state chairman Cale Holder, Senator Homer Capehart, and Taft's state chairman Lisle Wallace seated Pulliam and Hutcheson as far away as possible from her and the other delegates who were the most susceptible to switching.

He continued to use the *Star* in behalf of the Eisenhower campaign, and the *Times* continued to battle for Taft. When Mrs. Harden, a national committee member, along with former Governor Ralph Gates, did vote with the Eisenhower forces in the settlement of the Texas delegation, giving Eisenhower sixteen and Taft twenty-two delegates, the *Times* ran a story about "pressure" and threats that Pulliam had brought to bear on her. The *Star,* on the other hand, praised Mrs. Harden for her courage in voting independently of the rest of the Indiana delegation. The *Star,* in Pulliam's subsequent front-page editorial, complained about the "boss rule" of the Taft supporters:

> One of the shining exceptions to the boss-rule puppets on the National Committee was Indiana's own congresswoman Cecil Harden. Although Mrs. Harden was sent to Chicago as a Taft delegate, although she was under tremendous pressure to vote the dictates of the Taft machine, she

stood her ground and voted what she knew to be right. "On the merits of the case" she voted against the "Texas steal." Unlike Ralph Gates, Indiana's Republican national committeeman, who lay down supinely in the tracks of the Taft steamroller, Cecil Harden bravely stood up for principle rather than partisanship, for justice rather than political advantage. Her action stands out in sharp contrast to Gates' cowardly surrender to the machine.

His efforts to get the rest of the Hoosier delegation to vote for Eisenhower failed. After Eisenhower won the presidential nomination on the first ballot, Holder and Jenner still refused to allow the Indiana delegation to join the bandwagon. Pulliam tried to take the Indiana standard into the march for Eisenhower, but Holder managed to take it away from him in a pushing-and-shoving match. "That son of a bitch, he wouldn't change," Pulliam later growled at Ziegner.

In the fall campaign he seemed to try to make up for the way he had used the *Star* as his political instrument for Eisenhower. He gave Democrats front-page space in the *Star*. He wrote a memo to the *Star* editors, complaining that the headlines on Eisenhower stories were too big. The *News,* run by his son, Gene, had always been more balanced than the *Star,* and ran an investigative story in the fall campaign revealing a Republican party plan to slow down the voting on election day in Democratic wards.

There was one exception to balanced coverage in the *Star*— the stories, and lack of them, on the Democratic candidate for William Jenner's Senate seat—Governor Henry Shricker. Shricker was the only man ever elected to governor of Indiana twice. As the system prevented a governor from holding two consecutive terms, he had been elected in 1940, then again in 1948, and he was a formidable challenger to the controversial Jenner, who had denounced former Secretary of State George Marshall in a Senate speech two years earlier, calling him an "errand boy, a front man, a stooge, or a conspirator for this administration's [Truman's] crazy assortment of collective cut-throat crackpots."

Jenner was a stubborn man with firm convictions. He still did not like Eisenhower and his internationalism, and after the national convention, he sulked and fumed. Without the help of Eisenhower and Pulliam, he was probably headed for defeat. He recalled Pulliam's postconvention advice:

When it was over, we were leaving, and he [Pulliam] said, "Jenner, you go home and keep your mouth shut and you'll be all right."

At first he did not heed the advice: he denounced Pulliam and Eisenhower. Pulliam wrote to Taft, asking him to talk to Jenner about his attitude. In defeat Taft had been magnanimous toward Eisenhower. On the national level the Republicans began to pull back together with unusual unity, considering the bitterness of the primary campaign. Jenner, in compliance, began to keep his mouth shut. He quit denouncing Eisenhower, although he insisted he was not going to alter his own nationalist foreign policy convictions. "Fundamentals never change. I'm going to continue with the same fundamental principles that I've stood for for twenty years," he declared in a postconvention interview. The venom he had directed at Eisenhower and his supporters, he now doubled and redirected at the Democratic presidential candidate, Adlai Stevenson.

This friend of Alger Hiss and central figure in Illinois horseburger scandals pretended to be playing a coy game of hard-to-get until the blunders of the young alley fighters of the New Deal Millionaires Club compelled Stevenson to reveal his long-rehearsed plans.

He was reconciled to Eisenhower also—"I met a real American," he announced after meeting with him in early September. He needed the popular general's support to win in the fall. He also had the *Indianapolis Star,* front-page coverage and editorials. "He gave me the *Star,*" Jenner acknowledged. "I got the play." Editorials praised him, one saying he was needed in the Senate to continue the fight against internal communism, "regardless of what the pink professors from Harvard and elsewhere may wish." His opponent, Henry Shricker, was almost completely ignored in the *Star*'s news coverage except for a long critical front-page editorial just before the election. Pulliam was angry with Shricker, partly because as governor, he had pushed a bill through the state legislature continuing the political control of liquor licenses that Pulliam had denounced so often in the *Star.*

Also, Gene Pulliam's two closest friends in Indiana politics, Democrats Roger Branigin and Frank McHale, who were Catholics, told Pulliam that Shricker was anti-Catholic, which they based on Shricker's complaint that Catholics were in control of the

Democratic party. In the *Star*'s political coverage, former Governor Paul McNutt, campaigning for the Democratic ticket, received more coverage than Shricker, whose name was mentioned primarily when someone else was criticizing him. The result was a Jenner victory, yet he ran far behind Eisenhower and the Republican candidate for governor, George Craig.

Although he balanced the Eisenhower-Stevenson coverage in his newspapers, Pulliam did not tone down his personal involvement in the fall campaign. Sometimes he directed the news instead of reporting it. The assistant managing editor of the *News*, Wendell Phillippi, called him one day during the campaign to tell him about a story that state chairman Cale Holder was going to resign. Pulliam changed the story by changing Holder's mind:

> You tell Cale Holder he can't resign. We've got to have Republican unity and he can't resign. Tell him I said so.

Pulliam went out barnstorming for Eisenhower, making speeches in Indiana and Arizona, writing front-page editorials. One Bloomington newspaper story said he was "displaying a wide range of old 'fire and brimstone' oratory." In Phoenix, he told a Republican campaign breakfast: "God has brought Eisenhower to the fruition of his career in time to save freedom for America and for the entire world." He tried to win over the nationalists or isolationists who wanted to restrict American involvement in the world:

> I wish we could build a wall around America, but it's too late for walls. We must elect the man who inspired confidence in all of Europe, the one man who has the respect of the Russians, the one who can halt the creeping socialism that threatens our freedom.

He claimed that Truman and the Democrats had been too soft in the Korean War. "A year ago General Ridgway told me he could end the war in ninety days, if Washington would stop ramming its policies down his throat."

When the Eisenhower landslide came in November, he was ecstatic. He wrote in a front-page editorial:

Here the roots of the tree of liberty have grown deep and strong, so deep and strong that the totalitarian winds that have swept across Europe and Asia in the past twenty years have not been able to break them or tear them loose.

Yesterday's election has proved again how strong and how deep those roots have grown and how the tree of liberty still flourishes in our land with renewed vigor. Our people, with a surge of divine insight, have reasserted the principle that "man does not live by bread alone." They have said to their government, "There's more to life for free men than just free groceries." There is liberty, there is integrity, there is honor, there is faith.

He also compared Eisenhower to Lincoln:

Just as God raised up Abraham Lincoln to save the Union in 1861, so has God raised up Dwight Eisenhower to the peak of his career in time to lead us on this great crusade for freedom, for righteousness and for peace.

He was happy about Eisenhower's election. But he had been uncomfortable in his own partisan role, his conflicts in promoting a political candidate and running his newspapers. An AP reporter asked him if he would take a job in the new administration and he replied:

I am a newspaperman. It is our job to report and print the news objectively and to present editorials based on serious convictions that cannot possibly be suspect of political self-interest. To be really true to this policy, newspapermen must remain free and independent of political obligations.

He was constantly accused of job-hunting. Political professionals couldn't believe he meant what he said.

Some assumed he wanted to be an ambassador, as when he was asked on a Chicago radio interview about rumors that he wanted to go to Italy in that role: "Why, the only place I want to go is Heaven."

The moderator replied: "But, Gene, do you really think you'll get there?"

26

Phoenix Politics

IN ARIZONA, EUGENE C. Pulliam was interested in more than just reforming the Phoenix city government. As the morning newspaper in the state capital, his *Arizona Republic* automatically had statewide readership and impact. He did not like the one-party political system in Arizona, not because it was liberal—the Democratic party was actually very conservative, much like the party in other southern states—but because he disliked the lack of competition in politics. Elections were settled in Democratic primaries and conventions. The Republicans had never controlled either house of the state legislature and seldom could elect a governor.

After World War II, the state was ripe for change. Postwar economic growth, the campaigns of Pulliam's newspapers and a major Republican organizational effort, combined to rearrange the political structure of the state in a short twenty years. By 1964, the state was a conservative Republican stronghold, sponsoring a conservative Republican nominee for president, Barry Goldwater. Out of the same party came another conservative senator, Paul Fannin, and conservative representative John Rhodes, who became the Republican House minority leader in 1974.

Two men helped make possible the political change—Pulliam and Goldwater. Pulliam's papers provided a forum for a daily, articulate statement of the views he had developed by 1950. The new Arizona population, which stemmed largely from the Midwest, already had conservative instincts. The successful experience with charter government in Phoenix showed what businessmen could do to build a city without the state or federal government aid liberal

Democrats favored. Charter government also provided a springboard for Goldwater and others, like Phoenix mayor Jack Williams, to go on to statewide office.

In the early statewide races in Arizona, the conservative-liberal debate had not come to the surface. The young Republicans, Goldwater and others, emphasized their new blood and youth in politics and their good-government background in Phoenix charter government campaigns. They contended that Democratic opponents were too entrenched as an old political machine.

The first race in the new Republican effort came in 1950, when the Republicans named radio executive Howard Pyle to challenge the Democrats for governor. For the Democrats, Mrs. Anna Frohmiller, the state auditor since 1927, won the primary. Pyle won a close race, with the endorsement, constant editorial support and favorable news coverage from the *Arizona Republic* and *Phoenix Gazette* providing him with a winning margin. Goldwater had been named to run Pyle's campaign, and Pulliam applauded the choice in an editorial.

> One of the hopeful and refreshing aspects of the appointment of Barry Goldwater to work with Howard Pyle is the fact that neither is a saddle-galled politician who has spent his life at the public trough. Both are young businessmen, with a fresh viewpoint and progressive ideas.

The Pyle victory set the stage for 1952, when Goldwater decided to run for the U.S. Senate in what appeared to be a hopeless cause. He took on the majority leader of the U.S. Senate, Ernest MacFarland. A young attorney named John Rhodes was also running in what he thought would be a losing race for Congress against incumbent Representative John Murdock, the chairman of the House Interior Committee. The Eisenhower landslide, combined with editorial support from the *Republic* and *Gazette*, helped Goldwater and Rhodes win their upsets. Ironically, Goldwater's victory gave his future presidential opponent, Lyndon Johnson, the opportunity to move up to majority leader of the Senate.

The Republican party was well established in Arizona after the 1952 race. No longer could the Democrats settle statewide races in a primary. The Republicans were still far behind in voter registration, but they could no longer be ignored.

By the next election, in 1954, Pulliam was hesitant about backing Republicans again. Goldwater pleaded with him to throw his newspapers behind Pyle's reelection effort. Pyle was being seriously challenged by the well-known former Senator Mac-Farland, and a Republican loss would set back the GOP efforts to build a party in the still predominantly Democratic state. But Pyle had disappointed Pulliam.

The governor had ordered the National Guard to invade a polygamous Mormon colony in northern Arizona in the summer of 1953. The governor went on statewide radio to announce that he had declared a state of insurrection in Short Creek. The National Guard and police were sent in, arresting thirty-four men and fifty women. "It was like a military assault on an enemy position," wrote Associated Press reporter James Cary. Pyle had put $30,000 in the state budget for quelling the "rebellion." Gene Pulliam, like Pyle, was a preacher's son and was not going to defend polygamy; but Pyle's approach annoyed him and he let loose in one of his characteristic front-page editorials:

> There can be no doubt that Governor Pyle's coup made the front page of every newspaper in the nation, but certainly it was a humiliation to the citizens of this state.
>
> Most assuredly the guilty men in Short Creek should have been locked up long ago for their licentious misuse of children and their flagrant flouting of the laws of decency. But what of the women and children? Their lives now bear an indellible tag—words that are too cruel to print.
>
> The only life they know has been disrupted in a bewildering raid that resembles too closely the hated police-state roundups of the Old World.
>
> But why in the name of decency was it necessary to enlist the aid of more than a hundred law enforcement officers, armed to the teeth, in serving warrants on people who are so isolated they couldn't run any place anyway?
>
> By what stretch of the imagination could the actions of the Short Creek children be classified as insurrection?
>
> Were those teenagers playing volleyball in a school yard inspiring a rebellion?
>
> ...Nobody condones the illicit activities of the little core of sensualists. But our heart goes out to the youngsters who have been branded for the rest of their lives as outcasts because of coercion practiced on their misguided mothers. And the state plans to tear them apart!

> However wrong a way of life may be, it cannot endure for years without building up some ties of human affection. Nor can the disruption of these ties be entirely remedied by providing food and shelter.
>
> Again we say—officials of the state of Arizona have humiliated its citizens by a pistol and shotgun raid that resembled an operation to subdue Pork Chop Hill.

By fall of the next year, Pulliam had decided not to support Pyle, to have his newspapers remain neutral despite Goldwater's pleas. Pyle's Short Creek operation was the reason. Pyle had an independent spirit. Some thought he was arrogant. He was not inclined to bow in the direction of the state's most powerful publisher or anyone else.

"I was kind of an independent thinker," Pyle later commented, adding:

> I didn't seek more than a casual relationship with him [Pulliam]. I was well established in public and didn't have to work the newpaper angle. I was very determined not to be obligated to anyone.

The 1954 race may have been the beginning of Pulliam's break with Goldwater, a break that did not surface in public until 1964. "We can always start another paper," Goldwater told Pulliam after MacFarland beat Pyle. *Republic* reporter Avery explained:

> That falling out [in 1964] might have gone back to Pyle and 1954. Barry made remarks. He's kind of an intemperate guy. The roots were in things that Barry said about Gene for not supporting Pyle. Barry popped off at him privately.

Pulliam resented anyone telling him how to run his newspapers, whether it was a political figure or a minority stockholder or a journalism school professor. He was the boss and he resented anyone who treaded on that authority. Avery thought the conflict had roots in Goldwater's expectations of Pulliam.

> Gene let Barry Goldwater know that the Republican party wasn't running the *Arizona Republic*. Barry expected more blind loyalty. Everything was black and white with Barry. He felt the *Republic* should be a Republican party newspaper.

Gene Pulliam also expected gratitude, rather than bitterness, from someone he had helped along the way. It bothered him when one of his boys grew independent of him, and Goldwater would always be his own man. They were both blunt, independent, forceful men and were perhaps bound to clash at some point, as they did ten years later.

27

Businessman

PULLIAM AND HIS wife, Nina, slowed down their world travels in the 1950s, after Eisenhower's election. However, he was still going at a hectic pace, speaking in California, Texas, flying to Chicago and New York City frequently, shuttling back and forth between Phoenix and Indianapolis. When he was applying for a television station license, he was asked how he divided his time between the two cities:

> I don't know. I have never even thought about it. I am there when I am required to be there and if I have to be in Phoenix, I can leave my home in the morning, and eat dinner in Phoenix, and get back the same day, so I am one of the business commuters in America.

He always wanted to be a newspaperman first and businessman second. Still, he could never abandon his business suit—only a man with the wealth of a William Randolph Hearst could spend and spend without worrying about a balance sheet.

Pulliam nevertheless maintained a general policy of spending to improve news coverage instead of maximizing profits, as, for example, keeping a large and expensive newshole in his newspapers instead of using the space for more advertising.

He put in an opposite editorial page over the objections of his business advisers, who pointed out that it would cost at least $500 a day considering the loss of advertising and cost of newsprint. He poured $2 million into plant expansion in Indianapolis in 1950. Sometimes his spending policies caused disputes with other stockholders who lacked a newspaper background. These disputes made him more determined either to buy them out or to keep them out of decision-making positions.

"The only thing which is not clear is his tendency of not paying dividends," said a memo from an investment company as part of a reference for a loan application. He kept dividends low to put money back into the newpaper, and he could always win arguments with stockholders. He held majority control of Central Newspapers, which in turn held a majority of the stock in Indianapolis Newspapers, Inc., Phoenix Newspapers, Muncie Newspapers, Inc., and the *Vincennes Sun-Commercial*. The *Lebanon Reporter* went to his second wife Martha in the late 1940s. In 1964 he sold the *Huntington Herald-Press* to his son-in-law James Quayle, who had worked for him in Indianapolis, Huntington, and Phoenix and later was publisher of the Muncie newspapers.

Minority stockholders included the Ball brothers in Muncie and Indianapolis—he had bought their preferred stock in 1951—and, in Indianapolis, the Fairbanks family. In Phoenix, the most troublesome setup, other stockholders included author and political figure Clarence Buddington Kelland, actor Gene Autry, Los Angeles broadcast executive Robert Reynolds and New York advertising executive Bruce Barton.

By 1960 Reynolds and Autry asked for more regular and larger dividends, and they wanted a representative on the board of directors in Phoenix. Pulliam restricted the board membership tightly—in Phoenix, to himself, Nina, and one of the ranking executives from the newspapers. He ran board meetings with an iron hand, tolerating little dissent or argument. He replied to their requests for bigger dividends and board membership by arguing that the company had to maintain the lower dividends to hold cash reserves for plant expansion. He added that they didn't know enough about newspapers to be on the board:

> The problems involved in operating a newspaper are generally conceded to be rather peculiar to the newspaper business. A newspaper operates, by and large, in the public interest. Its success, in the long run, is measured by the success with which it meets its continuing responsibilities to the public in the community it serves. The demands made on the newspaper are inconceivable to anyone not actively engaged in or long familiar with newspaper operation. As the high cost of staying in business has forced newspapers to consolidate, this has become increasingly true.

He said that he wanted to maintain the separation from radio and television, having sold his radio interests a year before in anticipation of increasing government interference in broadcasting:

> I am very thoroughly convinced that newspapers should be divorced from both radio and television. As you know, our newspapers have no connection whatever now with either radio or TV. Our public relations have improved immensely since we have taken this position and our own personnel is free from having to compete with itself. Also, we are completely free from government interference of any kind, which is not true in the radio business. Therefore, it would be highly inconsistent for us to consider bringing any person actively identified with radio into our management. It took us five years to convince a lot of people in Phoenix that Gene Autry didn't own the newspapers there. That wasn't Gene's fault, but nevertheless, it certainly didn't help the Phoenix newspapers.

His past experience with lawyers and bankers made him antagonistic to them. His will decreed that neither lawyers nor bankers could be involved in running his newspapers after his death. Lawyers, he observed, seemed quick to kill stories for fear of libel; bankers were too interested in profit.

He had become a wealthy man. But he had not succumbed to the temptation to make money his only ambition in life. He told *Time* magazine:

> Why in hell should I want to sell newspapers? If I wanted to make money, I'd go into the bond business. I've never been interested in the money we make but in the influence we have.

He also lost his ambition to buy more newspapers. He was content with Phoenix and Indianapolis, Arizona and Indiana. He made a few efforts to buy other newspapers after 1948, including the *San Francisco Chronicle* in 1949. He also looked into a purchase of a Cincinnati newspaper. In 1953, he made a halfhearted try at buying a San Antonio, Texas, paper, but he gave up. "I don't have chainitis any more," he would remark to friends when asked if he wanted to expand his empire.

He didn't like the trends toward groups and chains after World War II, although he had been a part of it before. He couldn't see how Gannett, Knight, Ridder, and Newhouse executives could supervise ten, twenty or thirty newspapers. Seven seemed like a big enough job to him. "Otis has got conglomeritis," he complained about Otis

Chandler, publisher of the *Los Angeles Times*, who bought up major newspapers like *Newsday* and the *Dallas Times-Herald*. Chandler tried to buy Phoenix from Pulliam, offering $60 million at one point, and *Los Angeles Times* stock in other informal offers. "You're not getting any younger," the middle-aged boyish-looking Chandler told Pulliam. "Well, neither are you," Pulliam shot back.

He told friends that if he did sell to anyone, it would be to John Knight. He admired Knight's newspapers and their emphasis on editorial excellence. He liked to print Knight's weekly notebook, a column distributed originally to Knight newspapers, and later reprinted in other newspapers. For Gene Pulliam, the price was an annual case of whiskey. As Knight explained:

> The "case of whiskey" price applied only to a few of my favorite and affluent publishers—such as your grandfather. Such gentlemen would ask me how much I would charge them for the column, and I invariably replied, "A case of whiskey at Christmastime, if you can afford it."

The man he was least likely to sell to was Samuel Newhouse, who bought large numbers of newspapers but took little interest in the editorial side, allowing local managers to run them. Newhouse made him several informal offers. In one encounter in the Waldorf Astoria in New York, Newhouse made yet another offer and Pulliam blurted out:

> You're just a damned junk dealer, Sammy. If I wanted to make money I'd go into the bond business. You're just a damned junk dealer.

Pulliam had other opportunities to expand after he had become a major publisher. He had joined with some midwesterners and westerners seeking to wrest control of the New York Central Railroad from representatives of stockholders from New York, including heirs of the Vanderbilt and Morgan fortunes. The new board included Gene Pulliam, Indianapolis banker Frank McKinney, and two Texas oil men, Clint Murchison and Sid Richardson, who offered to buy him the *New York Herald Tribune* when it was losing money in the late 1950s and early 1960s. They were seeking a conservative alternative to the *New York Times*, they told him. Their offer was tempting—New York was the capital of the world in many ways.

> It was a losing thing. You needed a backlog of $25 million to compete
> with the *Times* and not ape the *Times*. So I told the Texans, I could buy
> it for $5 million, but I wouldn't give 5 cents of my own money for it. I
> told them I needed $25 million to do it. Sid said, "Clint, have you got $25
> million?" Clint said yes, he did. "Well, if you can get $25 million, I guess
> I can." So they asked me, "Will you buy it?" and I said, "I wouldn't get
> involved in the newspaper business here even if you gave me the *Times*."
> You'd have to run a yellow paper. I didn't give a damn about New York
> and didn't want to compete with the *Times*.

He also added that he didn't want to be in business with the two men
from Texas breathing down his neck.

At another time, he had an opportunity to buy a morning
newspaper in Washington, D.C., an opportunity to influence
national policy more directly. The *Washington Times-Herald* was
up for sale and he was approached about buying it. Eventually the
Washington Post bought it.

> It would have been too late in life for me; and you needed unlimited
> resources. I had the *Star* and *News* and Phoenix and had lost whatever
> ambition I had to have one in Washington. I could have borrowed
> money, but sold my soul with it. Or I could have raised a bond issue.
> Several times I could have made big deals, but that would have given the
> bankers a veto over editorial policy. I said nuts to that.

28

Disillusionment with Ike

W HEN GENE PULLIAM was roasted in the Gridiron dinner of the
Indianapolis Press Club in 1965, the speaker declared: "The last
radical thing he did was to support Eisenhower in 1952." His
crusade for Eisenhower was indeed the last time he teamed up with
insurgents in a major race. The rest of his life he would be fighting
the liberals, mostly Democrats, and above all, fighting the
bureaucracy and the growth of ever bigger government. No longer
was he hesitant to call a spade a spade, no longer was he going to
worry about being called old-fashioned. He had hesitated to oppose
the drift of the New Deal during the 1930s, as he suggested in a
commencement speech at the University of Arizona in 1954.

> We discovered we had thrown a cloak of respectability about the
> shoulders of a little group of politicians, social planners and thugs who
> were taking control of our affairs. We had come to the place where we
> actually curried their favor. We thought it was cute to go along with the
> bright young men who ridiculed the old-fashioned virtues which are the
> deepest-down foundations of our country. We didn't want to be accused
> of being patriotic for fear we would appear to be provincial hicks, and
> we wouldn't be caught dead getting thrilled by the words and music of
> anything old-fashioned and reactionary as the "Star–Spangled Banner."

He had thought Eisenhower was the man to save America from
the communist threat, to save freedom within America, to slow the
growth of the federal government and roll back the New Deal. Ike
proved to be a disillusionment, a shattering one because Pulliam
had thrown his whole heart and soul into the campaign.

His first disappointment was the appointment of John Foster
Dulles as secretary of state. He wanted General Lucius Clay, the hero
of the Berlin airlift, although he realized that one general in the
administration was probably enough. He feared Dulles would just
continue the policies of Truman's secretary of state, Dean Acheson,
easily influenced by the British Foreign Office. He was unhappy
with Dulles' rigid and inflexible approach to diplomacy.

He poured out some of his misgivings in a letter to the new
Arizona senator, Barry Goldwater, who shared similar concerns:

> I wish I could tell you that your misgivings are without foundation, but
> having been in about sixteen states during the last six months, I can tell
> you that you have correctly felt the pulse of the people. Everybody was so
> enthused and so hopeful about Eisenhower that they have been giving
> him the benefit of every possible doubt. He started off with a great deal of
> courage. His move in the Pacific in taking the wraps off the fleet is what
> brought about the demand for a Korean truce on the part of the
> Russians. Since then, however, we have allowed our foreign policy to
> become completely dominated by the British Foreign Office. Dulles is as
> much a tool of the British Foreign Office today as Acheson ever was. He
> is simply another Chamberlain, and because our foreign policy is so
> inescapably interwoven with our domestic policy, people are beginning
> to ask questions which are serious and pertinent. I hear on every side
> that the Republicans have substituted a New Deal for the Roosevelt Old
> Deal, and of course there is a great deal of foundation for this feeling.
>
> If we could have an ideal situation in this country, it would of course
> follow the pattern you have indicated. The conservatives would be in
> one party and the starry-eyed liberals in another, but because of the
> situation in the South that happy day is a long way off, if I correctly
> judge the behavior of politicians.
>
> In the meantime, every person who honestly believes in the destiny of
> America must also stand firm for a strong America, with preservation of
> the Constitution at all costs and for the free enterprise system. We have
> proven by very drastic and expensive experiments that we cannot buy
> friendship throughout the world. All of our global do-gooding has
> brought us not one sincere friend, and of course in the end it would
> bankrupt this nation.
>
> In the meantime, I think we must support Eisenhower as far as we
> possibly can. We must disagree with him when the chips are down and
> basic principles are at stake. At heart, I know he feels exactly as you and I
> do, but he has been surrounded by a group of bureaucrats and foreign
> diplomats to the point where he must be confused. At least his policy
> creates the impression that he doesn't know exactly where he is going.

Pulliam was also disappointed with Eisenhower's willingness to go along with traditional political pressures. He had warned him not to let the political advisers around him manipulate him.

"The Republican party did not elect him," he told the Associated Press after the meeting with Eisenhower. "He's got to remember that he elected the party instead of the party electing him."

With respect to Indiana politics, Eisenhower quickly ignored the advice. Within a year, he nominated Indiana State Republican chairman Cale Holder to a vacant federal judgeship. The two Indiana Republican senators, Jenner and Capehart, demanded Holder and no one else. They threatened to oppose all the Eisenhower programs. Jenner was a stubborn enough man to make big trouble for Eisenhower in the Senate.

Pulliam didn't care about political reality. He thought Holder was unqualified. To what extent he was motivated by the bitter Taft campaign is difficult to pin down. Undoubtedly it played a part. But he denied it constantly and his own assertions that Holder was unqualified and the appointment a flagrant political payoff were true, although Holder turned out to be a competent federal judge, as Pulliam would later acknowledge.

Pulliam pulled out all the stops in an attempt to block Holder's nomination. He sent a telegram to Sherman Adams, Eisenhower's chief of staff:

> Appointment of Cale Holder as federal judge in Indiana would be complete repudiation of everything Eisenhower's administration stands for. I have no candidate but I will oppose to my last breath such an unconscionable appointment.

He wrote front-page editorials. He called congressmen from Indiana, and even Arizona, frightening the new representative from Arizona, John Rhodes. Rhodes was not accustomed to dealing with Pulliam, and he was not sure what to do. Pulliam threatened that if Holder were nominated, "I'll be mad at Republicans, and not just in Indiana." Pulliam tended to exaggerate when he was on the rampage. If you worked for him, you might learn that over the years. But it was still a scary experience to face his wrath, even for a long-time and high-ranking executive like Indianapolis *Star* editor

Jameson Campaigne, a former marine, who remarked, "It was kind of terrifying to have him mad at you." Pulliam wrote to Adams again about the Holder appointment:

> In all the years of defaming the judiciary, Roosevelt never did anything as bad as would be the appointment of Holder to the federal bench. He has no qualifications for the job.

But his appeals were of no avail.

Another early disappointment was the nomination of Earl Warren as chief justice of the Supreme Court. Pulliam had liked Warren in the 1940s for his independence and nonpartisan record as governor of California. But by 1952, Pulliam had grown more conservative and Warren was moving in the other direction. Warren asked Pulliam to support his appointment to the court, but Pulliam refused and vowed to oppose him.

> He tried to get me to support him for the Supreme Court. I said I would be a committee of one to stop him. You're a socialist and you'd change the whole complexion of the Supreme Court, I'd tell him.

He did not campaign heavily against Warren, because Brownell had told him not to worry about it, that Warren wouldn't be appointed.

By 1956, Eugene C. Pulliam was no longer a starry-eyed, idealistic crusader for Eisenhower. He still supported him, but with reservations and criticism. Again, he went to the Republican convention, in San Francisco, as a delegate, and was appointed to the Republican Platform Committee, the foreign policy sub-committee. He advocated a strong civil rights platform, but did not want the 1954 Supreme Court decision directly mentioned because it might drag the court deeper into politics.

> I'm for a strong civil rights plank. I think we should have one. But I don't believe it is up to any political party to approve or disapprove of any decision of the Supreme Court. In this case, that would be political expediency.
>
> And it might tend to make the Supreme Court biased. We shouldn't do anything to put the Supreme Court in politics. The court should be concerned only with what's right—what's constitutional.

He wanted foreign aid placed on the basis of loans rather than outright grants. He had found in some of his travels that countries resented the paternalism of U.S. foreign aid. But his proposal was blocked by Eisenhower administration officials and he left the convention early, and unhappy. His advice was rejected again and again.

He still supported the administration in the election. He kept his personal faith in Eisenhower, often assuming he was misled by people around him. He told the Scottsdale Rotary Club in 1956:

> Eisenhower is a different type from any man we have ever had in the White House, except possibly in the early days of our country. I don't think there ever has been a man in the White House so utterly devoted to what he thinks is right.

He began to question Ike's "divine mission" after the 1956 election, telling the Huntington Chamber of Commerce in 1957:

> For at least six years I felt that God had raised up Eisenhower to save freedom and the Republic from the federal bureaucracy—but I'm not sure. He still is a great man and understands America.... I know what is in his heart, but what the bureaucrats have sold him is another question.

Ultimately he never really blamed Eisenhower. Later in life, he continued to blame the people around Eisenhower, telling a questioner:

> I thought Eisenhower's experience as the executive of the greatest army in history would give him a wonderful background for the presidency. I was wrong. Eisenhower was a good president because he was a good man, but he knew nothing at all about politics and was the victim of petty political intrigue time after time. It was a game in which he had no experience, and he did not know how to play it successfully because he was always forthright and frank—something a successful politician seldom is.

29

Conservative Democrats

GENE PULLIAM'S BEST friends in Indiana politics were Democrats, although, for all of his fights with the Republican party, he was still clearly a Republican and a conservative. Frank McHale, McNutt's right-hand man in the 1930s, became his closest friend in politics in the years after World War II.

Pulliam's other close friend among the Democrats was Roger Branigin, later elected governor in 1964. Pulliam had wanted Branigin to run against Republican Senator Homer Capehart in 1950, but Branigin didn't want to run—he liked Indiana and didn't want to spend time in Washington, D.C. Branigin had been born in Franklin and was a teenager when Pulliam ran the *Evening Star*. One of the wittiest men in Indiana politics, he had a blunt edge that Pulliam didn't find in many other political candidates who sought his favor. The three men would all die the same year—McHale in January, Pulliam in June, and Branigin in November.

To the extent that Pulliam socialized among Indiana political figures, it was with Democrats. "They were better people," Republican lawyer Kurt Pantzer said, explaining why Pulliam preferred McHale, Branigin, and another Democratic political figure, Frank McKinney, to Republicans like Jenner, Capehart, and Gates.

Gene Pulliam always put a lot of stock in what he thought was a candidate's personal ability to perform the duties of office. Although he generally shared and supported Capehart's conservative views, Pulliam complained privately about Capehart's bumbling tendencies. He liked to call him "Senator Cupcake" and tell stories to illustrate his ineptness in public. In Capehart's race for a fourth term in 1962, Pulliam kept his newspapers neutral, giving his Democratic opponent, Birch Bayh, a chance to win by a narrow margin. It was hard for Republicans and Democrats to grasp the subtleties of his politics. He remained an enigma. Republicans thought he was a traitor who deserted the cause too often. Democrats were angry because the editorial policies of the newspapers criticized so many of their proposals to expand government. If he could be identified with any political group in Indiana in the 1950s, it was with conservative and moderate Democrats like McHale and Branigin, and in Indianapolis politics, with Mayors Phil Bayt and Charles Boswell, who were equally opposed to federal programs.

Bayt was elected in 1955, then switched over to become Marion County prosecutor. Boswell, having succeeded to mayor, was elected on his own in 1959. Both grew up in Indianapolis and worked their way up the ladder in Democratic party politics. By 1950 they could see Pulliam was going to be a major factor in Indiana politics.

They began to visit him, play golf with him. And they began to oppose federal aid to Indianapolis, a stance that endeared them to Pulliam, who thought federal aid would lead to greater federal control over the city.

Opposition to federal aid had become a kind of test of loyalty to Indiana in the 1950s. Liberal Democrats mocked the opposition as old-fashioned. Conservative Republicans and Democrats thought they were taking an important stand, drawing a line and firmly saying no. The state's stance drew national attention in a *Saturday Evening Post* article—"They Don't Want Uncle Sam's Money." The city had already done a great deal for itself before federal money became increasingly available after World War II. Indianapolis developed its own slum clearance program, and received no federal aid until 1951.

Although the city and state turned down a number of federal grants, preferring to do things their own way, the most controversial issue arose when the legislature, backed by the *Star*, voted to make welfare recipient rolls open to the public. Federal Security Administration's Oscar Ewing threatened to withhold the state's $20 million in annual federal funds. Jenner and Halleck were finally able to get federal legislation approved to stop Ewing and they had vigorous support from the *Star*.

The welfare records controversy, combined with the opposition to federal aid, naturally made Pulliam and his newspapers very unpopular among professional social workers. Boswell, who had come from a professional social work background, thought much of this criticism was unfair, arguing that:

> He was basically the biggest do-gooder in all of Indiana. He criticized the federal government for its failures, but he always helped the local community. The greatest push for these programs came from these newspapers.

"In my time he did more for the agencies trying to help people than anyone else," Boswell continued. "It was part of him. He knew that he, Gene Pulliam, had a responsibility like no one else in the state of Indiana."

Bayt, who moved up to become mayor at the death of Al Feeney, ran against Republican Alex Clark. He found himself caught in a trap in the 1951 election. As a Democrat, he felt he had to give nominal support to Ewing and the Truman administration. But it cost him the election in the fall. By 1955 he was opposed to federal aid.

When Pulliam received a Sons of Indiana award from Hoosiers living in New York City, he spoke of Indiana as a model for standing firm for freedom, for withstanding the encroaching powers of the federal government.

> We neither pass the hat nor the tin cup. We believe in paying our own way and not in expecting handouts from the government. . . . We have no state debt. We are opposed to federal aid to education. We are opposed to socialized medicine. We are opposed to public power and we have held the line on the right-to-work law.

When Bayt ran for mayor again in 1955, Pulliam did not come out with a ringing endorsement, but neutrality in the major Republican newspaper was enough to give him a chance. He won the election. Then, unable to succeed himself, he gave up the mayor's office to his city comptroller, Boswell, in 1958 and ran for Marion County prosecutor with the *Star*'s endorsement. Boswell was elected mayor on his own the next year.

Boswell looked up to Pulliam as a kind of father figure. He had ideas, and vision, said Boswell, adding:

He'd give us counsel, he'd help us have philosophy. We needed help. Phil's parents were from southern Europe. I was from the rural South. We had to have help. We wanted to do the right thing. He helped me more than any other man in the city. Some of that old John Wesley was left in him from his father. My uncle had been a preacher too. Everything was black and white to them. The world had to be saved.

Meanwhile the *Star* was uncovering information about Marion County Eleventh District Republican chairman Dale Brown's activities, including accusations of payoffs for liquor licenses he obtained for others. Local Republicans blasted Pulliam and his newspaper crusades, sometimes through the *Indianapolis Times*. The *Times* front-paged a story on one political meeting when local Republicans backed Brown against the findings of the *Star*.

> *Indianapolis Star* publisher Eugene C. Pulliam today was condemned as a frustrated dictator by local Republican leaders as they unanimously reaffirmed their confidence in H. Dale Brown, Eleventh District chairman.

A deputy prosecutor and Eleventh District Young Republican chairman, Charles Daugherty, suggested that the Republicans must "rise up against the oppression of King Gene."

Democrats also made him their target. Former Democratic representative Andrew Jacobs, Sr., singled him out along with McHale when he sought the Democratic nomination of the U.S. Senate seat held by Republican Homer Capehart. McHale, the national committeeman, opposed Jacobs. Jacobs was crusty, belligerent, outspoken, independent. "Andy was just an unwashed, hypercritical populist,"said Charles Brownson, a Republican who succeeded to Jacobs' congressional seat in 1950. "Andy needed a big target."

Jacobs picked on Pulliam and McHale, denouncing McHale because of his friendship with Pulliam, as well as the legal work he had done for the *Star*. Pulliam tried to be fair to Jacobs for a while, as Jacobs recalled, calling him to come and complain if he felt he had been treated unfairly in the *Star*. "He was conciliatory, but I had a hard on for Frank McHale. I say what I think. I enjoyed the fight—it was fun."

"McHale prided himself on being the attorney for the *Star*, and I made a speech at the Athletic Club about McHale not being a genuine Democrat, playing footsie with the *Star*," Jacobs said. "It didn't win me votes, but it made me feel good. And I said the *Star* had Republican connections and was trying to control both parties. I was spoiling for a fight."

The *Indianapolis Times* entered the feud that emerged, taking the side of Jacobs, calling the *Star* a Republican house organ, and the two newspapers went to war against each other with a series of front-page editorials. Pulliam retaliated with an order he had seen William Rockhill Nelson issue against a number of people in the *Kansas City Star*, a strict order never to allow Jacobs' name to appear in the newspaper. Eventually the order was eased, as Jacobs' son entered politics and became a congressman in the 1960s and Jacobs himself ran successfully for a judgeship in 1974, the year before Pulliam died.

Pulliam didn't hesitate to use his influence when he was angry about something. Elected in the 1952 Eisenhower landslide, Republican Governor George Craig proposed that deaf children be transferred into the public school system early in his administration. Pulliam heard about the plan from a friend, Butler University trainer Jim Morris, who gave him rubdowns and enjoyed the close friendship Pulliam had with his barbers and doctors in Phoenix and Indianapolis. Morris had heard about the bill that would end the separate Deaf School in Indianapolis, providing for their special needs from a deaf neighbor. Pulliam had employees who had been to the school. He made some calls to his newspapers to check on the bill, then called Craig from Morris' rubdown room at Butler. Craig told him he thought it was a good bill, although he acknowledged he had not read it. "I don't want to hear another damn word about it," Pulliam told him, and that was the end of that bill.

He was not always so bossy and demanding, and grew much less so as he grew older. He surprised political figures with his charming, gracious manner on social occasions. His temper tantrums were exaggerated, though the rampaging style of his editorials suggested he would be a cantankerous, difficult man to confront in person. Instead, candidates were frequently greeted by a friendly, warm man who had a way of putting them at ease in his home.

"I couldn't believe this was the guy who published the *Star* and the *News*," commented Democratic state chairman Gordon St. Angelo, recalling his first meeting with Pulliam in 1965 after Branigin had been elected governor. "Democrats thought he was a boss, a Boss Crump, a power broker type," St. Angelo said. "But he never demanded anything, he'd just make a few suggestions. I was never told to do it his way; he treated me more like a son. And he didn't always take the conservative position."

Sometimes Pulliam could be conned and manipulated. He tended to listen to the last person he talked to, or sometimes the wrong person. Once an aide to Governor Craig, Jim Gregory, told Pulliam that former state chairman Holder was lobbying against part of Governor Craig's legislative program. In the factional politics after the Eisenhower landslide, Holder and Jenner were opposing Craig. Pulliam instinctively sided with Craig and against the Jenner faction. He came out swinging in a front-page editorial the next day, denouncing Holder, accusing him of trying "to wreak personal vengeance upon his own party."

> Cale Holder is getting even with the Republican party for nominating Dwight Eisenhower and George Craig against his personal wishes and the wishes of a political minority of his party. When Republican members of his own party deliberately slap the governor in the face in this manner, who benefits? Sure, Democrats benefit. But does the state of Indiana?
>
> When Republicans play factional politics to the ready tune of a deposed and vindictive political has-been, whom do they serve? The people who elected them to do a job of running the state government efficiently and honestly? Of course not. They serve selfish party factionalism and the cause of the Democratic party in 1956....

The next day a small but embarrassing item ran on the front page, stating the *Star* had been wrong. Holder was not in the state legislature lobbying against the Craig program. Jameson Campaigne, the *Star* editor, asked Pulliam, "From now on, do we take orders from Jim Gregory, or do we do it the way we think is right?" Pulliam blew his stack, but finally growled, "Dammit, do it any way you please." Campaigne noticed that Pulliam interfered less often in local editorial matters after the incident.

Sometimes he was bitter toward a political figure who told him one thing, perhaps because he thought it was what Pulliam wanted to hear, and then did the opposite. "He never lied to you at all," said Lisle Wallace, a factional foe during the Eisenhower-Taft fight. "You never had to go through a third party to know where he stood," added Charles Brownson. He expected the same sort of candor from political figures, but often he didn't get it and became embittered.

Sometimes he was naive. "Well, he's the president of the United States and he wouldn't lie to me," he blurted out to Campaigne and *Star* foreign editor Michael Padev after they tried to persuade him that President Kennedy had misled him about his future foreign policy plans.

30

Turkey, 1958

AGE DIDN'T SLOW him down much. Eugene C. Pulliam turned sixty-nine May 3, 1958. He had bought fifty-one newspapers in thirteen states. He had lived through the Spanish-American War, World War I, World War II, and the Korean War. He had survived the depression to rise to the top of the newspaper world after World War II and became a major political figure in Arizona and Indiana. For another man, it might have been time to retire and take life easy, or at least settle back in semiretirement. But for Pulliam, his life was his newspapers, and he continued to travel around the world.

He seemed to be everywhere at once in 1958; fighting Democratic Senate candidate Vance Hartke and his organized labor supporters in Indiana one day; swinging back to Arizona to argue in front-page editorials with Tucson publisher Bill Mathews; blasting the Menderes government in Turkey; criticizing the inflexible diplomacy of Secretary of State John Foster Dulles under a byline from Cairo, Egypt; golfing with President Eisenhower in Phoenix; pleading the cause of freedom from government when receiving an award from the journalism school at Columbia, Missouri; and telling a *Kansas City Star* reporter about business conditions in Arizona during a stopover in the city where he got his start in newspaper reporting.

The articles on Turkey revealed the independent streak in his nature, his unwillingness to be boxed into an ideological framework that totally colored his view of the world. Many who read his newspapers or knew him personally had cast him into a firm conservative, anticommunist mold. It was a fairly accurate picture of his views—he wanted freedom from more government interference at home and abroad, and he wanted to check the spread of communism and promote the capitalistic way of life. But the Turkey experience showed another side, the ability to call them just as he saw them, without being blinded by ideological commitments, the capacity to size up a man without being taken in by his ideological stance. The same streak would explain, at times, why he seemed to forsake conservatives and Republicans in politics, why he deserted Barry Goldwater in 1964, or the Republican party in Indiana after World War II. He was a conservative, but not an ideological one. He came to his convictions more by experience and observation than by philosophical reflection, and further observation could lead to new convictions.

The irony of the Turkey articles was the fact that the Turkish government, whatever its faults, had been a strong ally of the United States in the Cold War, firmly opposed to the Soviet Union and communism. And generally he looked for that kind of ally—his defense of Spain and Franco had been based on anticommunism, despite Franco's dictatorial ways. He and Nina had visited Turkey previously, coming away with favorable impressions. In 1951 he noted, "If American assistance to Europe had been as successful in the other thirteen countries as it has been in Turkey, the defense of Western Europe would be much further advanced than it is." He also approved of the way Turkey was emerging into the modern world:

> Turkey is proud of her troops' record in Korea. General MacArthur described them as "magnificent fighting men." One of the greatest but also most spontaneous demonstrations ever held in Istanbul developed here recently when a group of wounded Turkish soldiers was brought home. It was a welcome from the Turkish people, not the government. It was typical of the new Turkey which is evolving after centuries of dictatorial rule into one of the really genuine and progressive democracies of the Middle East.

Pulliam was disturbed by a number of things when he and Nina visited in the fall of 1958. The economy was sliding downhill, a black market was developing. Menderes was becoming dictatorial, manipulating the court system, surrounding himself with yes men and passing laws that made it a crime for newspapers to publish anything that "could harm the prestige of the government or any official." Pulliam concluded:

Power and personal authority have gone to his head. He has abandoned the program under which Turkey was making noteworthy progress when he took office. He has led her to the brink of disaster.

The loss of freedom of the press disturbed him. He talked to Turkish newspaper editors. They told him about other editors who had been jailed and fined for criticism of the Menderes administration.

The story we are writing could not be written by an American correspondent or any other foreign correspondent inside Turkey. He would be thrown out of the country or thrown into jail.

Pulliam never intended to write articles that would lead to a coup and a revolution. His purpose was to encourage Menderes to change his ways. "Despite all his grandiose failures, Menderes still is the key to recovery in Turkey because he is the duly elected prime minister and, barring a revolution, cannot be replaced until 1961 — and this will be too late," he and Nina wrote in the second article.

They suggested that the United States use its foreign aid to Turkey as a lever to straighten out Menderes.

The United States already is being censored throughout Turkey for the Menderes dictatorship and the Menderes failure. We can save Menderes and ourselves if we will bring him to his senses. He was an able and trusted leader before power went to his head.

He must be made to realize he has one last chance to restore freedom to Turkey, to revive the economy of his country, and to save himself. The new loans should be used exclusively for the purchase of raw materials and the restoration of industrial production.

He should be prevailed upon to dismiss the hordes of ineffectual yes men from the government. Capable administrators—there are many of them in Turkey—should be brought in to put the economic wheels in motion. America's position in this connection should be expressed with firmness, courage and tact.

More than one Turk, both officials and private citizens, told us they fervently wish American representatives sent to Turkey had more "guts."

It is not too late, but it is about half past 11 o'clock for both Menderes and Turkey. Unfortunately, that includes the U.S.A.

The two articles were much more mild than what Pulliam had written about Republican party affairs in Indiana after World War

II. But, when they were reprinted in Turkey by a number of newspaper editors during the next few months, the impact of the Turkey stories was startling. Ulki Amman, editor of the *Ulus* in Ankara, was fined $444 and sentenced to sixteen months in jail for printing the articles, according to the official sentence for "belittling those in an official capacity." His paper was suspended for a month at the same time, March 1959. In July, Shap Bulcioglu, copublisher of the weekly *Kim* newspaper in Istanbul, got the same sentence for reprinting the articles. Two weeks later, the man the Associated Press called the "dean of Turkish journalists," Emin Yalman, was sentenced to eighteen months and sixteen days in jail, and fined $1,388 for running the articles. Yalman, seventy-two, educated at the Columbia University Journalism School in New York City, was the owner of the *Vatan*, an Istanbul daily. He developed a heart ailment a few days later, delaying the full sentence until the next year. In December, four other dailies reprinted parts of the article, and a government prosecutor ordered them to stop. The next day the editors left black spaces where the articles had been scheduled to appear.

The opposition, led by Ismet Inonu, protested, but to no avail. Menderes' Democratic party set up a commission of inquiry into "opposition activities," empowering it to exercise press censorship, shut down newspapers, and jail people who hampered its work. Inonu was expelled from the assembly during the debate on the commission in April 1960.

Meanwhile student demonstrations, joined in by professors, started at universities in Ankara and Istanbul, protesting the commission. At one point government police fired on them, killing one student. The press was forbidden to publish reports of the demonstrations. In late May, fighting broke out between members of Menderes' party and the opposition in the assembly. The fabric of the constitutional republic was coming apart. On May 27, between midnight and 4 A.M., the army seized power throughout the country.

It was an unusual revolution—only three persons were killed. Menderes was hanged the next year for crimes against the Turkish constitution. The new government, led by General Cemal Gursel, freed two hundred students and nine newspaper editors from jails, and allowed fourteen newspapers that had been shut down by the Menderes government to start publishing again.

A month before the coup, Pulliam had set up newspaper fellowships for Turkish newspapermen at his newspapers, working through the Turkish Editorial Association. "I caused these people a lot of trouble," he said in announcing the program.

> At least we can show them what America is like and that we do have a free press.
>
> The real reason I did this is because of my admiration for the courage of these newspaper people. They're the most courageous newspaper people in the world.
>
> How many newspapermen would print a story if they knew they would go to jail the next day because of the story?

He became a kind of folk hero among Turkish newspaper editors. *Indianapolis Star* foreign editor Michael Padev, already traveling in Europe, headed for Turkey after he got the news of the coup, and was greeted enthusiastically by editors. Pulliam's accusations against Menderes had been vindicated by subsequent events. "Pulliam's name is an honored name in Turkey," Padev heard from Yalman, now out of jail. "Your publisher and your newspapers made Turkey's fight for freedom an international issue." Another editor, Dogan Nadi of the *Cumhuriyet*, added:

> This revolution was made by the press, the university people and the army. But if it weren't for the press perhaps nobody would have acted. And the Turkish press had very important and powerful allies—your newspapers.

An intellectual who was brought into the new government, Professor Husenin Kubali, was even more ecstatic in his praise:

> Tell publisher Pulliam your newspapers have made history in modern Turkey—in a most positive and honorable way.

Observers of the Turkish events were more guarded in their analysis, but few doubted Pulliam's impact. Thalia Donas, working for the Associated Press, reflected:

> The articles undoubtedly helped the opposition press in its struggle against the tyranny of the Menderes regime. They triggered a series of legal proceedings against well-known journalists which came to be known as "The Pulliam Trials."

All these developments made front-page news. Added to his other troubles, they created an unwholesome atmosphere toward the end of 1959—just a few months before the coup d'état which toppled Menderes in May 1960. They were one more thorn in his side.

31

1958

W HEN HE WASN'T trying to reform the government of Turkey in 1958, Gene Pulliam was mixing it up in a series of the roughest political brawls he had been in since his attacks on the Republican party in Indiana after World War II. This time his opponents were Democrats in Indiana and Arizona, supported by national labor representatives. He threw his morning newspapers into the fight.

U.S. Senate seats were up for reelection in both states. Both were targeted by labor as key spots for electing Democrats favorable to their cause. In Indiana, Republican William Jenner, tired of politics and Washington, stepped down after two terms. Jenner had never voted the labor line, nor had the Republican candidate who hoped to take his place, Governor Harold Handley. Handley was a special target of labor because he had refused to veto a right-to-work law approved by the Indiana legislature in 1957, despite pressure from organized labor.

In Arizona, Barry Goldwater was warming up to run for his second term. His election was far from the sure thing it became in the 1970s. Arizona was still a Democratic state, and Goldwater had been elected in the Eisenhower landslide of 1952. He was being challenged again by the man he had upset in 1952, Ernest MacFarland, who had proved he was still popular by being elected governor in 1954 and 1956. Labor wanted MacFarland to win— Goldwater had consistently voted against their recommendations.

To some extent 1958 was an ideological battle. Despite Pulliam's discontent with Republicans in Indiana and his occasional minor differences with Goldwater, he thought the AFL-

CIO's political arm, the Committee of Political Education, was pushing for the kind of socialism he had seen in England and other European countries after World War II. He wanted to stop it. The Republic, he was convinced, was in danger of losing its freedom if a European form of socialism, embodied in some of the proposals of the liberal wing of the Democratic party, were established in the United States.

> Newspapers have got to debunk the idea that socialism ideology is progressive. It is neither progressive nor liberal. It is the most diabolical idea that has arisen in the world in the last 500 years.

Pulliam used the same strategy in Arizona and Indiana. His efforts in Indiana failed, because Handley was already governor and his opponent, Vance Hartke, capitalized on resentment that the governor was not finishing out his term. Hartke's campaign was not completely blacked out in the *Star*, but stories on his speeches were repeatedly put in inside pages while Handley was regularly treated to a front-page story. The thrust of the *Star*'s campaign was to show Hartke as a tool of outsiders, out-of-state labor bosses.

Toward election day, the coverage was more balanced, with Hartke stories on page one along with Handley. Pulliam's son, Gene, Jr., complained to his father that the *Star*'s coverage was way out of hand. "I'll take care of it," Pulliam responded. The *Star*'s coverage reflected the personality of the managing editor, Robert Early, who was an old-fashioned fighting newspaperman like Pulliam, Sr. The *News* covered the Hartke-Handley campaign in a balanced manner, giving equal space to the two candidates. As it turned out, the *Star*'s campaign was not enough for Handley. Hartke beat Handley by 200,000 votes.

In Arizona the Goldwater-MacFarland race was rough on both sides, and the *Republic* jumped in on Goldwater's side. MacFarland claimed he had not received any contributions from COPE, but the *Republic* revealed that he had. MacFarland came back charging that the *Republic* was running a "vicious hate, smear and fear" campaign. MacFarland linked Goldwater with Senator Joseph McCarthy, saying he was using the same techniques "as his old friend and teacher, the late Senator Joseph McCarthy." The Sunday before the election, handbills appeared linking Goldwater with Stalin.

State Democratic chairman Joseph Walton claimed that the Democrats were not getting outside help from labor. The *Republic* ran a picture of Walton outside a restaurant with Charles Alva Green, a COPE worker with a criminal record, coupled with a story that started off:

> One of Walter Reuther's political musclemen, who has a record of criminal violence, has moved in on Arizona Democrats and is directing the COPE campaign to beat Goldwater, elect Morrison, and win control of the Arizona State Legislature.

Walton came back with an attack on Pulliam, accusing him of trying to destroy the two-party system in Arizona. The next day Walton had to back down at a Phoenix Press Club Forum, acknowledging that Gene Pulliam had helped develop the two-party system in Arizona since World War II. But Walton insisted that Pulliam was not an independent but a Republican, whose candidate for governor was Paul Fannin, a Phoenix businessman. Republican state chairman Richard Kleindienst shot back:

> Unless a meeting was held at 5 o'clock tonight, to my knowledge Paul Fannin has never met with Mr. Pulliam, was not asked to run by Mr. Pulliam, nor did Mr. Fannin consult Mr. Pulliam when he ran. Secondly, I personally have had only two or three meetings with Mr. Pulliam; consequently this is not a personal situation. I wish I had the privilege, like Joe Walton, of playing golf with Mr. Pulliam out at the Paradise Valley Country Club. That has not been accorded me. Maybe that is my status in the Republican party.

Walton misunderstood Pulliam. Pulliam was independent. But in 1958 he threw his entire newspaper into a fight he cared about, with little effort to step back and seek some sort of balanced approach to the controversy.

Critics had a case against Pulliam in the coverage of the Senate races in Indiana and Arizona. But the complaints about another race in Arizona were questionable. In the Democratic party, State Attorney General Robert Morrison was running in the Democratic primary against a conservative real estate man from Phoenix, Richard Searles, a former Truman administration official in the State Department.

Morrison blasted away at Pulliam from the start of his campaign. Searles blasted Tucson Democratic publisher William Mathews. Pulliam and Mathews got into an old-fashioned editor's duel. Morrison started attacking Pulliam in 1957, criticizing the political bias in his newspapers, calling him a carpetbagger from Indiana, finding fault with the extent of his growing political influence in the state. He told a Phoenix Young Democrats meeting, for example:

> The main external problem we have is creeping Pulliamism. It has taken over the Maricopa County courthouse and is headed for the capital. And to achieve that end he (Pulliam) is running candidates on the Democratic side as well as the Republican side.

After Morrison announced he was running for governor, Ben Avery, a quiet *Republic* reporter who had heard rumors about Morrison's criminal record in the 1930s, went to see Pulliam, later recalling:

> That was the thing that made me really love Gene Pulliam. He called me in, and asked my opinion of Morrison. I said he had not been truthful. So he sent me to California, and I tracked down the background to the rumors. I told Morrison about the information I had, and he threatened to sue. The story that Morrison told was an outright lie.

Avery's story ran in the *Republic* a month before the primary election. It detailed Morrison's record of passing bad checks, abandoning his wife, who had sued him for desertion, changing his name and leaving California. Morrison's response was a threat to sue, although he never did. He labeled the series "an act of sheer desperation by an opponent who could find no fault with my spotless record in Arizona."

In Tucson, *Arizona Daily Star* publisher Bill Mathews was outraged. He was supporting Morrison for governor. He and Gene Pulliam were fighting newspapermen, and had quarreled before. Mathews was also the son of a Protestant preacher and a hero to the Democrats in Arizona. Like Pulliam he used his newspapers to promote his political objectives. "Once convinced, he carries his ideas in one hand and a hatchet in the other," a personality feature described him.

Pulliam and Mathews were colorful and belligerent figures, although Pulliam was considered slightly less arbitrary and cantankerous than Mathews. "Bill was openly arbitrary," explained former Govenor Howard Pyle. "Gene was arbitrary too but Gene was more subtle about it."

Mathews was more parochial in much of his approach to Arizona than Pulliam. To Mathews, it was Tucson against the world. And Morrison was the Tucson candidate for governor in 1958. Mathews blasted the *Republic* for the series on Morrison, arguing that Morrison's background in the depression should be forgotten.

> *The Arizona Republic* of Phoenix has stooped to a new low in journalism by invading the early married life of Bob Morrison, who like many couples in the 1930s suffered family and business misfortunes.

Pulliam came back the next day in the *Republic:*

> Mr. Mathews must be naive indeed to believe the story about "youthful indiscretions" and "overdrawn accounts" which Mr. Morrison has tried to peddle. The record extended over five years. It is clear and the facts are unquestioned.

The *Republic*, responding to Mathews' attack, summarized Avery's findings, concluding:

> 1. On June 28, 1933, Morrison was accused of "making, passing, uttering and publishing" a fictitious check on the Fresno Main Office, Bank of America, signed with the name of "J. Larson." The complaint said, "There was no such person in existence."
> 2. On Sept. 8, 1933, Morrison was accused of writing a bad check Aug. 26 of that year on the Fresno Branch, Security First National Bank of Los Angeles.
> 3. Morrison pleaded guilty to these two checks and was given sixty days.
> 4. On Feb. 8, 1934, he was mugged and fingerprinted in connection with a charge of writing a bad check on the Fresno Main Office on the Bank of America.
> 5. On Aug. 21, 1935, Oakland police picked up Morrison for the Contra Costa County sheriff's office on a felony warrant accusing him of writing checks without funds in the bank.

6. Oakland police picked up Morrison on Dec. 29, 1935, on a charge of writing checks in Tracy, Calif., and he was delivered to San Joaquin County officers the following day.

7. Not long afterward, a complaint was filed against Morrison asking the court to evict him from his farm for failure to meet payments despite harvesting a crop.

8. On March 26, 1936, a bad check complaint was signed against Morrison by Frank Hickman. A felony warrant was filed on April 1.

9. On Oct. 11, 1939, Morrison appeared before the Alameda County Superior Court and was sentenced to thirty days in jail.

10. On April 2, 1945, the Fresno Superior Court held that Morrison had done nothing to support his daughter by his divorced wife for the previous twenty months. It denied his application for part-time custody of the child. It ordered him to pay $500 in unpaid support money to his previous wife, and to resume payments of $25 a month.

Here are ten separate items in Morrison's record. They cover a period of twelve years. Any criminal lawyer will tell you that hot check artists usually pass off many more checks than ever get into police and court records. But there are enough in the Morrison record to prove it was no childish prank, no mistake in arithmetic that led him to overdraw an account.

Millions of Americans lived through the depression without making the passing of bad checks almost a way of life. Hundreds of thousands of Americans never went to jail, or had their debts "disposed of as misdemeanors." Mr. Morrison, who beats his breast, says he has told the people everything when he hasn't, and asks them to elect him governor of the state.

No one was arguing with the facts that Avery presented. Morrison didn't challenge them—he attacked Gene Pulliam instead. Mathews didn't challenge the facts either, but instead initiated a theological argument:

As a Christian I believe in the doctrine of forgiveness and the atonement of sins. Mr. Morrison has more than atoned for his sins by the exemplary life he has lived since he has come to Arizona.

He added that:

As one who went through the Big Depression I know how desperate I and others were at times. I used some bum checks in those days, but fortunately I was not prosecuted for such criminal acts.

Pulliam came charging back:

> If a man pays a debt to society and is truly penitent, he is entitled to live his life as a private citizen without further harassment. But if he misrepresents his record, continues to dismiss it as unimportant, and actually lies about it, then we believe the criminal record of a candidate for public office deserves careful consideration in the voting booth.
>
> The Christian virtue of forgiveness requires that the erring sinner have a certain amount of sincere repentance. We haven't seen the slightest indication that Bob Morrison thinks he did anything particularly out of line in issuing bad checks, deserting his wife, failing to support his daughter, and living in Arizona as a fugitive from justice.

The publishers of the state's two major newspapers were having an old fashioned political duel on their editorial and front pages. Searles had taken to attacking Mathews for supporting Morrison, charging "Mathewism." Other candidates in Tucson were criticizing Mathews. *Nogales Herald* editor Hanson Ray Sisk got tired of it all and wrote:

> All of this is political rot and should have no bearing on the campaign. Important public issues are seemingly forgotten and the campaign is directed against the publishers of Phoenix and Tucson.
>
> As a matter of fact, Mr. Mathews and Mr. Pulliam have a perfect right to express their opinions and to endorse or oppose any candidate seeking public office. American newspapers have done this since the nation was founded.
>
> When a candidate for office sticks his neck out and enters a campaign for public office he can expect to be criticized or lauded. It is as it should be.
>
> The trouble is many candidates are thin-skinned and should they be opposed by the press, they immediately charge the press is trying to dominate the party or the election.
>
> We know both Mathews and Pulliam. They are fearless American newspaper publishers and are successful in their journalistic enterprises. Arizona is fortunate to have men of their caliber and newspapers which are not dominated by political parties. We know they are independent in their judgment and are staunch, loyal citizens of our great state.
>
> The people are interested in issues, not tirades against newspapers who have the right to a free press.

Morrison won the primary, despite the stories. But in November, Fannin won the election and Goldwater defeated

MacFarland. Some Democrats were bitter about the Morrison stories. "I thought it was a low point," said Stuart Udall, then a congressman and later secretary of the interior. Other Democrats disagreed and thought Morrison deserved what he got from the *Republic.* Charles Pine, later a Democratic state chairman, says, "Morrison was not an ethical man. He shouldn't have got the nomination in the first place."

A Democrat who worked for Pulliam, Tom Sanford, an assistant managing editor at the *Republic,* often didn't like the treatments Democrats got from the *Republic* in the 1950s. But in the case of Morrison, "I think Robert Morrison asked for everything he got. He should have made it public himself. . . . "

32

Employer

LABOR UNION REPRESENTATIVES had a hard time figuring out Gene Pulliam. Here was a man who fought them tooth and nail in the 1958 elections, in Indiana and Arizona. Here was a man who had backed right-to-work laws in both states, at a time when a chief goal of organized labor was to abolish the laws that forbade compulsory union membership. Here was a man who denounced organized labor's efforts in politics, and got denounced in return. Before the 1958 campaign, the Phoenix chapter of an international machinists union had asked for a congressional probe of "abuses of the press" in Pulliam's newspapers.

Yet here was a man who never had a strike at his major newspapers in Indianapolis and Phoenix from 1944 to his death in 1975—a period when nearly every other major metropolitan newspaper that was unionized had several strikes. And here was a publisher who was given award after award from his unions. "He's unparalleled in terms of employers I've seen," said Darwin Aycock, a stereotyper at the *Republic* and *Gazette* in Phoenix who went on to become head of the state AFL-CIO. "You can be angry with him for the editorial page, but you know you'll be treated fairly at the bargaining table. He said he'd join a union if he wasn't the publisher."

He believed that the major responsibility for the well-being of the employees was that of the employer. He tried to provide an example of how it was supposed to work in his own newspapers.

In Indianapolis and Phoenix, it was harder for his unions to go on strike when they knew the publisher cared about their welfare.

"As a publisher, he's offered more on a personal basis, always helping out. Like the 'Fourth Estate' [recreation area]—no one had done that before in newspaper publishing. He has built up a lot of loyalty this way, especially among the back shop people," said *Indianapolis Star* assistant managing editor Charles Griffo. He was often the first to call after someone was injured or became ill, choosing the best doctor in town, the right hospital, picking up bills which were not formally covered by company insurance. He paid for the college education of employee's children, eventually establishing a foundation to finance formal scholarships. He provided scholarships for newspaper carriers.

It was hard to go on strike when there was a company swimming pool and recreation area for the family. It was hard to go on strike against the man who golfed with your union representative or brought you over to his house or danced with your wife at a company party. He had an impulsive desire to do things for employees. "My fondest memory is a phone call I made telling him I was a grandfather," recalled Ross Garrigus, his editor for a number of years at the *Vincennes Sun-Commercial.* "My son was in Pakistan at the time and he said I should go to see him. Mr. Pulliam footed the bill for the trip."

He knew more about the details of his employees' jobs than most publishers. He had been poor, he had known life without medical insurance, he had struggled to make a dollar. And he had carried paper routes, laid out papers, run presses, sold advertising. When the life of *Indianapolis News* reporter Fremont Power was threatened for writing a series about Negroes in Indianapolis in 1949, Gene Pulliam could respond sympathetically. He had been through the same sort of threats with the Ku Klux Klan in the 1920s.

Part of his quarrel with organized labor and the liberal approach was that they wanted government to force business to do what he was already doing. He was ahead of his time, ahead of his unions at times—they hadn't even thought of asking for the benefits he gave them. "He's done things before he had to do them," explained *Star and News* general manager William A. Dyer.

Soon after he bought the *Star*, he ran up against Joe Shepard, a reporter and guild organizer, a Eugene Debs socialist who was threatening to call a strike on the new publisher. Mark Ferree, then an executive at the *Indianapolis Times* and later a top figure in the

Scripps-Howard organization, was impressed by Pulliam's ability to handle Shepard, recalling:

> He [Shepard] was a crackpot. I had to negotiate with him with the guild. He was a police reporter for the *Star*, surly, and they never gave him a raise and wouldn't fire him. We told him to go organize the *Star*. Joe threatened Gene with a strike, and then Gene called me and said Joe's okay. He gave him a raise and some recognition on reporting and an office. Joe had told Gene, unless he did certain things, we'll strike. Gene replied, I just bought the paper. If you want to strike, do it now. We'll take the strike rather than your bum recommendations. He called Joe's hand. Management used to pussyfoot with him.

Shepard would never forget Gene Pulliam, always asking about him until he died. And Pulliam didn't forget Shepard. He kept him on the payroll long after Shepard could do a full day's work.

Receiving the John Peter Zenger Award in 1966, he complained about publishers who did not treat their employees as fellow human beings:

> Let me give you an example of publisher oversight, aloofness and stupidity for which there is no justification. Some weeks ago the heads of the various printing trade unions and the labor relations committee of the American Newspaper Publishers Association held a joint meeting in Phoenix. Nina and I had a dinner party in our home for the union officers and the publishers' labor committee, together with their wives. In the course of the evening the president of a union which is represented in the majority of the newspapers throughout this country told me this was the first time in his life he had been invited to a publisher's home.
>
> Here was a man with the same feelings and ambitions as other men, a man who has reached the top of his chosen profession, yet never before had a publisher thought to invite him to his home. Was this inexcusable oversight deliberate? I don't think so. My personal opinion is that too many publishers fall into the human error or thinking in terms of friends and foes, rather than in terms of human beings.
>
> Instead of constantly fighting each other, I believe the printing trade unions and the publishers should get together on a program of mutual advancement and self-protection. Thousands of mechanical jobs may be at stake if the federal government ever brings the newspapers under federal regulation. The unions and the publishers have so much in common that I cannot help but believe that tolerance and common sense and willingness on each side to see the other's viewpoint will solve almost any problem confronting us. And we need a united front—the

printing union and the publishers—in this fight to head off federal domination of newspapers, for ours is a common cause versus government.

His aid in emergencies was hard to forget—he was there so often when an employee needed help. Apparently no one ever kept a record and only a few of the stories are known. Usually employees were instructed to keep it to themselves when they received help. *Indianapolis Star* cartoonist Charles Werner had a ruptured appendix, and Pulliam paid all the bills, provided twenty-four-hour nursing care. "It would have broken me," Werner said. *Arizona Republic* reporter Don Bolles had a daughter who was deaf.

> At age one and a half we learned that she was deaf and I began enquiring how much our medical plan would pay. The price of hearing aids was fierce—$1,000 a pair, and schooling more so. Gene found out about it somehow and I was sent to Cleo Smith, who informed me that the boss wanted to take care of any expenses I couldn't handle. And he did— buying two sets of aids.

In another case, he paid all the expenses of a costly lung operation for advertising manager Lee Hover. "He paid it all. It happened to reporters, it went on all the time. None of us were allowed to talk about it," Hover said. "In the press room you'd run into guys who were loyal to him for this. We'll fight for him, although he's ornery."

"He'd go further for you than Charles Stauffer," said *Republic* reporter Ben Avery, comparing Pulliam with one of the previous owners of the Phoenix newspapers.

> When Gene backed you, he backed you all the way. If you got sick [under Stauffer], it was your hard luck. Under Gene Pulliam, if you got sick, it would be the same as if you were his son. Usually the first person we heard from was Gene Pulliam when anybody got sick. This was just unheard of.

He kept people on the payroll when they were sick, he put widows of employees on the payroll, sometimes at full pay. He wanted to reward loyalty of employees. Seldom was anyone fired for incompetence. A few were fired in his thirty years, but usually for other reasons.

He made many threats to fire people though, and his overbearing, domineering manner led to a certain fear of "the old man," a tendency to try to please the publisher at all costs. Some older employees thought their coworkers took Pulliam too literally and seriously and would water down his orders, assuming he had exaggerated, and ignore his threats to fire them. "It was just his way of being emphatic," said a long-time employee, *Republic* assistant managing editor Tom Sanford. Strong personalities like Bolles or Ed Murray or his son Gene were not afraid of him, but few had the guts to stand up to his withering blasts. He could be irascible and cruel when he was angry about something, and would seldom apologize directly for a temper tantrum. Hover found that he did so indirectly:

> If you made a stupid mistake, he had a short fuse. He could be a rough customer. Then he'd forget it, and ask you to play golf the next Saturday.

He became a kind of patriarchal figure in his later years at annual company picnics. He always wanted to establish a family atmosphere for his employees, and the picnics were the highlight of it all, in Indianapolis and Phoenix, with a day of free food, drinks and entertainment. "Anyone else, it would sound corny. He really sees it that way," said Don Bolles.

Shortly before his death the International Typographers Union was trying to organize the newsroom and other nonunionized departments in Phoenix. He responded with an emphatic letter to all employees, defending his record:

> You know that salaries, benefits and working conditions have improved year by year. The record proves our policy of paying the best possible salaries and providing the best possible benefits. We always have and we always will. The record speaks for itself. It is a record which includes the best pension plan, the best medical plan and the best recreation program of any newspaper in the country. The R&G ranch is an outstanding example.
>
> A union can promise you more but it cannot get you more. And obviously the union itself cannot pay you. There is no money to pay salaries except what we get from advertisers and readers. Increases have to come from the money we get from advertisers and subscribers and from greater efficiency.

> If the papers cease to publish because of a strike, advertisers and subscribers would turn to other media. Some would never come back. And then there would be fewer jobs and less money for salaries and benefits.
>
> You and I have built great newspapers together and we have established a great relationship. We all have benefited from our trust in each other and from our teamwork.
>
> Let's not break up the team.
>
> Let's not destroy what we have built.

The ITU effort failed. But three years after his death, the same departments were organized by the Newspaper Guild.

Awards from his own unions meant something special to Gene Pulliam. When he got the first honorary membership in the seventy-four-year history of the Phoenix Typographic Union, Local 352, in 1974, he said it was better than any honor "from any president or king." The year before, the Phoenix Stereotypers Union, Local 151, awarded him a plaque, "Best Damned Employer Ever." Perhaps the most significant award was honorary membership in the pressmen's union international in 1964, when the international president, Anthony J. DeAndrade, wired him:

> There is no one in the newspaper industry who is more deserving of the honorary membership being presented by our international union. Your years of service to the newspaper industry have been outstanding and you will go down in history as one of the greatest publishers and journalists of our time.

33

TV, Out of Radio

GENE PULLIAM COULD see that television was going to grow after World War II, just as radio had before the war. But he had doubts about the broadcasting industry. He had a growing distrust of the federal government and the Federal Communications Commission. The FCC was essential for its original purpose, he agreed, to organize and regulate the airwaves. But the idea of government regulation was anathema to him. He abhorred the idea that a bureaucrat might instruct him on how to run his business, what to put on the air. The shift from regulation to political censorship seemed close, even when no one was seriously proposing it.

He did not like the channels of authority. He was impatient and liked to have things done immediately. He didn't want to bother with chains of commands, least of all in his own newspapers. Older employees got used to phone calls at odd hours from the publisher, but occasionally a newer employee who didn't know his habits and procedures would be surprised to wind up talking with the Boss. One skeptical copy boy answered a telephone and heard a voice bark: "This is Gene Pulliam."

"Yeah, and I'm Christopher Columbus," the copy boy supposedly replied, hanging up on a startled publisher.

Pulliam's doubts about the radio industry began as far back as World War II and influenced his decision to get out of Phoenix radio station KPHO in 1943. One of his KPHO partners had been Tom Chauncey, who later was president of KOOL television and radio stations, as well as a prominent civic leader in Phoenix. Chauncey recalled Pulliam's fears about holding both newspapers and broadcasting interests. "He thought it would change from entertainment to news. 'The government will be more and more involved. As government gets more involved, newspapers will have problems in holding both,' he would say," Chauncey recalled. By the time he sold WIRE in Indianapolis and all his other broadcast interests in 1960, his fears had multiplied.

After the war, however, he still owned WIRE. He had also become interested in television, buying equipment and setting up studio space in the *Star* and *News* Building in Indianapolis. Three television stations were already established in the Indianapolis area by 1950. Pulliam applied for the fourth, channel 13, and by 1954 he was competing with three other groups who also wanted the channel. Richard Fairbanks, representing his family interests, had taken WIBC radio station out of the *News* when the newspaper was sold to Pulliam, and now, representing WIBC, sought channel 13, as did Crosley Broadcasting Company, owned by AVCO Corporation of Cincinnati. But it was an unlikely candidate because FCC regulations made local ownership a key consideration. Another local Indianapolis group of businessmen, calling themselves Midwest TV and led by George Sadlier, joined the competition.

The FCC application hearings confirmed Pulliam's fears of political interference with government regulation of the broadcasting industry. Crosley attorney Duke Patrick questioned him closely about his aggressive editorial policies, focusing particularly on his opposition to the nomination of former Indiana State Republican chairman Cale Holder to a federal judgeship. Patrick and Pulliam went back and forth, arguing about Eisenhower, Taft, the federal judiciary, Holder's reputation among lawyers in Indiana. Presiding officer Basil Cooper got exasperated. Confused by what Patrick was trying to establish, he blurted out: "I know, but some places they play politics a little harder than others."

Pulliam, observing it all, broke in to ask a question: "Do I understand Mr. Patrick to say that under the FCC rules a man who has a radio license cannot have any interest in politics, for God's sake?"

Mr. Patrick: No.
Pulliam: You said a licensee has no business being in politics.
Mr. Patrick: You are not answering any question now. You are not making any speeches and you are not writing any editorials.

They argued some more. Cooper declared that he did not want to retry the confirmation of a federal judge. Finally he tried to wind up the matter by telling Patrick:

> I think you have demonstrated that he [Pulliam] is not Casper Milquetoast, if that is what you are trying to demonstrate.
> Mr. Patrick: That was one of my purposes.

Pulliam didn't fit into the decorum and propriety of an FCC hearing. It was all too proper, the formal questioning with all the courtroom language that obfuscated obvious points. "That is right, I am the boss," he growled at one question.

"I never inherited a dime from anybody," he barked at his own lawyer, Dowd.

The opposition did win one point against him when he was shown a column written by Irving Leibowitz of the *Indianapolis Times*, which noted: "The whirling dome, publisher-politician Eugene Pulliam and his charming wife, Nina, announced in Phoenix the other day that they intended to make their home in Arizona at least six months of the year."

"That is about as correct as anything Leibowitz prints," Pulliam shot back. But the lawyer pointed out that the story originated in his own Phoenix newspapers and was picked up by the Associated Press. "I didn't authorize the story," was his response.

Cooper ultimately recommended that the license go to the Midwest Television group, partly because of the *Star*'s aggressive editorial policies, specifically citing Pulliam's editorial on Holder. The recommendation bothered Pulliam. He was annoyed, being told he couldn't have a television station unless he would tone down his editorial policies. Who was the FCC to tell him how to write editorials?

Despite Cooper's recommendation, the FCC awarded channel 13 to the Crosley-AVCO applicants of Cincinnati, even though Cooper had specifically eliminated AVCO because it was from out of town. Fairbanks sued AVCO and the FCC for the ruling, and later settled the suit when AVCO agreed to sell him an Atlanta station.

The whole experience left Gene Pulliam even more fed up with government regulation. Now he had seen what he had feared, what he had observed in other countries, the political manipulation of the media, the tendency in the FCC to punish a strong editorial stance. He made plans to get out of broadcasting. He told friends, "No damn bureaucrats are going to tell me how to run my business." He sold his interest in a Richmond radio station, sold his Vincennes station to his editor at the *Sun-Commercial*, Howard Greenlee, and sold WIRE in 1960, formally announcing:

> Our association with the radio industry has been interesting and pleasant. But I feel that we can serve the public with greater objectivity and freedom if we devote our energies exclusively to producing good newspapers.

He increased his attacks on the threat of federal censorship, accusing President John Kennedy of having a "dictator complex" in a speech before the Texas Press Association in 1961. He charged that the new president was "a tailor-made pushover for the Washington bureaucrats who have been running this country just about as they pleased for the last twenty-five years."

> Even before President Kennedy made his now infamous attack on the press at the publishers convention in April, his own secretary of defense, Robert McNamara, had gone far out in front of the president in his effort toward censorship. The secretary of defense actually suggested that officials deliberately release false information about defense matters. This isn't secrecy in the interests of national security. It is another move toward thought control.
>
> Then the administration took after TV stations. FCC chairman Newton Minow attacked television programming and told station owners they would have to devote more programs to cultural and public affairs—such as what the Kennedy administration is doing for the people, for instance. To force them to do this, Minow said the FCC would have to exert pressure on individual stations through the power to revoke licenses. If the FCC can tell broadcasting stations what they can and cannot broadcast, how long will it be before this Congress controlled by bureaucrats will pass laws giving some bureau in Washington the right to tell newspapers what they can print and cannot print.

He was equally critical of the Republicans:

> On its record for the past six years, the Republican party has stood for deficit spending, bigger budgets, higher taxes, more foreign giveaways,

more appeasements to the Soviets, federal aid to and control of the schools—in short, everything against which it was fighting from the days of the two deals until the American people got sick of the two deals and threw Harry Truman out of the White House.

No wonder the Republican party got dumped in the ash can last fall. It is no longer a national party with definite principles.

All the presidents beginning with Franklin Roosevelt came under his attack:

Roosevelt, Truman, Eisenhower, Kennedy, Johnson, all contributed to the expansion of the federal bureaucracy. None of them ever did a thing—not a thing—to curb its growth.

The year he sold WIRE, he told congressional candidate Don Bruce, a Republican, that he wanted to spend the rest of his life fighting for the principles of freedom. As it turned out, he was not just crying wolf about the threat to freedom from government. The administration that came the closest to doing what he predicted was, ironically, Nixon's, which he supported almost until its end, in the summer of 1974. The two previous Democratic administrations, it was later revealed, were likewise using the FCC regularly for their own political purposes.

34

Friends

GENE PULLIAM ALWAYS had a wide range of friends and
acquaintances, and the circle widened after World War II. It
extended from the eccentric architect Frank Lloyd Wright and world
citizen Garry Davis to leading postwar conservatives like Herbert
Hoover and General Douglas MacArthur. He had known Wright in
the 1920s and thought about having him design a radio center for his
Indianapolis radio station WIRE.

> We considered this for about six weeks, but Frank's ideas were pretty
> highbrow and the expense was out of line for our resources since we
> didn't want to go that far in debt, so we gave it up. The church he
> designed in Columbus, Indiana, gave us the idea, but I doubt if it would
> have been a practical thing to do.

After Pulliam bought the Phoenix newspapers, Wright, living
at his nearby Taliesin West, often came to see the publisher, arguing
with him about anything and everything. They were two irascible,
combative men, each with his own eccentric life. Pulliam always
suspected that Wright wanted to be the architect for public projects
in Phoenix and was hoping the publisher would use his influence to
give him the opportunity. He also suspected that Wright had a hard
time finding anyone who would argue with him so much.

In visits to New York City he began to span a wide ideological
spectrum. He visited Herbert Hoover or General MacArthur, then
called on left-wing acquaintances like Garry Davis or Amy
Schaeffer. Hoover became something of a hero to him, although
Pulliam had rejected him as a candidate in 1932 as a hopeless loser.

By 1950 Hoover appeared to be a victim of economic circumstances that he had not created, and that the Democrats never corrected with the New Deal. By Hoover's death in 1964, he had come around to this perspective:

> In the broad field of public services, Herbert Hoover was the greatest mind of our times. He had felt the spontaneous adulation of the crowd and he knew the cruel ridicule of selfish-minded political enemies, yet he was never vain and he was never bitter. Judged by any standard of eternal values, he was the greatest American of our times.

On the same day he met with Hoover or MacArthur, he might also visit Jane Allison, who had worked at WIRE and later was part-time New York-based correspondent for the *Indianapolis News*.

"He loved to be included in what I was doing," she recalled. "He enjoyed meeting people and he'd grill them with questions. He liked interesting work." Sometimes he stayed on Jane's couch in her East Side apartment—midtown hotels were filled, and he didn't want to go all the way to the Carlyle at Seventy-second Street in Manhattan. "I'm not gonna stay way out there. I like to stay in the heart of things," he would tell her. At her apartment, he met a young man she was dating in the late 1950s, Garry Davis, who had renounced his American citizenship in an effort to establish the brotherhood of man, catching "the imagination of some idealists and many screwballs," *Newsweek* magazine observed.

Before they met, Davis made no sense to Pulliam. He was just "that little son of a bitch who turned in his passport," he would tell Jane. In their first encounter, he and Davis stayed up until 4 A.M. talking, arguing. Finally, as they were leaving Gene Pulliam put his arm around Davis:

> Young man, I think you are 1,000 percent right in what you say, but your timing is 1,000 percent wrong. You're one of the most interesting persons I've met.

Davis declared that Pulliam was one of the most open-minded men he had ever met.

Pulliam also met a friend of Jane's from her Voice of America work, Amy Schaeffer, a Phi Beta Kappa from Barnard College and an active member of the liberal Americans for Democratic Action.

They would argue and argue about politics—Jane was surprised at how well they got along because they were miles apart politically. He would call her on trips to New York City.

> While I was gone [on a 1954 trip to Europe] I had a letter from Amy saying that much to her surprise the Boss had been in town and called her several times and they had had dinner and chatted until the wee hours, drinking and arguing about everything political . . . and though she had never had much use for right-wing people, she found him one of the most fascinating men she had ever met.

The same year he ran for the board of the New York Central Railroad. Normally he refused to join the boards of other businesses—he would sit on civic committees, but he wanted to keep his newspapers untangled from business alliances. Joining the proxy fight for control of the New York Central was an exception.

It was an attractive kind of fight for him. Some midwestern and western businessmen who had set up their own financial empires were challenging old money easterners, especially the heirs to the Vanderbilt and Morgan fortunes, who controlled the railroad. Pulliam always resented their kind. The easterners seemed pompous, aristocratic, and out of touch with the reality of the practical business world. The purpose of the proxy fight was to establish ownership management, with the directors owning stock, having a direct interest in the business.

Persuaded to run by James Rogan, president of the American National Bank in Indianapolis, he bought stock, and joined the slate led by Robert Young of Texas, who had built a career in stock promotion. Also on the Young slate were two Texas oil men, Sid W. Richardson and Clint W. Murchison, who controlled the Indianapolis Water Company; and Indianapolis banker and political figure, Frank McKinney, who, with Frank McHale, had run Governor Paul McNutt's presidential campaign in 1939 and 1940.

They were running against representatives of the Vanderbilt, Whitney, and Morgan fortunes—the Vanderbilts had been on the board since the 1850s. Their president was William White. As the proxy fight heated up, White accused Pulliam of making a deal with Murchison, suggesting that Pulliam was dropping editorial opposition to a water company rate increase in return for being on the slate. It was an odd accusation. Editorial opposition to the rate increase was continuing even on the day, April 16, that White telegraphed Pulliam to explain what he had told newsmen:

> A question was asked of me by one of the newsmen whom I do not know, asking if I knew why Mr. Pulliam was on the Young slate of nominees and was it to rally the strength of the great Midwest in favor of Mr. Young. To the best of my recollection, my response was to the effect that I did not know and to get the real answer someone would have to ask Mr. Young or Mr. Pulliam; that I was sorry I had not seen Mr. Pulliam when I was in Indianapolis a few weeks ago and Mr. Pulliam was in Arizona. I stated further that I did not know Mr. Pulliam, but of course had heard about him and that it was possible Mr. Murchison had gotten Mr. Pulliam to go on Young's slate because Mr. Murchison, along with Allegheny, controls Indianapolis Water Company. Further I stated that I had been told there had been quite a row in Indianapolis about the fact that the water rates had been increased and that there had been a good deal of opposition in the Indianapolis newspapers. Further, in view of the *Indianapolis Star* and *Indianapolis News* it was rather strange that suddenly Mr. Pulliam's name would appear on Young's slate along with Mr. Murchison. Further, I stated that perhaps careful scrutiny of the Indianapolis newspaper files might be enlightening.

Pulliam called a news conference in New York, announcing:

> This is the first time in my life that anyone ever accused me of selling out to anybody. My position is that a man so careless with the truth is either desperate or irresponsible. I can only conclude that we need a new president of the New York Central.

He added, "I am still opposed to the rate hike. It is inconceivable to think White would make such an utterly false statement about a man he has never met."

The *Star* maintained its opposition, with a front-page cartoon on April 17 following the April 16 editorial. And Lester Hunt, a reporter, was writing daily front-page stories mocking the water company's rate increase.

The Young slate managed to win the New York Central proxy fight, and Pulliam stayed on the board until 1966, through the merger with Penn Central. He was convinced that railroad problems were primarily the fault of government regulation.

But he turned for real, private enjoyment and relaxation to a small group of golfing friends in Indianpolis: his son, Glen Warren, and Bill Shumaker. With them he could just be himself and have a good time, wearing his red slacks and a red floppy hat. "I think old Gene could relax more with Bill Shumaker than anyone else," said one-time Indianapolis mayor Charles Boswell, who sometimes played with Pulliam, Shumaker, and Warren.

He had not met Shumaker, who had a construction business, or Warren, who ran a hotel, through his newspaper work or politics, but happened to golf with them by chance one day at Highland Country Club in Indianapolis. They were not in awe of him, in contrast to others he met, nor did they seek any favors. They liked to tease him, and it wasn't hard for them to find ways. He was intensely competitive, in fishing, card games, whatever he did, including golf. "He always smoked those $1 cigars," Shumaker recalled. "He'd get so busy with the golf and lay down the cigar in order to tee off. Warren was always trying to get his goat so he'd take his cigar. Gene would cuss and cuss, but he never caught on. You can get his goat in a minute. He used new dimes to mark the ball. We'd steal them and he'd get so angry. Everything upset him. We'd tease him about his politics. We'd say he would lose with a certain guy and he'd get mad and argue. He'd enjoy the teasing. We kept him in a turmoil—he'd just storm. We'd take his clubs, his putter. He'd cuss and swear and rave. He was a delightful man."

In Phoenix, he liked to play with former touring professional Johnny Bulla, whose son became a key executive for Pulliam in the Phoenix newspapers. "I was just a friend. I didn't want anything from him," Bulla said. Bulla once persuaded Pulliam to play as his partner in the one-day pro-am competition that preceded the Phoenix Open and recalled:

> He's got to be good in everything he does. He shot a 76, even with those 175-yard drives. It was ten strokes under his normal game. He'd play good because it was a tournament. He always wanted to tee it up on the fairway. He'd use a putter from fifty yards out and I never saw anything like it. He'd get it close always.

Playing with his friends, Gene would go to great lengths to win. He developed his own handicapping system to assure him and his partner of victory. He gave himself long putts, always played winter rules, and set the ball up for a better lie. "He thinks it's his last dollar he's playing for," noted Mike Fennell, a Phoenix Democrat and businessman who played with Pulliam frequently. "He always picked the best player for his partner." His handicapping system was notorious, with a mysterious adjustment after nine holes. "We often asked what his logic might have been, but his answers were never quite clear," said Robert Jaap, a golfing friend and Phoenix bank executive.

He would "give" himself putts of three, four, five feet. He just assumed he would make the putts and pick up the ball. That is a common procedure on very short putts that are "within the leather" of a putter; less than two feet. Friends once gave him a long putter with an extended shaft to provide for "gimmes" up to six feet. Verlie Haldiman, a Phoenix insurance man, once tried to make up for Pulliam's gimmes.

> I remember one time when I was playing with him and his son, Gene, and Forest Whitney; he had been particularly bad about picking up putts that were out of the leather.
> My ball landed in the water in front of the ninth green at Phoenix Country Club and Gene got it before I did and pulled it out from the hole. When I got there, I picked the ball up and started for the green. He yelled, "Where the hell are you going?" I said I was going up to the green to put my ball in the hole to make up for all the long putts he had picked up. Of course the fight was on. I finally came back and attempted to make a shot to the green, but was chuckling to myself so much that I pulled it into the trap and then we all had a good laugh.

35

1960

By 1960 Gene Pulliam was a major force in politics in Indiana and Arizona. His feisty front-page editorials, his candid and sometimes helpful advice to aspiring politicians, his use of the news columns to promote his political strategies, all combined to make him influential in both political parties.

Within the GOP, Pulliam was no longer in league with the East Coast Republicans, the liberal and internationalist group he had joined in the 1940s and in 1952. By 1960 he was at home with the heirs of Robert Taft, led by Arizona Senator Barry Goldwater. He was convinced that Richard Nixon, the Republican presidential candidate, would win only with an aggressive conservative campaign. He was afraid Nixon would repeat the 1948 mistakes of New York governor Thomas Dewey, trying to be above the battle rather than slugging it out wholeheartedly. He wrote the vice president:

> I hope I am not too pessimistic, but I am concerned for fear you will find yourself in the same kind of trap which Dewey built for himself in 1948 when thousands upon thousands of Republicans didn't vote at all. They wouldn't vote for Truman and they were too disgusted with Dewey to vote for him. Dewey lost.
>
> You must have the wholehearted, enthusiastic support of all Republicans—not just the international group on the eastern seaboard. Your reported position on the International Court amendment has disturbed many Americans. Also, the continued rumor that you are looking with favor on Lodge as your running mate is another thing which is causing no end to comment—all unfavorable.
>
> I am for you 100 percent, but for the first time I am a little concerned about what you are for.

When Lodge was being promoted as Nixon's running mate, Pulliam protested. He wanted a more conservative candidate, Goldwater, Republican national chairman Thurston Morton, Representative Gerald Ford or House minority leader Charles Halleck of Indiana. He rolled out his complaints in a long front-page editorial.

> The "international set" inside the Republican party has begun its move to name a running mate for Richard Nixon. The call was sounded last week when *Life* magazine, finding 1960 to be a "foreign policy year," heartily endorsed UN ambassador Henry Cabot Lodge.
>
> Such support as Lodge can gather will rally under the frayed banner of the "independent voter." According to the me-too logicians of the East, the GOP needs Lodge to make inroads among the Democrats and the uncommitted.
>
> Unfortunately, elections are not won by fastidious images beamed from Madison Avenue, but by the exertions of dedicated party workers. The party which wins is the party which does the best job of turning out its own faithful at the precinct level.

He sent Nixon the editorial, telling him:

> I've been for you all the time and I am still for you but if you allow a group of New York bankers to force Lodge down your throat I think it will be the fatal mistake of your political career and I certainly don't want that to happen.

Nixon's direction was unclear—he seemed to be setting up a vaguely moderate campaign rather than a conservative one. Pulliam had come to know Senate majority leader Lyndon Johnson on visits to Washington, D.C. He liked Johnson's earthy character, his rise from a poor background in Texas. He could sit back and enjoy a drink with Johnson in a way he never could with Nixon. But he could never adequately explain his friendship with Johnson to his conservative friends.

By late spring, he was telling Democratic friends he might support Johnson over Nixon, if Johnson could get the Democratic nomination. He tried to help him in two states, but with little success. He greeted him at the Indianapolis airport in May of 1960, promoting him with Democratic friends like Marion County prosecutor Philip Bayt and Mayor Charles Boswell. What he learned was what so many Johnson supporters would discover—that Senator John Kennedy had been there first and gained commitments from Bayt and Boswell.

In Arizona, Pulliam threw his newspapers behind the efforts of former governor Ernest MacFarland, who was seeking support for Johnson. News coverage and editorials took the side of Arizona old-line Democrats led by MacFarland, but they were trounced by the younger men working for Kennedy, led by Representative Stuart Udall, who became the secretary of the interior. It was too late for Johnson. Kennedy won in a walk.

Once the Republican Nixon-Lodge and Democratic Kennedy-Johnson tickets were set, Pulliam backed the Republican alternative. He wrote a number of spirited blasts at Kennedy, including one rouser that backfired with many readers. "You Can't Buy the White House" was the title. Pulliam charged that Kennedy was using his Catholic religion to attract sympathy.

> Nobody has persecuted Jack Kennedy, and it is unlikely that anybody will.
>
> Why won't Kennedy be frank enough to admit publicly that it was his Catholic friends who gave him the nomination? The five big states were for Kennedy? Mayor Wagner, who led the New York delegation, is a Catholic. Governor Lawrence of Pennsylvania, who turned Pennsylvania over to Kennedy, is a Catholic. Governor Mike DiSalle of Ohio, who gave the entire Ohio delegation to Kennedy, is a Catholic. Mayor Daley of Chicago, who controlled the Illinois delegation, is a Catholic. Governor Pat Brown of California, another Kennedy state, is a Catholic. The delegations from these five states, led by Catholics, put over Kennedy's nomination.
>
> Why should Jack Kennedy be ungrateful and hypocritical? These influential politicians had a perfect right to be for Kennedy if they so chose. The very fact that these men have been elected to high office shows that the American people do not let religion influence their political voting. The people in these five states believed that these candidates were good men and they voted for them regardless of their beliefs. When they were running for office these men did not go around whimpering that they were being persecuted.
>
> The truth is, Jack Kennedy has deliberately set out to make a martyr of himself on the Catholic issue in order to get sympathy and to glamorize himself as a candidate.
>
> Jack Kennedy has been shouting and crying persecution, but if anybody else says anything about his religion, then that is "bigotry."

Well, we think it is bigotry to inject religion into this campaign. It has nothing whatever to do with the real issues on which the American people are going to vote. Anybody who uses religion either as a shield or a sword is guilty of bigotry, and the greatest offender in this nation at the present time is Jack Kennedy himself. He never misses a chance to keep the religious issue alive. It can't be kept out if Jack Kennedy himself is going to bring it up every time he makes a speech. Such hypocrisy seldom has been practiced in American politics.

We are not opposed to Jack Kennedy because he is a Catholic. We do not believe many Americans will be opposed to him on that basis. Certainly nobody has ever accused this newspaper of being anti-Catholic.

Catholic voters, however, were enraged—some turned against Nixon as a result. "It sounded overtly Ku Klux to a sensitive Catholic," said Democrat William P. Mahoney, a Kennedy campaign worker in Arizona who used the editorial to stir up support for Kennedy. Gene Pulliam had no prejudice against Catholics. No one who knew him ever accused him of it. He had put them in high executive positions in his newspapers, especially the *Star,* and socialized with them. He simply didn't realize that his vigorous editorial would be construed as anti-Catholic.

His editorial the Sunday before election was a long attack against Kennedy, with only a bare mention of Nixon at the end.

We are opposed to Jack Kennedy because he is completely lacking in administrative experience to assume the responsibilities of the presidency in the handling of foreign policy and domestic issues. During this campaign he has revealed himself as being totally unaware of administrative responsibilities. He is impetuous and inconsistent in his comments on foreign relations. As president he would have this country in deep trouble within thirty days if he continued this impulsive carelessness in what he says and advocates.

We are opposed to him because it is obvious that he has no understanding whatever of labor and wages. He doesn't know anything about earning a dollar. He doesn't know anything about spending and saving a dollar. He has had no business experience—either on a large or small scale. Every sound economist says frankly that Jack Kennedy sounds like a high school kid when he starts talking about economics. He proposed to increase the national budget by whopping billions, but either through ignorance or dishonesty he says it will not be necessary to increase taxes. This is pure hogwash.

This was the last presidential election that Gene Pulliam waded into with both fists swinging. In the three elections before his death he played a more balanced role.

He changed partly because he wanted to be respected—he grew tired of being constantly criticized in both parties for trying to be a dictator. In Arizona he was tired of being called a Republican—he was an independent and wanted everyone to know it. He wanted to be respected as a good newspaperman—with good newspapers.

He never toned down his own editorials—but the news coverage did shift to a more consistent balance. He told his editorial writers to become more issue-oriented, with fewer bitter personal attacks. He bawled out *Star* cartoonist Charley Werner and *Star* editor Jameson Campaigne for a front-page cartoon of President Kennedy a few months after Kennedy's election. After consulting with Campaigne, Werner drew a picture of a smiling Nikita Khrushchev looking at an X-ray of Kennedy's back, with a Soviet official standing by and declaring: "Kennedy's Back Trouble Is Big Capitalist Lie. Secret X-ray Intelligence Shows As Having No Spine." Pulliam did believe that Kennedy was not taking a firm enough stance with the Soviet Union. But he had his own back troubles, and he talked to Kennedy about his. He noticed the president's nervous tension and inability to sit comfortably at White House luncheons. "He gave Jamie [Campaigne] absolute hell," *Star* foreign editor Padev recalled. "He called me and said, never make fun of people's physical afflictions or personal life. Just attack the policy."

He was invited to a White House luncheon soon after Kennedy's inauguration, and he was surprised. He was even seated next to the president. He found the new president had a good sense of humor. Kennedy told him that the editorial "You Can't Buy the White House" was one of the roughest he encountered in the campaign. Pulliam shrugged his shoulders. What could he say? But Kennedy added with a smile, "I did, didn't I?"

He knew what Kennedy was trying to do. He was bringing editors and publishers into his fold, telling them his problems and trying to get them to tone down their criticism. Pulliam warned other publishers and editors:

> I do hope in this battle with the bureaucrats against censorship and suppression of news, that American newspapermen are not going to be seduced into silence by engraved invitations to official dinners in Washington.

He kept on making speeches, writing editorials, thundering against the liberalism of the new administration. Occasionally he would come to Kennedy's defense; for example, in the Berlin Wall crisis when the president called up the military reserves.

Our president and commander-in-chief, John Fitzgerald Kennedy, needs your help and ours. He is making a determined stand against communism abroad. But at home he and the military effort are being harassed by the civilians who have been called to military duty because of the Berlin crisis.

In his press conference, Mr. Kennedy pointed out that a soldier on duty in the cold of Ft. Lewis, Washington, is just as important as a bomber on fifteen-minute alert status at an air force base. How true!

But a few Americans have decided the best way is to complain to Washington. So some of our congressmen are running around playing politics with the military and our country's defense.

It is true undoubtedly we are short in matters of supply. We Americans are accustomed to luxurious accommodations and three-course meals. We are short of weapons. But this time we're carrying good Garand rifles and not broomsticks. Army life is at times unpleasant, boys, but this is the cold war 1961.

He was frequently critical of the new administration's foreign policy, complaining that "old-fashioned American patriotism is unwelcome on the New Frontier, where the United Nations and not the United States is considered the hope of the world."

But after the Cuban missile crisis and the successes of the blockade of Russian ships, Pulliam was impressed with Kennedy's personal judgment. He wrote him reminding him that he was an independent publisher, not necessarily a Republican. He noted:

At your luncheon late in the spring, I told you I would support [Democratic] Senator Hayden for reelection, but would not do one thing for [Republican] Senator Capehart. Senator Hayden will tell you he would have lost without our support. Senator Capehart is bitterly complaining that he would have won if we had supported him. The returns prove that I kept my word.

Also, let me say again that you have the ability and the unique opportunity to be one of the country's great presidents. You have a clear, concise mind. You know history. When you make a decision on your own, it is always clear and understandable, and usually a good decision. But when you allow yourself to be confused by the urgings of that little coterie of well-meaning but impractical theorists who frequently infest the White House, your decisions are confusing and the whole country is confused. On your own, your judgment is damn near infallible.

I sincerely hope I can support you as enthusiastically in 1964 as I opposed you in 1960.

Above all, get some rest every day. I would be dead if I had not acquired the habit.

Foreign policy issues landed Pulliam in an argument with columnist Walter Lippmann. The dispute found its way into *Time* magazine. Lippmann, spending a week in Phoenix, cited Pulliam's Phoenix newspapers as a prime example of the "War Whoop Party" that favored "the fruits of a successful war without having to fight."

"I have learned," he wrote from Phoenix, "that we must distinguish between a war party—of which I have seen no traces out here—and a war-whoop party, which likes to be warlike but does not want war." Pulliam shot back a quick reply to the *Washington Post*, noting, "I wonder if Mr. Lippmann has read any of our editorials carefully. We do not advocate an invasion or an occupation of Cuba. What we do advocate—and have done so for many months—is a forceful American policy aimed at Castro's isolation and eventual overthrow. We think that an American partial blockade or quarantine can be one of the effective instruments of such a policy, especially as it has the support of the Latin American states."

> We don't believe—as Mr. Lippmann thinks we do—that the Russians "will not go to war no matter what we do to them." The Russians will certainly go to war to defend themselves from attack. But we do not believe that the Russians would go to war to defend Castro. We believe that Soviet Premier Khrushchev is a very shrewd politician—the shrewdist the Communists have had in Moscow for a long time. Beset as he is with very serious internal troubles, Mr. Khrushchev would not, in our opinion, do anything reckless in order to challenge an American naval blockade of Cuba. Still less is he likely to risk a nuclear war in order to save Castro from an American-supported anti-Castro uprising.

Pulliam concluded by saying his newspapers had predicted that the Soviet Union would not go to war over the blockade. Lippmann and other liberal commentators had suggested they might. *Time* gleefully ended up its item:

> Whooped publisher Pulliam in conclusion: "I dare say we proved to be right, which is, perhaps, one of the reasons Mr. Lippmann doesn't like us."

36

An Odd Couple

In Arizona Robert Morrison was determined to avenge his 1958 loss at the polls. He wanted to get back at Gene Pulliam for ruining his political career. He couldn't get revenge in politics, so he tried journalism. He started an alternative newspaper in Phoenix, a liberal voice designed to offset the conservative stance of Pulliam's newspapers.

Morrison dismayed a lot of prominent liberal Democrats when he started a public stock sale campaign to get a newspaper, the *Arizona Journal*, started. They knew he had no professional newspaper background. If the liberals were going to have their newspaper, they reasoned, let someone like Bill Mathews from Tucson run it professionally, with enough money to make it work. They were afraid Morrison might blow all future opportunities for their dream. "I was sick when he started it," recalled then Secretary of the Interior Stuart Udall. He had tried to interest the Kennedys in putting money into a liberal newspaper for Phoenix.

Nevertheless, Morrison's effort did reveal widespread discontent with Pulliam's newspapers. He managed to raise $1.5 million by selling stock publicly. Circulation ranged over 50,000 on the first day. There was clearly a demand for another newspaper. But Morrison could not supply it.

His newspaper did have a professional look. It was the first metropolitan daily to use the photocomposition and offset printing used increasingly by small and medium circulation newspapers in the 1960s and 1970s. It won awards for layout and typography, including the Ayer Award for layout after only a month of publication. But the management was weak. Morrison made the mistake of starting publication before raising the capital; composing room employees were untrained; and mechanical equipment had not arrived on publication day in 1962.

The *Journal* hit the newsstands in time to provide a balance in news coverage in 1962. The *Republic* was tilting its stories in favor of Republican Governor Paul Fannin against his Democratic challenger Sam Goddard. But the *Journal* never got beyond the point of being against the Pulliam newspapers. In the end, in desperation, the *Journal* even took out after the prize-winning investigative reporting of Walter Meek and Don Bolles. Bolles and Meek had written a series of stories on the state Corporation Commission, particularly E. T. Williams, who was later impeached by the Democratic Arizona House of Representatives but cleared by the senate on bribery and other charges. Bolles and Meek were told to come to commission offices one day in 1964. They said they would come. Then they decided against it, thinking it might be a setup. But the *Journal*, by then a weekly, came up with a front-page story about how the reporters tried to break into the building, with the story starting off:

> The Pulliam press came under fire yesterday for alleged "Gestapo" tactics as Eddie T. Williams, Jr., member of the Corporation Commission, told the *Journal* of attempts to rifle their files on a holiday.

Bolles suspected the incident had been set up by Williams and the *Journal*: "This piece is made up out of whole cloth—Bill Meek and I weren't anywhere near the place that day," Bolles recalled.

One *Journal* editor, Robert Zimmerman, thought the newspaper might have survived if Morrison had taken a different approach: "My opinion is that it might have survived if Morrison had not been obsessed with his personal vendetta against 'Pulliam.' Morrison was a real Captain Ahab. He insisted on being editor and publisher of the paper when he was competent to be neither. He became very secretive about the true financial condition of the paper—even to the point of issuing payroll checks when he knew there was no money in the bank to cover them. It was as if he could not admit to anyone that he had failed."

Zimmerman and other *Journal* staffers were convinced that they had forced some changes in Pulliam's newspapers.

> To some extent it probably helped "make them honest." When the *Journal* folded, the *Republic* picked up a number of the more liberal columnists we had been running and began publishing them on a new op-ed page. I would like to believe that "Pulliam"—whether your grandfather himself or his management in Phoenix—was impressed by the fact that an opposition paper did get started, that the enthusiasm for it was widespread prior to publication, and that it did survive for more than a year. This may have broken down a barrier to the expression of contrary points of view in the Pulliam papers, and made them more mindful of an obligation to cover news more fairly.

Those changes were coming with or without the *Arizona Journal.* Pulliam was tired of being cast as the villain of Arizona politics. During the 1962 campaign Phoenix Democrats put out the kind of sheet that local Republicans had issued in the late 1940s in Indianapolis. The Democrats called Pulliam "a man who likes to play God." Their election newspaper, the *Arizona Crisis*, published by the Maricopa Democratic Central Committee, said, "He is in every sense of kingmaker, a man who operates behind the throne.... And like all kingmakers, he is ruthless in his quest for power."

He was growing tired of such attacks, he was in his seventies and he wanted some respect. He had always wanted good newspapers, not their fruits of political influence.

He asked his son, Gene, Jr., for suggestions for a good managing editor for the *Republic.* Gene, Jr., was more moderate than his father and much less of a crusader. He didn't like the way his father used the news column for political purposes and wouldn't allow it in the *Indianapolis News.* He had earned respect for his fairness, for a consistent personality, for avoiding the quick and sometimes mistaken judgments his father would make. He had revived and extended some of the earlier editorial excellence of the *Indianapolis News*, helping it recover from its downhill slide after World War II.

Pulliam's purchase of the *News* in 1948 had not been greeted with cheers in many quarters, especially among Republicans who had relied on the *News* to defend them from Pulliam's onslaughts in the *Star*. The staff of the *News* also did not know what to expect. His son's immediate appointment as managing editor helped the troubled atmosphere at the *News*, according to Fremont Power, then a reporter, later a columnist:

> Before the merger, we had a lot of fluff in the paper, for advertisers; it all stopped when the Boss came in. It had stopped in the *Star* when he took over also. That's one of the things I liked—the Boss and Gene are newspapermen. Not all publishers are like that. After the merger, the staff was unhappy. He invited all the employees to the Claypool Hotel for a big banquet and assured them of their jobs. The banquet helped, and Gene became the managing editor. He reassured the city staff, he was hard-working, available.

It was a convenient arrangement—his father played most of his politics in the morning paper, the *Star*, where the managing editor, Robert Early, was more like the elder Pulliam, feisty and belligerent.

Active in the Associated Press Managing Editors Association, Gene, Jr., had come to know J. Edward Murray, then the managing editor of the *Los Angeles Mirror* after a career with the United Press. He suggested several names to his father, including Murray.

Murray was an impressive man. He could talk about anything and everything, yoga, Jung, logical positivism, technological ethos. He had been a foreign correspondent for the United Press during World War II, in London, Paris, and Rome, before moving to the *Mirror* in Los Angeles. Like Pulliam, he had come out of a rural background in South Dakota. Some thought he was pretentious, with his Jung and his positivism, but no one questioned his abilities as an editor. After meeting him, Pulliam decided to hire him, insisting their political differences would not be important. Together, they formed the odd couple in American journalism for ten turbulent years. Here was a very conservative publisher, who hired leading conservative thinkers like M. Stanton Evans to write editorials, teaming up with a liberal and sometimes avant-garde managing editor in a fast-growing and conservative state in the Southwest. Newspapermen who knew Murray and Pulliam were puzzled to see them working together and wondered how long it would last. "I was always surprised that he [Pulliam] put him there in the first place," commented newspaper publisher John Knight, who knew both of them.

The odd couple survived for a couple of reasons. The first of these was that Pulliam always liked a fighter, conservative or liberal. Some of his top employees hastened to agree with him no matter what—they were frightened of him. Others would disagree, quietly but firmly, without any loud shouting—his son, *Star* editor Jameson Campaigne, and William A. Dyer, the general manager in Indianapolis, tended to take that sort of approach along with assistant publisher Harry Montgomery in Phoenix.

"You could always talk straight with him," said Howdy Wilcox, Jr., the son of a 500-mile race winner, who joined Pulliam in 1952 to do some promotion work after running the Indiana University foundation. "When he was hiring me, I told him, I want to ask you now, a lot of people think you're a son of a bitch. He replied, well, you don't know anyone who works for me who says I'm a son of a bitch."

"He was always very blunt, even when he was playing gin rummy," added Wilcox, who later established his own business in Indianapolis. "You never had to guess where in the hell he stood. I don't think he had a devious bone in his body."

A few of his executives were like Pulliam, table-pounding, argumentative, cantankerous, bossy, and demanding. They could get away with a lot with the Boss, Robert Early in Indianapolis especially, and, as it turned out, Murray in Phoenix. Early lasted longer than Murray. He was named managing editor of the *Star* right after World War II and held the position for the rest of Pulliam's life. He was more willing to do Pulliam's bidding in slanting the news coverage for political purposes, but in his personality he and Murray were similar—abrupt, abrasive, arguing and shouting at the Boss. Stories about Early abounded, some perhaps apocryphal, but at least one was true. The *Star* and *News* switched to plastic desk tops at one point because Early had broken so many glass tops by pounding on them.

Murray survived with Pulliam because he also fought with him openly, about almost everything. "He and Ed would fight like cats and dogs," recalled Montgomery, who as assistant publisher found himself frequently mediating between the managing editor and the publisher. "Ed was hard to handle, just like Gene." Montgomery remembered asking Murray not to do something, but Murray went ahead and did it. Montgomery confronted Murray with the matter and Murray, realizing at last that Montgomery really had meant it, blurted out, "Why didn't you pound the table and tell me, dammit, don't do it!"

Pulliam was a bully also—he would push someone as hard as he could until the other person pushed back. When, for instance, he was trying to buy the stock of Phoenix newspapers in the early 1960s from Gene Autry and several others, he worked through broker Vincent Manno, who told him he should be willing to pay $1,800 a share. Pulliam got angry, complaining that the price was too high, but when Manno got angry in return and said he could find another broker, Pulliam backed down quickly and apologized.

The other reason Murray lasted so long was he produced the quality newspaper Pulliam was seeking. Murray was a stimulating man to work for, and he built up an excellent staff and a high morale at the *Republic*. "He was a leader, good with the staff. Life was never dull. He was involving the staff in decisions," recalled *Republic* political writer Bernie Wynn. Murray established more balance in the *Republic*'s political coverage, and he gradually put an end to the extremely partisan coverage typical of the 1958 campaign. He set up new investigative reporting teams, added writers for science, religion, education, and other areas, brought in the *Washington Post–Los Angeles Times* news service. Pulliam didn't like the liberal slant of the *Post-Times* news service at times, and he still wanted to use the *Republic* for political ends in the 1960s. But he also knew Murray was a good newspaperman. "What allowed it was that Ed had a tremendous professional capability, and Pulliam respected it and wanted that caliber running his newspaper," said Tom Sanford, then the assistant managing editor.

Pulliam and Murray could also work together at this particular time because Pulliam had become less a crusader for and against certain candidates in politics, at least in Arizona.

Toward the end of the 1960s, however, the union between the odd couple became shaky. A youth revolution was under way. Pulliam didn't like it, and didn't see why it deserved so much coverage. Murray tried to understand it, and to present it to the readers. Pulliam was growing older—he couldn't take the fights with Murray as he once had and he wasn't about to consider retirement.

In the 1960s, Gene Pulliam was changing, mellowing. "He didn't seem so hell-bent on saving the world," commented Charles Boswell, who was mayor of Indianapolis in 1960.

> He wasn't sure if his great crusade was so great. He hadn't lost the interest or concern, but he wasn't so brash or gung-ho.

His *Indianapolis Star* editor, Jameson Campaigne, also noticed the subtle change in the 1960s in Pulliam, recalling it ten years later:

> When you are young and liberal, you think everything can be solved with the liberal answers, but then you see they can't really work. And when you are young and conservative, you want to abolish the public schools, oppose all federal aid. Then you see it's impractical, to be so ideological. His views aren't quite so strong now, he has friends on the other side and has seen some of it work out okay. And as he got older, he wanted to be liked. He liked the recognition, the awards, being honored. He always had been called a fascist pig before that.

Now the Democrats were in power, perhaps to stay for a while. Pulliam was becoming more friendly with Lyndon Johnson, his doubts about Barry Goldwater were mounting. Politically he was no longer so quick to turn to Republicans. In 1962 he supported Democratic Senator Carl Hayden over the very conservative Republican candidate, Evan Mecham, helping the Democrats both in news coverage and with advice on the side. In Indiana that same year, he purposely held the *Star* to a neutral stance when Republican Senator Homer Capehart was challenged and defeated by the Democrat Birch Bayh. The neutrality was a bonus for the young and active Bayh, who won a startling upset with vigorous campaigning. In 1964 Pulliam endorsed the Democratic candidate for governor in Indiana, Roger Branigin, and in Arizona he wrote a halfhearted endorsement of Barry Goldwater's presidential campaign, while privately helping the Johnson campaign.

The political circumstances were ripe for Pulliam to opt in favor of balanced news coverage. Murray and Pulliam's son, Gene Jr., who became assistant publisher of the *Star* and *News* in 1962, took advantage of it.

Though Pulliam's instincts were against it, the effort to balance coverage was bringing him the respect he wanted in the newspaper industry. In 1966 he received the John Peter Zenger Award and was featured in favorable stories in *Time* magazine and *Editor and Publisher*.

It was an unusual shift for *Time*, which had mocked his conservative views in the past on a number of occasions. His editorial policy was descibed once as "on a bearing somewhat to the right of Warren Gamaliel Harding," after he hired conservative M. Stanton Evans as an editorial writer at the *Indianapolis News*. A few years later *Time* acknowledged that Pulliam "has always been portrayed as more of an intransigent conservative than he actually is." He had been elected and overwhelmingly reelected to the prestigious Associated Press board, first in 1961, then in 1964 and 1967. One friend was disappointed in the change in Pulliam—John Knight, who enjoyed Pulliam's crusty and feisty spirit because he shared much of it with him.

Knight had voted for Gene Pulliam and a more liberal publisher, Mark Ethridge, Sr., of the Louisville newspapers, in the AP board election, hoping they would both shake up the board meetings.

> He had a strong mind of his own. I thought he'd be more aggressive that way on the board. I told him I thought he was too tame for the AP. I'd tease him, telling him to kick up some dust.

Others on the board, though, had assumed that Pulliam would try to impose his conservative views on the AP news report. He never did. AP deputy general manager Harry Montgomery explained: "A lot of publishers don't understand newspapers. They'd like the AP report to fit their views. He'd stick up for the liberal side, or presenting all sides." He did offer strong opinions on some matters, though. General Edwin Walker sued the AP and several newspapers for coverage of his opposition to the enrollment of a black student, James Meredith, at the University of Mississippi. Several newspapers settled privately with Walker, but the AP went on to win the case in the U.S. Supreme Court. AP general manager Wes Gallagher, checking with board members on how the AP should respond, was pleased with Pulliam's gruff but brief advice: "Tell 'em to go to hell."

Part III

The Boss

37

Muscleman

To THE YOUNGER reporters and editors at his newspapers, Eugene Pulliam seemed to be an erratic, odd publisher. One minute he would manage the news for purposes of his own political wheeling-and-dealing. The next minute he'd stand by a series on air pollution that named top businesses and might cost his newspaper considerably in potential libel suits and loss of advertising. The work of an *Arizona Republic* investigative reporter, Don Bolles, revealed that side of Pulliam.

Bolles came to the *Republic* in 1962, after eleven years with the Associated Press in New York, New Jersey, and Kentucky. He knew Pulliam only by reputation when he came to the *Republic*. So Bolles was a little nervous when he got a special assignment from the Boss to check up on the Indiana income tax system, which, Pulliam had been told, was so good it should be adopted in Arizona. Pulliam wanted a series of stories on it. Bolles went to work, later remembering:

> About 1963 or 1964, Gene got touted onto the claim that Indiana had a super income tax system which could be adopted in Arizona. He sent a *Gazette* reporter and myself to Indianapolis for a week to do a detailed series on it. He set up our meetings with the governor, top aides, top businessmen, and even came out to Indianapolis to make sure nobody was ignoring us, and had us to lunch with Gene, Jr., and himself at the Athletic Club.
>
> When we had finished, the *Gazette* guy and I had the identical thought; the Indiana system stunk. Then came the question, how are we going to tell Gene? Would we get fired if we expressed our true opinion? The cost?

> When we returned, we went into his office and he chatted awhile with
> us about Indiana, then asked how we were going to present the series. I
> gulped and gave him the news that we, and any businessmen with
> whom we had talked, believed that the tax system stifled initiative and
> should be repealed. He said okay, and that was it.

Bolles started to get more assignments in investigative
reporting. He began looking into corruption in the state
Corporation Commission and Tax Commission. There had always
been rumors about the commissions, but no one had ever been able
to pin them down. Bolles started with the Tax Commission. He
came up with a list of persons who allegedly contributed to the
incomes of tax commissioners. The commissioners were indicted for
bribery, but when Bolles refused to reveal his sources for the list in
court, the indictments were dismissed.

After the Tax Commission stories, Bolles, joined by reporter
Walter Meek, began to look into the Corporation Commission. He
discovered evidence for a wide range of charges, including bribery
and hidden campaign contributions. The case went to the state
legislature, where Democrats controlled both houses, as well as the
commission. The House of Representatives voted for impeachment
proceedings for two Democratic commissioners, E. T. Williams and
A. P. Buzard, but in the Senate the Democrats had a 24-4 majority.
The Senate subpoenaed Bolles' notes on the Corporation
Commission, so Bolles went to Pulliam to ask what to do.

"Don, I'm not going to let you give up your notes. If anybody
goes to jail, it's gonna be me," Gene Pulliam told him. When
Pulliam, Bolles, Meek, and other executives were called as witnesses,
Pulliam had every copy of the newspapers for the previous sixteen
months trucked over to the Senate in response to a broader subpoena
for material on the case. "They never had the guts to find us in
contempt," Bolles said. Neither were the commissioners impeached.
However, Buzard lost a reelection attempt in a primary and
Williams did not seek reelection.

The series on tax and corporation commissions led to a Pulitzer
Prize nomination for Bolles. He went on to delve into a wide range
of areas, particularly land fraud and the Emprise horse-track racing
firm headquartered in Buffalo, New York. Bolles had often heard
that Pulliam protected his friends from unfavorable publicity, but
he said he never encountered it himself. "This loyalty to his friends,

I haven't seen it. If he knows he's a bad guy, he won't defend him. The word doesn't come down to lay off his friends." Bolles named some of Pulliam's friends in the stories, at one point revealing that a leading lawyer was one of the contributors to the tax commissioners' income.

> One of my fellow reporters told me, "Man, if you get that name out in public, you don't have a job."
>
> I decided that if the *Republic* was that kind of a paper, I didn't want to work for it.
>
> And when his name finally came out in court, Gene expressed his admiration for our work in turning it up, without fear or favor. He said, "I always wondered how long it would take."

Bolles grew to enjoy working for Gene Pulliam and managing editor Ed Murray. Sometimes he was summoned for a special project by the publisher. Pulliam went directly to certain reporters when he wanted a story done, and Bolles found that Pulliam's own sources and tips were helpful. "He knows an awful lot," Bolles said. "His instincts are impeccable." In a 1970 series, he named a number of prominent figures in connection with organized crime's entry into Arizona.

> I remember on one occasion I took to him the fact that we had information about a top Republican being involved in syndicate activities. His specific instruction was—"Go get him, but be sure we have it nailed down tight." I would have to say that I felt uneasy sitting there, but he always tried to make reporters feel that their opinions were worthwhile.

Bolles was always aware of Pulliam's tendency to want to manage the news in political campaigns if he was interested in stopping or helping a candidate. But he also concluded that some editors took Pulliam's "rockets," as he called the publisher's blunt memos on news coverage, much too literally. He learned how to handle the rockets. When Senator Robert Kennedy was running for president in 1968 and came to Arizona to seek delegate support, Pulliam told Bolles to do a story on how Kennedy was going to buy the state. Bolles didn't take the publisher's order too seriously. "I only embellished the story a little," Bolles said. "Others would go all-out."

Reporters or editors who did not know the publisher except by reputation could not dismiss his rockets so easily. After all, he was the publisher, with the authority to hire and fire. When he was upset and angry, he rattled off threats that created fear and trembling in his newsrooms. "Heads are gonna roll," he would tell *Indianapolis Star* city editor Larry Connor when he didn't like the way a story was handled in the *Star*. Like a few others on the staff, Connor learned that "it was just a figure of speech. No one was ever fired. Some should have been. He talked big, but he could never tell someone, you're through."

Once Pulliam sent down orders that Senator Birch Bayh should not get any major publicity in the 1970 Indiana Senate campaign, when Senator Vance Hartke was being challenged by Representative Richard Roudebush. "Heads are gonna roll," Pulliam threatened, when he complained to Connor. He demanded to know who had put Bayh's picture on the front page of the second section of the *Star*. Connor later wrote to Pulliam, putting the blame on himself. Pulliam wrote back, telling him not to worry about it, he was a fine city editor and it was just a minor matter.

Pulliam's son, Gene, Jr., occasionally got an order to fire someone. He would ignore it, waiting for his father to forget it or realize later that he was wrong. Charles Griffo, the *Indianapolis Star* assistant managing editor, who had worked for Pulliam since World War II, understood the Boss's thinking. Sometimes he'd encounter a friend of Pulliam who would tell him that "Gene says to do this" in the *Star*. "I'd just say, Gene who?"

Often the best way to respond to Pulliam was to be as blunt and direct as the publisher was, but few dared. Daniel Ben-Horin, a young *Republic* columnist who had been hired by Murray to voice the aspirations of young people and was later fired by Pulliam, observed:

> Actually, and ironically, if all the people who worked for him were as tough and ballsy as he is, the invidious effects he wreaks would not be possible. But alas, they ain't and they are.

Another *Republic* columnist, Paul Dean, once left a note on a malfunctioning cigarette machine in the *Republic* and *Gazette* building saying he felt like "kicking the son of a bitch to pieces" because it stole his money. Someone decided it was obscene and had no place in the R&G plant. The note found its way all the way up to Pulliam, who sent it back to Dean, asking for an explanation. Dean wrote an answer, not apologizing, but saying he got mad and would have kicked someone who had stolen a quarter from him. Pulliam called him and congratulated him, saying, "I'd do the same thing if that machine stole fifty cents from me." Dean later noted:

> He appreciated the same kind of bluntness that he had himself. He had absolutely no time for ass kissers.

Pulliam did not make the situation easier with his direct approach to the newsroom. A copy boy never knew when he might be talking to the publisher. "He'd call and bawl out anybody on the phone," said reporter Walter Meek. He ignored any chain of command, creating problems for some editors. Others learned to tolerate it and were occasionally amused by it.

Sometimes he wandered into the newsroom just to talk to a reporter, share stories, surprise an employee who wasn't accustomed to chatting casually with a publisher. Or, he might run into an employee on other odd occasions. *Indianapolis Star* reporter Bill Anderson, who was part of the team that won the newspaper's 1975 Pulitzer Prize for reportage on police corruption, was only a *Star* cub reporter on the police beat in December 1952 when he was sent out to Pulliam's home to pick up an editorial the publisher had written. Nina was typing the editorial, one of his longer ones, so the publisher invited the cub reporter in, offering him a drink. At first Anderson said no. "Are you saying you don't want a drink or you mean you don't want a drink because I'm Gene Pulliam?" the publisher asked. Anderson agreed to have one. Pulliam gave him a big highball and entertained him with stories about his days as a police reporter at the *Kansas City Star*. After a few stories Nina was still working in the other room and he asked Anderson if he wanted another drink. Anderson thought to himself, how can I say no to my publisher? So they had another drink, and he heard more stories. Later came a third drink. Anderson finally returned to the *Star* with the editorial, slightly dazed, after more than an hour of drinking with the publisher. "I wasn't used to drinking that much," he said.

Six months later, Anderson was crushed under a truck while on a police story. He suffered seven broken ribs, a ruptured liver and spleen, and a broken ankle and shoulder. He returned to work in August, assuming he had spent his vacation in the hospital.

> I told him [city editor Lowell Parker] my vacation was over—it was supposed to be in July when I was in the hospital. He told me that didn't count. I said something about mid-September but it didn't matter because we weren't going any place. (Reporters in my grade were getting about $65 a week then.) Parker told me it would do me good to get away for a week or so and I replied that we couldn't afford it. That was early in the week and I was off on Thursday and Friday. When I returned to work Saturday there was a letter addressed to me in my mailbox. Inside was a note from Mr. Pulliam saying, "Enjoyed our talk, have a good time on vacation. From one police reporter to another. (Gene)" Enclosed was a check for $200.
>
>   In 1975 the *Star* won the Pulitzer and Mr. Pulliam sent Dick Cady, Harley Bierce and myself a nice letter and check for $1,000. He said it was his proudest moment. I replied, thanking him and reminding him of the night in 1952, how it had influenced my feelings, my love affair with the *Star*. He answered with a very warm letter. He died just two weeks later.

After the death of one of his Republican Arizona friends, Clarence Buddington Kelland, Pulliam ordered the city desk to collect eulogies from around the country for the next day's paper. Five minutes before deadline, Pulliam called the city desk without identifying himself, asking, "How are you doing on the Kelland obituary?"

"We're doing fine," answered rewrite man Colin Deacon. "Who wants to know?"

"This is Gene Pulliam."

If you're Gene Pulliam, you should know better than to call me five minutes before deadline," Deacon answered, hanging up on the publisher.

The rebuked publisher called the managing editor, asking the name of the rewrite man. "Give Deacon a raise," he said, "he's a good newspaperman."

If that story revealed one side of Gene Pulliam as a publisher, some innocent pigeons in downtown Indianapolis revealed another side.

After he and Nina sold their Indianapolis home, they kept an apartment at the downtown Athletic Club, a block away from the newspaper. He was staying there one night in 1966 when some pigeon-shooters in University Park fired and hit the club building. In past editorials, the *Star* had supported the Jaycees' pigeon-shooting program, but all rules were off that night. The publisher was irate at seeing his apartment building under siege. He called the city desk, angry, ranting about how absurd and dangerous it was for grown men to be firing shotguns into downtown Indianapolis. He wanted it stopped—right now. That was no time to argue with the Boss. Richard Cady, who later lead the Pulitzer Prize-winning team of reporters for the *Star*, was working that night and recalled:

I was working rewrite and Al McCord was on the night desk. The "hot line" started ringing. Al answered. It was the Old Man. I could hear him shouting over the line, and I was six or seven feet away. McCord's face got red, and about all he could get in was "yesses," "uh huh," while he scribbled notes. As I recalled, Al hung up and said ECP was furious because the Jaycees had fired a shotgun blast that struck the side of the Athletic Club, they being in University Park. We were supposed to get a story saying it was dangerous and silly for men to be going around shooting shotguns. I believe I got the police reporter working on it, he called Mayor Barton, I called the Jaycees, and I also checked the clips and found, ironically, *Star* editorials supporting the Kill a Pigeon program. Anyhow, the story was written and went on page one.

The first story, referring to Mayor John Barton, was headlined: "Barton Vows Probe in Downtown Killing of Pigeons, Starlings."

Gunfire echoed through downtown Indianapolis again last night as the Junior Chamber of Commerce resumed its city-approved war against pigeons and starlings.

A squad of five Jaycees armed with shotguns blazed away at starlings in University Park, north of the Federal Building and in the vicinity of the World War Memorial.

Other shots had shattered the calm of a Sunday afternoon two days earlier as Jaycees attired in red hunting coats directed their fire at the pigeons in University Park.

They kept firing despite the protest of some children playing in the park who started crying at the plight of the besieged birds.

The Jaycees boast that they have bagged 20,000 pigeons during the last nineteen months.

Stories continued for several days, with the state attorney general John Dillon jumping in and calling the Jaycee program "a pretty dangerous thing." The editorial position of the *Star* suddenly was reversed. "Gunfire in the Streets," was the headline on the editorial announcing the new position.

Walter Meek was assigned to write about the growing air pollution in Phoenix in 1969. "I got called into managing editor Ed Murray's office one day and he said we were going to do air pollution. I said, good. But he said, no, I mean, we're really gonna do air pollution. I said, 'Oh, you mean *Gene* wants to do air pollution.' The apocryphal story was that Gene walked out on the patio one day and couldn't see Squaw Peak or Camelback Mountain." Meek started a series, and the *Republic* ran a picture of air pollution every third day for three months, under a headline, "It's Your Air." The state legislature began to respond, ultimately approving some of the tightest air pollution laws in the country. "We created such a storm. We went too far," said Meek. He was later public relations director of the Arizona Public Service Company, where he saw some of the laws from the other side. "We picked on everybody. The tough political issue was the mines. The mines tried to take me on personally." Mine representatives were going to Pulliam, complaining about Meek. "Gene never said one damn word to me and never told me to stop doing anything. I know it was going on because there were business people out at the legislature telling people I was going to be stopped any day."

When Bolles, who had the same kind of support at key points, was killed a year after Pulliam's death, *New Times* Magazine noted how Bolles had fit so well into Pulliam's newspaper:

> Almost from the start, Don Bolles seemed to thrive in the rarefied atmosphere of Phoenix and Eugene C. Pulliam's newspaper. An arch conservative, Pulliam would often outrage his reporters by inveighing against creeping socialism and bolshevism on his front page; but he felt no less strongly about the enemy nearer at hand, the creeping criminal element that was invading his media province. As a result Pulliam created one of the best climates for investigative reporting of any paper in the country.

38

Conservative Movement

GENE PULLIAM WANTED to help the conservative cause grow. It had emerged with new strength and youthful followers in the early 1960s. The leaders of the movement were William F. Buckley, M. Stanton Evans, Frank Meyer, and those who established Young Americans for Freedom and similar groups dedicated to the cause. There was a strong intellectual and philosophical framework for their convictions, a framework that American conservatives had rarely shown in twentieth-century politics.

They were not mere defenders of the status quo. Rather, they had a broad vision for America and could trace it to philosophers, economists, thinkers and writers like John Locke, Adam Smith, and Edmund Burke. In contrast to so many conservatives who opposed the New Deal, they were not satisfied to hold the line, to preserve America as it was or had been. They wanted to go farther back, or forward, to a new way of life, with all government strictly limited to certain functions, nothing more, and a free economy unregulated by the government except in the most necessary areas. Freedom from government was the essential thrust of the movement. Some of the young conservatives were strict libertarians, truly believing in maximum personal freedom. Some would later advocate, for example, the legalization of marijuana. Most of the conservatives also favored a strong defense posture, aimed at blocking the spread of communism, and where possible, overthrowing it.

Pulliam shared many of these views. His chief goal had become freedom from government, particularly the growing federal bureaucracy. But he came to his conclusions, not from reading Burke, Locke, and Smith and thinking about it, but rather from his business and reporting experience, his buying and selling and running newspapers, and traveling around the world and observing postwar socialism in Europe. The free enterprise way of life had worked well for him and others who were willing to work hard and use their initiative; government intervention, as far as he had seen, did not work well for anyone except those who got their hands on government power. He was occasionally drawn into conservative circles, especially in the early 1960s after he had hired one of them, M. Stanton Evans, as an editorial writer. He quickly promoted him to be the editor of his major afternoon newspaper, the *Indianapolis News*. Evans had followed William F. Buckley at Yale, schooling himself in the writings of conservative thinkers and working for conservative publications like *Human Events* and Buckley's *National Review* before he came to Indianapolis. Pulliam was looking for editorial writers like Evans, a Phi Beta Kappa at Yale. Well-educated conservative writers were hard to find. *Time* magazine noted Pulliam's search:

> "I've been looking for years to find a man like him," chortled Gene Pulliam, 71. "I've combed the whole goddamn country. There are lots of good journalists around, but they're all cockeyed left-wingers."

The Young Americans for Freedom honored Gene Pulliam in 1961 in New York City, giving him an award for distinguished service to freedom. He told them:

> You are the young people who must supplant the Galbraiths, the Stevensons, the Schlesingers and other New Frontiersmen who today are playing God with four-syllable words and in impeccable rhetoric are filtering away American freedom bit by bit.
>   I would not be concerned about these men who play God were it not for the fact that just recently they have been given the power and authority to play fast and loose with American freedom and American lives.

A few months later he introduced columnist William F. Buckley in Phoenix to an enthusiastic crowd of 1,200, who gave Pulliam a standing ovation for the introduction as he declared, "Conservativism is on the march in America."

But Pulliam was never able to put his whole heart and soul into the conservative movement the way Evans and others did. He wanted the same results, but he also had other goals that sometimes conflicted. He wanted to be close to those in power, Democrats or Republicans. He wanted good newspapers. His conservative friends could never understand why he hired Ed Murray, a liberal who was such a remarkable contrast to Evans, to be managing editor of the *Republic*. Some could not see the point of an opposite editorial page that Pulliam established, giving prominent space to liberal viewpoints.

He was a pragmatic rather than an ideological conservative; he wanted to know whether something would work in practice in politics, and was less concerned about whether it would pass the test of conservative ideology. He picked and chose among political candidates with an emphasis on their personal qualities. *Star* editor Jameson Campaigne noted the difference between Pulliam and the more ideological conservatives who were growing in influence and numbers in the early 1960s:

> He was a seat-of-the-pants conservative, not an ideological one. The kind who wants to preserve what is best, change what doesn't work, keeping always in the forefront the question, will this action enlarge or constrict personal liberty? I doubt that he asked himself why he took one position or another or considered what his "philosophy" was. But he did have a great instinct for issues that endangered personal liberty over the long run.

The conservative movement was particularly strong in Arizona, and Pulliam's newspapers gave the conservative movement a respectability and intellectual acceptance that it lacked in other parts of the country. Day after day the editorial pages poured out the conservative themes: oppostion to more federal programs and intervention in the economy, and support for a strong national defense posture. The Kennedy administration came under frequent fire for its liberal initiatives—urban aid programs, medicare, civil rights—as well as weakness toward communism in foreign policy.

As the conservative movement picked up steam, a more extreme movement developed, revolving around the John Birch Society. Pulliam turned against this extreme movement in 1962. The extremists tended to see a conspiracy, often a communist one, in nearly everything and everyone who did not agree with their particular approach, and they became a powerful force in the

Arizona Republican party. In 1962, their candidate for the U.S. Senate nomination, car-dealer Evan Mecham, defeated Goldwater's top aide, Stephen Shadegg, in a divisive primary.

Pulliam had already decided to support the aging Democratic senator Carl Hayden, regardless of who won the Republican primary. Pulliam thought Hayden had always carried the ball for Arizona when it came to getting bills passed, keeping the Arizona Water Project alive, getting the practical things done that were necessary for the growth of Arizona. Hayden was a Democrat and supported the kind of liberal programs that Pulliam opposed. But if he had to choose between conservatism and the growth of Arizona that Hayden stood for, he tended to pick the latter. This startled and confused his conservative friends.

Hayden was sick in 1962, and was expected to have a hard time campaigning. His top aide, Roy Elson, didn't know Gene Pulliam, except by reputation. Elson figured the conservative publisher, who had done so much to promote the Republican advance in the state, would be plotting to topple the vulnerable Hayden. Elson had polls indicating that 40 percent of the population of the state, with so many newcomers, did not even know who Hayden was. He had served in Congress since 1912, in the House until 1926, and in the Senate since. With congressional seniority and age, he had spent increasingly more time in Washington.

Elson mapped out a strategy for the 1962 campaign, figuring on the kind of rough-and-tumble opposition from Pulliam's newspapers that MacFarland had encountered in 1958. Elson sought to meet Pulliam, to try to neutralize him somehow. "If he couldn't support us, I was ready to make trouble, antitrust, prices, all that," Elson recalled. But Elson had a surprise when he met the publisher in his *Republic* and *Gazette* office. He asked Pulliam what his position would be in the upcoming campaign. "What a silly question," Pulliam answered. "I'm for Hayden, he's done everything for Arizona. What ever made you think I wouldn't be for him?"

> I asked his advice from then on. He was fun to talk to—he had a lot of balls. He had a lot of fun in that campaign. He'd call me up with ideas, he was interested in all the details.

Hayden went into Bethesda Hospital thirteen days before the election, suffering from a virus infection. Rumors started from the Mecham camp that the senator was dead. Pulliam called Vice President Johnson, told him to arrange a picture with Hayden and Senator Richard Russell of Georgia. It ran on the front page of the *Republic* the Sunday before the election, quashing the rumors effectively. It was an odd campaign for Pulliam, as he plotted behind-the-scenes strategy in behalf of a liberal Democrat.

Mecham and his supporters were angered by his rejection of the conservative movement. They expected more loyalty. Some accused him of selling out, making deals. Mecham was so irate that, like Robert Morrison, he started his own newspaper, first a daily and later a weekly, using it as a platform to attack Pulliam and the *Republic.*

The Hayden-Mecham campaign was the beginning of a subtle shift for Pulliam. The two-party system he had sought was well established. He could accept Murray's constant pleas and storming arguments for a more balanced news coverage in political campaigns. And he ran into the same problem he had in the 1920s and 1930s—Republican candidates, in some instances, were not as competent as the Democrats. And, too, the Republican party in parts of Arizona, especially Maricopa County, was gradually being taken over by the extreme conservatives. Finally, Pulliam had a strange, almost incomprehensible falling out with the man he had started in politics, the leading spokesman for the conservative cause, Barry Goldwater.

39

1964

BARRY GOLDWATER AND Gene Pulliam were probably bound to clash, just as Pulliam had with Senator Jenner. Goldwater was strong-willed and independent. He said what was on his mind, which Pulliam often liked, but not when he was on the receiving end.

Goldwater faced a dilemma after the assassination of Kennedy in November 1963. He had helped put together a strong national conservative movement with a momentum he could not personally control. He felt obligated to the young conservatives who had flocked to his side and were ready to do battle for him in his crusade for freedom from excessive government. But he could also see how difficult it would be to challenge Lyndon Johnson. He had known Kennedy since he had come to the Senate in 1953 and liked him. But to Goldwater, Johnson was slippery, always wheeling-and-dealing, hard to pin down on specific issues. When Johnson was nominated to be vice president in 1960, an *Arizona Republic* reporter called Goldwater for a quote, tracking him down at a party at Pulliam's house. "All whores don't wear skirts," Goldwater commented, whereupon Pulliam grabbed the telephone and ordered: "Don't print that."

After Kennedy's death, Goldwater started asking friends what he should do. He met with Pulliam in December 1963. Whatever was said at their meeting, which lasted most of the day, the result was misunderstanding and bitterness on both sides. Pulliam's memory of the meeting was that he advised Goldwater not to run. He said he would lose badly to Johnson and set the conservative movement back several years. Goldwater, for his part, remembers Pulliam telling him to go ahead and run in order to keep the eastern liberals from taking over the party. *Republic* political writer Bernie Wynn suggested, "While Goldwater privately claims that Gene 'encouraged me' to seek the Republican nomination, I believe he's reading a polite reply from Gene as encouragement."

It was understandable that Goldwater believed he had received encouragement from Gene Pulliam. Pulliam had helped him every step of the way to that point, from winning a seat on the Phoenix City Council through a startling upset victory in 1952, to his triumph over a severe challenge from organized labor in 1958. Pulliam's newspapers were conservative, and Pulliam shared Goldwater's basic political convictions. But publicly, after that meeting, Pulliam was not urging Goldwater to run. During an Associated Press board meeting in New Orleans, soon after Goldwater announced his candidacy, he told the *New Orleans Times-Picayune* that Goldwater was running only because he felt obliged to thousands of conservative supporters. "This is nothing I haven't said to Barry before. Personally, I feel he'd prefer to stay in the Senate," Pulliam said. "When the original cry for Barry went up, he was answering a demand for a strong conservative voice against the Kennedy administration. Now that demand, with Johnson in, has been diminished."

Clearly, Pulliam was not beating the drums for Goldwater. Nor did he have any personal antagonism toward Goldwater's chief challenger for the 1964 Republican nomination, New York Governor Nelson Rockefeller. He had met Rockefeller a number of times in New York, and came away convinced that he was a moderate rather than a liberal. During Rockefeller's 1962 campaign for governor, he suggested:

> I am delighted you are not letting people pressure you into an inflexible left-wing position. I think you know America well enough to know that this country does not believe in socialism and the people are far more conservative than the government, but there is a middle of the road which you seem to be occupying almost single-handed for the time being.

Pulliam was also close to the new president. He had promoted Johnson in Indiana and Arizona Democratic circles in 1959 and 1960, and was upset with him for taking the vice presidential nomination. But he congratulated him after the 1960 election, saying:

> There is no doubt in my mind at all that your work saved the southern states for the Democratic ticket. Of course you know I was never convinced that Kennedy was big enough or experienced for the job. However, I hope and pray to God I am wrong.
>
> I know you give him great help, and I feel a whole lot better about the next four years with you sitting in there at his right hand.

Wooed and enticed by the Johnson presidential charm, Gene Pulliam also must have dwelled on Goldwater's weaknesses as the campaign developed. Goldwater was rash, as the campaign revealed, delightful in his irreverent way, but almost suicidal as a presidential candidate under the hostile scrutiny of a national press. Pulliam had seen that side of Goldwater before.

Goldwater was also a visionary who dreamed the conservative dream and shared it with his admiring followers. Pulliam was nervous with dreamers and talkers. He wanted to see it worked out in real life and wondered if Goldwater could put it through from the White House. He wanted someone who would do things. He remarked in 1968, after Goldwater's move back to the Senate:

> There are a good many things about Barry Goldwater that the public doesn't understand. One of them is that he is a pretty self-centered man and really never has done anything for Arizona except build a national reputation for himself and give Arizona a lot of favorable publicity. I think he will do a lot better job in the Senate than he would have done in the White House.

Johnson was reaching out everywhere after the Kennedy assassination, pouring his charm on publishers, editors, businessmen. Friends of Pulliam later were sure he was being manipulated and used by the new president. Johnson would appeal for Pulliam's help, putting it on a patriotic basis—the need for national unity after the assassination, with a small war brewing over in Vietnam. One letter shortly after Kennedy's assassination suggests the approach that Johnson used with Pulliam and others:

> It is comforting in these difficult hours to know that I have your heart and your hand. Believe me I need both, and your prayers as well.
>
> I will never forgot your friendship which is a great sustaining force.

Johnson added in handwriting below: "Carl Hayden gave me your message—thanks much. He is going to watch Arizona for me and you all keep me informed."

By the spring of 1964, Pulliam was helping Johnson plot his campaign strategy. He invited him to Arizona in May. "I will guarantee you the largest crowd that ever greeted a president in Arizona," he promised, adding:

> A record-breaking crowd for you in Arizona will attract national interest, and the significance of such an Arizona welcome to you will be front-page news in every paper in the country. Incidentally, you will get credit for bringing the Lower Basin states together in a peaceful solution to their differences. Nobody will complain. The majority will applaud I earnestly hope you will do it. Also, I would like to prove to you that I was right about Arizona's deep feeling for you.

While he was helping Johnson, he also observed the more extreme conservatives who were organizing Goldwater's campaign, packing the Cow Palace at the Republican National Convention in San Francisco. "If you weren't with them 1,000 percent, you were part of the conspiracy. All the media was seen as part of the conspiracy," explained Bernie Wynn, an *Arizona Republic* political reporter who consulted frequently with his publisher on political matters. "The right wing played a big role in the convention. Gene was upset by it."

Pulliam began defending Johnson as a "conservative" to friends and he grew personally loyal to him. His conservative friends didn't understand it. How could a man of Pulliam's convictions and shrewd judgment be taken in by Lyndon Johnson? He seemed to be snowed by Johnson's charm. Johnson poured it on Pulliam in 1964, calling him frequently, meeting with him during the campaign privately, when he was supposed to be out talking to Democratic audiences.

Pulliam liked being close to those in power. Here was his chance. Johnson was going to win, he was sure. Why go out barnstorming in behalf of a losing cause, Goldwater, when he had doubts about him anyway? He kept on helping the Johnson campaign behind the scenes, giving him advice on what to say and what not to say in his presidential visits to Indiana. In October he suggested he avoid the civil rights issue because it would only

further the backlash that had emerged in northern Indiana when
Governor George Wallace made a strong showing in the May
presidential primary.

> I wouldn't discuss a word about civil rights. The law has been passed.
> There have been no demonstrations of any kind in Indiana. There may
> be a backlash, but there certainly would be if you discussed it. In
> northern Indiana where Governor Wallace made such a showing the
> situation is very much better, but any effort on your part to justify it
> would only hurt. It has been passed. Let it operate and let the people
> digest it before you discuss it any further.

While he was helping Johnson behind the scenes, he was
creating all kinds of confusion about his own stance, and that of his
newspapers. Whom was he for? In 1964, his newspapers were a maze
of confusion. They were generally praising Goldwater's stance on
the issues. *Indianapolis Star* editor Jameson Campaigne wrote what
he hoped would be an official front-page endorsement of
Goldwater, for Goldwater's October 1st visit to Indianapolis. But
Pulliam told him to sign it as a personal column and put it on page
one. Johnson came to town a week later, and the *Star* rolled out
another red carpet, with Pulliam's front-page editorial welcome. "It
is a rare privilege and honor for Indianapolis to have the president as
its guest."

In Arizona, he told *Republic* managing editor Ed Murray that
he was playing up campaign news on Goldwater too much. Murray
was surprised. Democrats were confused but happy, for once, with
Pulliam. Arizona native William P. Mahoney, the ambassador to
Ghana, came back to campaign for the Johnson ticket in the fall. He
had felt the wrath of the *Republic* before, in 1960, when he was
working for Kennedy while Pulliam was backing Johnson in the
preconvention delegate selection process in Arizona. He thought the
Republic would come after him again, for campaigning while he
was still an ambassador. Instead he saw favorable stories on his
appearances on behalf of Johnson. "I expected to be raked over by
the *Republic* and *Gazette*," he said. He went to see Pulliam, blurting
out with a grin, "What's going on here?"

"You're pulling for the right candidate, he's an old friend,"
Pulliam responded, adding some negative comments about
Goldwater.

Behind the scenes, Pulliam was advising Johnson on how to carry Arizona:

> You can lose this state and Roy [Elson—the Democratic candidate for Goldwater's Senate seat] can most surely be defeated if the foolhardy Democratic leaders persist in their plans to bring Franklin Roosevelt and Senator Pepper out to Arizona. You must remember that 75,000 to 100,000 Democrats have been voting Republican because they didn't like the socialism being preached by the Democratic candidates.
>
> They are going to vote for you this year because they don't think you're a socialist and they believe you have done a wonderful job as president, but they will forget all about this if Roosevelt and Pepper and men of that type come out here and begin to harangue them. They're good Democrats and they don't like to be reminded that they voted Republican.

In Arizona, rumors started that Pulliam had sold out his interests in the newspapers. He wrote a response in the *Republic* and *Gazette*.

> During the last several weeks, rumors of all sorts have circulated in Arizona and several other states regarding the *Republic* and the *Gazette*. Most of these rumors are so fantastic, so false and so obviously a natural outburst of election hysteria as to require no notice.
>
> However, one rumor has persisted and I feel it is necessary to nail it for exactly what it is—a completely false and silly rumor.
>
> It has been reported that the *Republic* and the *Gazette* have been sold to an eastern syndicate.
>
> There isn't one single word of truth in this rumor. These papers are not for sale now and never will be during my lifetime. And even in the event of my death they will not be sold. They will remain in the hands of the same competent executives who now manage these papers.

Pulliam's dilemma over Goldwater and Johnson was complicated by the statewide races in Indiana and Arizona. In Arizona, he was neutral in the senate and governor's race. In Indiana, Roger Branigin was the Democratic nominee for governor, and Lieutenant Governor Richard Ristine was the Republican nominee. If Pulliam was for anybody in 1964, it would be Branigin, his favorite kind of candidate, as well as one of his true friends in politics. Branigin was the exact opposite of Lyndon Johnson, the complete amateur in politics. He later let the party fall apart as governor; he often refused even to meet with county chairmen. He was an honest man, uninterested in personal power or higher office, as conservative as Ristine on most issues, and less awed by Gene Pulliam than other political figures.

Pulliam wrote a front-page endorsement of Branigin in the *Star*, the Sunday before the election, stating:

> Seldom has a man been nominated for governor who is so completely free of political commitments. Roger Branigin is under obligation to no man or any organization large or small.

Republicans were outraged. One wrote to Pulliam, canceling a subscription to the *Star* and calling the publisher a "Benedict Arnold." Democrats were happy. "It didn't turn it," said Branigin's campaign manager, Gordon St. Angelo, later the party's state chairman, "but it was worth 100,000 votes." Branigin won by 263,278 votes, running ahead of Johnson in his first run for public office.

In Arizona, Pulliam finally did endorse Goldwater the Sunday before the election, but the endorsement, as one *Republic* editor, Tom Sanford, noted, "damned him with faint praise." It was anything but a typical Pulliam editorial:

> Arizona's stake in the presidential election goes beyond its five electoral votes. For the first time in history, a native Arizonan is the candidate of a major party. The state's natural pride is enhanced by the knowledge that only one other westerner has ever been a serious contender for the presidency. Such an honor seldom comes to a small state, and we think natural state pride alone is a good reason to vote for Barry Goldwater for president.
>
> If the polls and other usually reliable indices are even partially correct, President Johnson will be elected by a rather large majority in the electoral college. Lyndon Johnson has been a good president. The country will be safe in his hands. Indeed, the nation is fortunate that two men of the caliber of Barry Goldwater and Lyndon Johnson are running for the presidency.
>
> But Arizona's five electoral votes will in no way be a decisive factor in the election.
>
> Barry Goldwater is not a political freak. His successful bid for the nomination grew largely out of his personal appeal across the nation, just as they have always had in Arizona.

It has been a rough campaign, much rougher than most. Goldwater has been called shallow, ignorant, trigger-happy, a racist, irresponsible, a psychopath and Heaven knows what else. His fellow Arizonans know that these epithets are utterly false. They know Goldwater as one of their own: an attractive personality with a deep and abiding faith in his state and his country. Arizonans are proud of their state and of the citizens in it. They are especially proud to have an Arizonan honored by being a candidate for the most important office in the world.

Down in your hearts you may know that Barry Goldwater has not always been right, but down in your hearts you also know that he has been right enough to deserve a vote of confidence from the citizens of his own home state.

Pulliam's long-time critic, *Indianapolis Times* columnist Irving Leibowitz, mocked his stance and speculated on the potential cabinets of Johnson and Goldwater. In Johnson's, Leibowitz wrote, Pulliam could be United Nations ambassador, since he has been an independent for Johnson. In Goldwater's cabinet, he could be secretary of Health, Education and Welfare, since he has been an independent for Goldwater. But then, Leibowitz tended to find fault with Pulliam no matter what he did. When Pulliam was for Eisenhower, Leibowitz was for Taft, when Pulliam was against Marion County Republican leader Dale Brown, Leibowitz was for him. Still, in this case, Gene Pulliam provided a vulnerable target for Leibowitz. For once he waffled and straddled the fence. He failed to support the man he had started in politics, the man who lifted the conservative movement into a national phenomenon. Conservative Republicans were bitter. They feared he had allowed himself to be taken in by the charms of the president.

Democrats and liberals, on the other hand, were seeing another side of Pulliam, his independent streak, and of course, they liked it since he was no longer beating on their heads. Arizona Democrats like Stewart Udall, a member of the Johnson cabinet, assumed he was simply aware of Goldwater's weaknesses and didn't want to support him for the presidency. Others thought his motives were personal, that he wanted to be close to those in power and was hesitant to offend them; or that he had made some sort of deal with Johnson and Branigin. But if he wanted something, he had never asked for it. From Johnson all he ever requested was that he meet his Phoenix doctor, Hayes Caldwell, during the summer before the election. He wrote Johnson:

As you know, I never ask personal favors. As a matter of fact, I think this might be of more advantage to you than to me; but because this man is my personal physician and has saved my life twice, I am imposing on our friendship to make sure that he and his two sons have a chance to visit the White House while they are in Washington July 28 to July 30.

From Branigin, he requested only that the governor clean up the bathrooms in the statehouse, after he got a letter complaining about how dirty they were, explaining to the governor:

We have lots of requests from subscribers to do this, that and the other, all the way from changing baby diapers to getting U.S. presidents fired, but I don't believe anybody ever asked us to censor the janitor service in a public building before.

Former Arizona governor Howard Pyle, also a radio executive, put Pulliam's motives in the best perspective in the 1964 race between Goldwater and Johnson. Pyle was not fond of Pulliam. He had enjoyed the publisher's support in 1950 and 1952, then felt his wrath for the Short Creek operation in 1954, losing Pulliam's support as well as the governor's office. Pyle had known Gene Pulliam for a long time, observing him in business also. He explained his motives in 1964 more simply:

Gene has always been his own man. He just thought that way. He's not anybody else's man.

40

Vietnam

GENE PULLIAM HAD been a harsh critic of Secretary of State John Foster Dulles and his habit of making treaties all over the world in the 1950s, establishing a wide range of Unites States military commitments. He had traveled all over the world and he couldn't see the point of all the treaties and alliances. Like Dulles, he wanted to stop communism, but treaties seemed to bind the United States too closely, robbing the U.S. of flexibility in foreign affairs. When Dulles was establishing the SEATO organization for Southeast Asia, Pulliam was cautious, fearing an association with former colonial powers as well as overextended commitments.

At the time, he was corresponding with another publisher, John Knight, who had similar and stronger fears about any U.S. involvement in Southeast Asia, fears that he voiced consistently in the 1960s. Pulliam reprinted Knight's 1954 warning in his own newspapers, entitled, "Is Dulles Preparing U.S. for War in Indochina?" and Pulliam noted to Knight his agreement with it:

> I didn't interpret our editorial as saying we ought to go it alone. I just don't think we ought to go at all under present circumstances. In fact, I think your editorial Saturday and what we've been saying are about as much in harmony as two newspapers could be.
>
> Nothing could be as disastrous as to begin pouring white troops into Asia. The only way Asia is going to be liberated is for yellow men to fight yellow men for their own liberation. I'm in favor of helping them, but not sending a single American boy into combat in Asia.

Pulliam was corresponding with Senator Barry Goldwater on the same subject, the same year. Goldwater told Pulliam how he inserted a *Star* editorial in the *Congressional Record*, calling on the United States to establish a foreign policy independent of England and France and take a stronger stand against the Soviet Union. Goldwater wrote about his own doubts about U.S. intervention in Vietnam:

> To me this whole subject of Indochina is extremely distasteful, and I wish that the president would come out with a reassuring statement to the American people that he has no intentions of engaging this country in war in that area of the world or, for that matter, in any other area that does not directly and closely affect the well-being of our citizens.
>
> I think one of the greatest contributions he could make to the people of the world at the present time would be to establish a committee that would work directly under him, which committee would be composed of Mr. Hoover and Mr. Truman and other men whose background and experience would enable them to come to a decision on where the United States should build its fences. Today we act like a young boy who has just felt his first muscles, who looks for a fight on every street corner, not knowing that he is only equipped to handle one.

Ten years later, Knight was voicing the same fears, still a critic of U.S. involvement and an early and consistent critic of the Johnson administration policies, calling for withdrawal long before it became fashionable and popular. Pulliam, meanwhile, had changed his mind. The doubts he had about U.S. involvement were apparently smothered by a combination of his sense of wartime patriotism, by his anticommunism, but most significantly, by Johnson's personal influence. Johnson had applied his treatment to a number of publishers and with Pulliam it was very effective. It came in the form of frequent phone calls, requests for advice, appeals to patriotism and for national unity. Pulliam received more personal attention than he had ever received from any other president, including Eisenhower.

Johnson's press secretary George Reedy thought their personal backgrounds developed a mutual attraction:

> About the best thing that I can suggest to explain the attraction between him [Johnson] and your grandfather is that both were very strong men

who were accustomed to making their own way in life. There is a fraternity of men who stand on their own feet and who have been through some difficult struggles. That is the only way that I can account for it, as otherwise the two were quite divergent.

Both of them disliked the polish and formal manners that they had encountered in many social settings, the "snobs," the aristocratic types who looked down with an air of paternalism on a Kansas boy who had made his own way in the newspaper world. Both felt insecure socially when they mixed with people of more refined manners. It was a game they didn't know how to play properly, and even should they learn it, it didn't look like much fun. Johnson's earthy personality, his coarse language and manners, appealed to him.

Gene Pulliam was growing susceptible to flattery and charm by 1964 anyway. He still liked to rock the boat, but not as hard as he had ten and fifteen years before. Johnson's treatment might not have worked so well in the past, but in the 1960s, it produced the results Johnson was seeking. Pulliam joined his team. He defended the administration's Vietnam policy, seeing himself as one of Johnson's lieutenants and trying to keep public opinion behind the administration politics. In 1966, on his last foreign reporting trip, he wrote a story from Geneva, Switzerland, on how Johnson was winning support for his policy in Vietnam among European leaders.

> If the U.S. wins in Vietnam—and almost everybody believes the United States will win—then America will emerge stronger than ever, unless, of course, President Johnson's efforts and policies are sabotaged by weaklings at home.

As the country grew more divided over Vietnam and Johnson's policies, Pulliam did all he could to shore up public support. He began to see himself as a personal adviser to the president. He wrote him to take naps every day, urged him to stand firm on Vietnam, offered strategy suggestions on how to maintain public support for the war. He advised him to speak at the Associated Press luncheon in New York in 1965 "to offset the irresponsible criticism of the yakkity-yak doves."

He extended his influence well into the Democratic party, especially in Indiana. Pulliam was the man the Democrats would go to if they wanted to bring Johnson or Vice President Hubert Humphrey to the state. "If I couldn't get a speaker in, he could," said Gordon St. Angelo, the Indiana state Democratic chairman after Branigin was elected, "He had more influence with Johnson than any party official I knew anywhere in the country." He was as close as anyone to the Democratic governor Robert Branigin, although he never exercised the influence he might have had over Branigin. In the 1965 legislative session, Branigin did ask his advice on two bills he had to approve or veto, an open-housing act and a repeal of capital punishment. According to St. Angelo:

> Roger said he'd veto one or the other, adding that Pulliam had advised him that we'd look too liberal if we did both. I said we shouldn't let Pulliam dictate to us. Branigin gave me a lecture then, saying one, we wouldn't be here without Pulliam and two, he's got a bunch of them coming. Roger said, no one will ever fry while I'm governor, so he vetoed the capital punishment bill and approved the other.

Gene Pulliam was seventy-six years old in May 1965, but age didn't seem to be slowing him down. In January, he started off with five days in Phoenix, then six days in Indianapolis, three days in New York City for Associated Press meetings, followed by four days in Indianapolis, five in Phoenix, two in Washington, including a meeting with Johnson, then back to Indianapolis for six days. He scoffed at rumors that he would retire, having announced at a *Star* and *News* picnic three years earlier: "I'll only retire to attend my own funeral."

He was surprised to hear that *Wall Street Journal* publisher Bernard Kilgore was going to retire—Kilgore had finished DePauw twenty years after Pulliam left in 1929. "I was rather shocked to learn that you are retiring from the *Wall Street Journal*," Pulliam indignantly wrote to Kilgore. "You're not that old. What the hell goes on?" Pulliam was still golfing at a good clip, although various physical ailments, particularly with his back, kept him from hitting the ball as far as he once had. Playing at the *Republic* and *Gazette* annual tournament in 1965, he knocked in an eagle two with a wood shot from 180 yards from the green on a par four.

He hosted a luncheon in Indianapolis and a dinner in Phoenix for Vice President Humphrey and urged Johnson to keep him out on the trail defending the administration's policies in Vietnam. He praised one of Johnson's Texas speeches, telling him in a telegram:

> Your speech at San Antonio was the best and most effective presentation you ever have made on Vietnam. I do hope you won't be influenced by the appeasing doves and the critics who are trying to make political capital out of the misery of the war.
>
> The American people always have responded to courage and the defense of freedom and they will support you in increasing numbers when they know you have no intention of backing down or appeasing anybody—red, brown or white.
>
> So forget the polls, ignore the doves, and let the American people know that you and not McNamara are running this war.
>
> By the way, Hubert Humphrey has made thousands of converts to your Vietnam policy in both Arizona and Indiana among Republicans and Independents by his brilliant explanation and defense of your Vietnam policy. I've had as many letters of commendation from Republicans and Independents as I had from Democrats, although the audience in both states was at least 60 percent Democrats. Keep Humphrey on the trail. He is doing you a tremendous service. I will bet you another ten-gallon hat that we will carry Arizona and Indiana for you next year and you will be reelected regardless of who your opponent is. In the meantime, keep your promise to get a nap every day.

One *Indianapolis Star* reader wrote Pulliam, suggesting that he was getting soft in his old age, when Pulliam scheduled a luncheon for Humphrey. The reader, Bill Dunn, said Humphrey was a socialist and how could Pulliam be hanging out with him? Pulliam wrote back explaining that he was merely giving a luncheon "for an old friend who happens to be vice president of the United States." Humphrey may be a liberal, he acknowledged to Dunn, but he is not a socialist and he believes in free enterprise. You can't doubt his patriotism, Pulliam added, and suggested that winning the war in Vietnam required the kind of unity the United States maintained during World War II.

Publisher John Knight was disappointed in the apparent mellowness he sensed in his fellow publisher. He had always enjoyed Pulliam's cantankerous bluntness and he was finding it among fewer and fewer publishers in America. "He was feisty. There was no cant or hypocrisy. We had a kind of gruff way with each other. I enjoy that sort of thing," Knight said. But Knight thought Johnson had snowed Pulliam.

> Johnson was a very pragmatic man. He could sit down with an adversary and use what we called the Texas charm. He cultivated people and in a cruder sense he used them. He wasn't above buttering you up. I think your grandfather kind of liked the earthy qualities of Johnson. And I think Johnson buttered him up.

He suggested that Pulliam was swayed by the presidential luncheons, the phone calls, all the attention.

> This was heady stuff. I think he held Johnson in a little more awe or respect than I did. To me, he was just a Texas politician. I never saw your grandfather in an argument with Johnson. Your grandfather was quite sold on him.

Whatever his relationship with Johnson, Gene Pulliam could still be outspoken and independent. He still had his past convictions about the federal government and freedom and showed his old vigor in carrying them out when he abruptly quit the DePauw University board of trustees in 1966.

He had served on the board thirty-five years. He helped the school in a variety of ways, fundraising, providing a radio station hookup through WIRE. He had always dealt with DePauw officials with his characteristic blunt manner, and it frightened those more used to a gentle approach, but many grew to like him. Elmer Carriker, who had worked in the DePauw administration and later went to Baker University in Kansas, noted that Pulliam "never talked for very long. He wasn't conversational, always very busy. His answer was always yes, no, or go to hell." Methodist bishop Richard Raines, an influential figure on the DePauw board, found him to be:

> A powerful aggressive fearless person, so loyal to his convictions as to sometimes seem lacking in diplomacy when contrary convictions were expressed.
> This aggressive side was balanced by a deep emotional and sentimental vein in his life. He used to send money with a Christmas message overflowing with gratitude and love for his parents. He was either very much liked and appreciated, or strongly disliked, depending upon one's relationship to him and his purposes and procedures. Those closest to him, his employees, he was proud to say, trusted and had real affection for him.

He had brought prominent figures to the school, especially former British Prime Minister Harold Macmillan in 1958. The Macmillan visit brought widespread national attention to DePauw.

"This is a rather feeble way of expressing what I have been thinking for many, many months," DePauw president Russell Humbert wrote Pulliam after the visit. "You have given DePauw its greatest experience in history. I do not intend to be a prophet, but I sincerely believe that this is the climax."

Humbert died in 1962, and William Kerstetter was named to succeed him. Pulliam didn't like some of the new directions at DePauw; liberal speakers were brought to the campus more and more often. He wrote a friend who later joined him in resigning from the board, Ernest Sims: "I can't understand how the faculty of a school which has been supported by free enterprise and by men who believe in free enterprise all these years, will continually bring in socialists and foreign ideologists as speakers."

But he kept helping the school. He mediated a potentially divisive dispute about fraternities and sororities on the board of trustees in 1965, working out a compromise statement that put DePauw on record against racial and religious discrimination.

The next year the board agreed to Kerstetter's proposal to accept federal financial aid. Gene Pulliam was furious. He decided to quit in protest, along with Sims and Don Maxwell of the *Chicago Tribune*. Bernard Kilgore, the DePauw board chairman and chairman of the *Wall Street Journal*, tried to persuade them to come back, but they refused. Pulliam told him:

> I have considered very carefully all that you have said, but so much of it just doesn't jibe.
>
> You say you have been as opposed as either Don or I, and that you have said so in the *Wall Street Journal*.... [You] write an editorial opposing federal aid, and then preside at a meeting of the Board of Trustees of DePauw University and take exactly the opposite view, with the protest that a meeting of the Board of Trustees is not the place to face the issue.

He added:

> Taking that first million dollars from the government will be like taking the first shot of heroin. DePauw's appetite for more and more federal aid will expand and expand until it will be just like any other college, subsidized, controlled and dominated by the federal bureaucrats.

Denison Kitchel, Goldwater's campaign manager in 1964, wrote him congratulations, having wondered about Pulliam's lukewarm response to Goldwater's presidential campaign. "I had no alternative if I wanted to sleep with myself or my conscience," Pulliam replied. The *Pontiac Press* (Mich.) took note in an editorial, declaring:

> In these spineless days of "gimme, gimme, gimme," it's doubly heartening and refreshing to run across a situation like the one that just unfolded at DePauw University.
>
> College officials were negotiating for a million-dollar handout from the federal government. However, Trustees W. D. Maxwell of the *Chicago Tribune* and Eugene Pulliam, who owns newspapers in Arizona and Indiana, filed objections. They refused to go along with collegiate boondoggling, in any form. And E.M. Sims, of Elkhart, joined them.
>
> The great bulk of all America has accepted current blandishments and federal handouts with a bow of humble obeisance and a majority of the DePauw trustees held out for the plum from the District of Columbia and the protesting trio was outvoted.
>
> That terminated the matter, but it didn't end the consequences. All three resigned. To them, the old-time American principles of independence and probity that built this nation far outweighed the million dollars. Honor hasn't entirely faded. I applaud them heartily.
>
> Here are three staunch and sturdy American gentlemen who believe that first things come first and the lowering of a college escutcheon smacks of decadence. Glib and specious arguments didn't make the slightest dent in the old-fashioned armor of these champions of educational integrity. It is highly refreshing to encounter individuals committed to these standards in our days of uncut beatniks, teachers parading shamelessly in defiant strikes, and malcontents brazenly demanding relief from the third generation.

The resignation didn't mark the end of his association with DePauw—he continued to help the school financially, coming back for a Sigma Delta Chi anniversary the next year, receiving another degree in 1969.

His conservative friends applauded the DePauw resignation. Still, his friendship with Johnson remained a mystery. In January, he urged Johnson to speak to the Associated Press luncheon in New York to help mount a comeback for the fall campaign.

I feel so strongly about this that I want you to make it a personal urgent request that you accept. I think you already know that I am going to support you in Indiana and Arizona. The polls you see about Indiana and Arizona are phonies. I wrote David Lawrence the other day and told him that his polls on Arizona and Indiana were phonies and that if the rest of the polls were as phony, he should begin all over again. In Indiana you have Governor Branigin, the most popular governor Indiana has had in many, many years, and who is a very close personal friend of mine. He has agreed with me that he will campaign in the state from the Ohio to Lake Michigan for you, provided we support you. And you know we are going to support you.

The same thing is true in Arizona. It is too bad that the Democrats are as badly divided as they are and that Carl Hayden is sick, but nevertheless, I feel absolutely confident that we can carry Arizona for you.

Pulliam assumed he had enough power in both states to bring Johnson through, save the administration's Vietnam policies, and help in the fight against communism. He had done it many times before; why not one more time? But the country was turning against Johnson and the war and he withdrew. Pulliam was still ready to fight, but now he had no candidate.

41

1968

GENE PULLIAM HAD gradually changed his newspapers in the 1960s. When he started supporting Democrats, he let everyone know that he was truly an independent. "Who are they gonna blame this time?" he would ask Democratic friends. "I told the Democrats, we've got to find another scapegoat. We can't blame Gene Pulliam anymore," said Arizona Representative Morris Udall, a Democrat. In Arizona managing editor J. Edward Murray told his staff to report and edit according to professional standards of fairness, instead of trying to second-guess the publisher's desires. In Indianapolis, Pulliam had named his son, Gene, as assistant publisher in 1962, with responsibility for the editorial operations of both newspapers. He was establishing similar standards of balance in political news coverage that he had applied as managing editor of the *Indianapolis News.*

The dwindling number of newspapers in America perhaps affected Pulliam's thinking. Fewer and fewer cities had competitive newspapers. Only twelve of one hundred cities in the 100,000 to half million size had them by 1968. Indianapolis was one of the few major cities of its size to have three daily newspapers in the early 1960s. But the *Indianapolis Times,* having lost money for several years, was folded by the Scripps-Howard organization in 1965, leaving Pulliam with the field to himself in Indianapolis. In Phoenix, Robert Morrison's *Journal* folded about the same time, after a year and a half of publication. Evan Mecham's effort to put out a very conservative daily also failed, and he switched from daily to weekly publication of his *American,* which he had started after Pulliam had opposed his effort to unseat Democratic Senator Carl Hayden in 1962.

Pulliam surprised some of his competitors with his interest in keeping competition going. He had run smaller newspapers before, faced the rough competition of Ed Howe in Atchison, and he knew what it was like to be on the bottom. He also knew the competition was helpful to his own newspapers.

In the early 1960s Pulliam had talked to Scripps-Howard executive Jack Howard and Mark Ferree about possible arrangements to save the *Times*. "He wanted to see the *Times* preserved. He could see the advantage of having two editorial voices," recalled Jack Howard. "We talked about a joint production setup." But Pulliam, on the advice of his lawyers, cut off the discussions because of potential antitrust action by the Justice Department, which annoyed Pulliam. To him it was another example of government meddling in his business. He complained in speeches that two Los Angeles publishers, Otis Chandler and William Randolph Hearst, Jr., had to go see Attorney General Robert Kennedy before they could fold the competitive Los Angeles newspapers, the *Mirror* and the *Herald*. When he received an award a few years later, he spoke about the major problems of the newspaper industry, including "the dogged policy of the antitrust division, which today makes it almost impossible for a newspaper publisher even to speak to a weak competitor, much less help him keep his paper going."

In Indiana, R. H. Blacklidge, publisher of the *Kokomo Tribune* fifty miles north of Indianapolis, found he could lean on Pulliam for advice after he took over the paper at a young age. "Whenever I needed advice and counsel I had but to pick up the telephone or go see him and he gave me whatever time I thought was necessary," Blacklidge recalled.

In Arizona, liberal Democrat Jonathan Marshal had bought the *Scottsdale Progress* in a Phoenix suburb. "I was a little bit nervous. I had been warned to be careful of him, that Pulliam was a tough guy and would try to squash me because I was a liberal," Marshal recalled. Marshal met him in 1963 soon after he came to Scottsdale and was surprised when Pulliam told him.

> Now I want you to know one thing. I know how hard it is to get started and I've run small newspapers. Anytime our people do anything you don't like, you come to me personally. I want to help you in any way I can and I mean it.

Marshal was skeptical. He complained several times about unfair tactics, once when an employee in one of Pulliam's women's departments told Scottsdale people not to go to the *Progress* first with news items or else they would not get publicity in the *Republic* or *Gazette*. Each time he found that Pulliam followed up and straightened out the matter to Marshal's satisfaction.

> A couple of lawyers told me we were his antitrust ace in the hole. But that was not his real motive. Although he was a tough guy, he was an awful sentimental person. A lot of people didn't see that side of him. It was a private side. He would always say, I remember the days when I had a small paper. I didn't feel he was as tough and hard as people said he would be. He was a very strong person, tough, dominating, and used to having his own way. I wouldn't have wanted to cross him, get in a fight with him.

With the death of the *Times* and the *Journal*, Pulliam wanted to provide a wider range of viewpoints on the editorial page, something Murray and editorial writer Ed McDowell had continually urged on him in Phoenix. In a startling move for the year 1964, he started opposite editorial pages in his Indianapolis and Phoenix newspapers. Very few other newspapers, liberal or conservative, had full op-ed pages which devoted columns and opinions that challenged the editorial policy of the newspapers. Among the nations's major newspapers only the *Los Angeles Times* had a full opposite editorial page.

At first, the op-ed pages in Phoenix were marked with a boldface memo to the editor, "Let's always remember that the other man has a right to be heard. Gene Pulliam, publisher." Later, the page was marked with the comment Pulliam had used in his talks on freedom of speech during the 1930s, Voltaire's remark to Helvetius: "I disagree with what you say, but will defend to the death your right to say it." In Indianapolis, Pulliam's top executives were surprised by his sudden decision to start the page, including his son, who recalled:

> I don't know just who really thought up the full-size op-ed page. I had started a one-column affair in the *News* way back when but it didn't amount to all that much. Somewhat out of a clear sky, Dad called a meeting of the top people and announced there would be full page op-ed

pages. There was some dissension. Bill Dyer thought it was too expensive, Bob Early and I were afraid we couldn't fill up that much space effectively, and I even talked Dad into letting me run the weather there for a while. He didn't like it and told me to run a full page.

The meeting in Indianapolis was a short one—Pulliam never did like long meetings, preferring to announce a decision rather than to survey opinions. "Everyone was against it," recalled *Star* editor Jameson Campaigne. "Then he just said, 'Well, we'll start it next week.' He was the 'majority of one,' as Bill Dyer used to say. It confused the people for a while—nobody ever condemned it though. On big decisions like that, he was always right."

"I was shocked by the cost—it was $500 a day then, with newsprint," added general manager William A. Dyer, Jr. "It turned out to be a good move. With a monopoly and being conservative, it helped with those who didn't agree with us."

The new op-ed pages and more balanced news coverage brought new respect for Gene Pulliam in the newspaper industry. Many conservative publishers and editors had always admired him for his climb to the top of the profession, for his outspoken manner, his worldwide reporting. Basil Walters, a Knight newspaper executive, ranked him as one of the great publishers of the Midwest, classing him with John Knight, Robert McCormick of the *Chicago Tribune,* and Roy Roberts of the *Kansas City Star.* "He did the things I didn't have the guts to do," Walters said. John Knight, who was not as conservative as Pulliam, looked on him as "a first-rate publisher and editor; a man of excellent business judgment and strong editorial opinions. His strength lay in the fact that he did not dissemble on any question, but was always forthright and readable."

To liberal editors and journalism teachers, Pulliam had always been something of an anathema. Now some of them were beginning to look on him with respect, if not fondness, partly because of the quality of the *Arizona Republic* under Ed Murray in the 1960s. Yet some *Republic* staffers felt the newspaper was still underestimated in *Time* magazine rankings, in the *Columbia Journalism Review,* and in many journalism schools, because Pulliam's conservative editorial views were not considered on their merits, but viewed as old-fashioned, not in tune with the times.

In the stiff competition for the Associated Press board Pulliam was reelected in 1964 by an overwhelming margin, running a close second in the voting to Benjamin McKelway of the *Washington Star*. He ran well ahead of other publishers such as Barry Bingham of the Louisville newspapers and Otis Chandler of the *Los Angeles Times*. He received a number of journalistic awards in Indiana and Arizona, as well as two of the top awards in the industry—the John Peter Zenger Award in 1966, and the William Allen White Award in 1970—putting him in the company of such past winners as Russell Wiggins of the *Washington Post* and James Reston of the *New York Times*.

Yet he had not really changed direction 180 degrees. Temperamentally he was still an activist. He couldn't sit on the sidelines or confine his fighting to the editorial page. He wanted to put everything he had into the battle.

He could still revert to his earlier form, and did in 1968 when Senator Robert Kennedy was running in the May Indiana presidential primary.

Pulliam had been all set to support a Johnson-Humphrey ticket in 1968 when Johnson withdrew from the race, leaving the field to Kennedy, Senator Eugene McCarthy, and Vice President Hubert Humphrey. Indiana's May primary was a key race, Kennedy's first primary and a test for Humphrey. Governor Roger Branigin was running as a favorite son and was expected to throw any support he had to the vice president, who was just beginning to set up his campaign. Pulliam wanted to stop Kennedy at all costs, and perhaps get Johnson back in the running with a Branigin victory.

Few could fully explain the depth of his antagonism toward Kennedy. He had grown to like John Kennedy—at least Kennedy seemed to have a sense of humor—but Pulliam maintained his resentment of the Kennedy money, the advantage it gave them in politics. He considered their wealthy background and upbringing as a mark against their character. Privately he expressed fears that Kennedy would use the Justice Department to move against his own and other conservative newspapers under charges of antitrust violations.

"Jack was different from Bob, who was honest," Pulliam once said.

But he [Bob] saw everything in black and white. You were either for him
or against him. You never could relax and just be with him, like you
could with Jack.

Kennedy had turned into a committed liberal by 1968, and
Pulliam was still a conservative, regardless of whether he had
mellowed temperamentally. Both were gut-level fighters who went
into political battles with everything they had. Neither could relax.
Both wanted to win badly.

The year before Pulliam had made a valiant effort to say
something good about Bobby Kennedy. He wrote to praise him for
some of his speeches on poverty:

> Because I have been rather quick to criticize you at times during the last
> few years, I am writing this letter to tell you how sincerely delighted I
> have been to read your statements recently regarding the cause and cure
> for riots, poverty, and social justice.
>
> You were so right in saying that the answer to these social problems
> will be found in providing education—especially vocational
> education—and jobs for the poor whether they be white, black, or
> yellow. And what heartens me most is your suggestion that the country
> can rid itself of the major evil effects of poverty only through
> enlightened extensions of the free enterprise system. I think you were
> right in saying that the business community will respond
> wholeheartedly if they are given this job to do without too much
> interference and supervision by the Washington bureaucrats....

Kennedy misunderstood. He took it personally and thought it was a
new policy for Pulliam. Perhaps he was turning into a liberal after
all.

Whatever the sources of his feelings toward Kennedy, Pulliam
went out to stop him in 1968. He called meetings with top executives
and political reporters in Indianapolis and talked about the need to
stop Kennedy and help Branigin win. His son, Gene, and general
manager William Dyer warned him that slanting and burying the
news coverage of Kennedy would only hurt the reputation of the
newspapers and probably not even help Branigin. At the meetings,
Pulliam would agree, but no clear policy was ever established. The
result was a mass of confusion on news desks, and disaster in the
newspapers. Pulliam sent out memos telling editors not to give full
coverage to Kennedy. "Give Senator McCarthy full coverage, but
this does not apply to a man named Kennedy," he said in one memo.

When Martin Luther King was assassinated a few weeks before the primary, Pulliam called the *Star* news editor and told him to put the story on the bottom of page one, not as a flag story at the top, because King had been a "rabble-rouser." His son Gene intervened and had the story put back on the top of page one, but the editors were confused. *News* political editor Edward Ziegner set out to cover Kennedy for a few days, but managing editor Wendell Phillippi called him back, saying Pulliam was upset and didn't want Kennedy covered. Editors were afraid to cover anything, wary of how Pulliam might react. The result was absurd primary coverage, with news on Kennedy or McCarthy buried in the newspapers, and puffy stories about Branigin in the weeks before the primary. News about Branigin got unusual prominence. The son of former governor Henry Shricker criticized Branigin opponents and made page one. A Republican congressman said his party would try to help Branigin defeat Kennedy and wound up on page one. But when Kennedy persuaded Indianapolis blacks not to riot the night of King's assassination in early April, the information was buried in another story about a new statewide youth group that had been formed in behalf of Branigin.

The coverage suddenly changed the Friday before the Tuesday primary. His son had won a running argument with his father and ordered the managing editors to give equal space to all the candidates. Stories about the three Democrats as well as the only Republican candidate, Richard Nixon, were given equal space and prominence across the bottom of the front page for the next few days.

To some extent Pulliam's papers were editorially reflecting the resentment of Indiana conservatives toward what the *News* editor M. Stanton Evans labeled the eastern liberal establishment. In a column on the primary, Washington-based columnist Joseph Kraft revealed some of the arrogance that eastern liberals showed toward Indiana. He labeled it "One of the Last Backwaters in the Country."

> Until very recently, to be sure, the modern America of Kennedy and McCarthy had bypassed the Hoosier state. Indiana had been populated less by immigrant masses from Europe than by migrants from Appalachia—itself a backwater.

Kraft described McCarthy and Kennedy as "intelligent and cosmopolitan," while deriding Branigin as a "a small-town lawyer with a taste for drinks at the country club and distaste for TV, newspapers and airplanes, not to mention Negroes and unions."

The *Indianapolis Star* editor printed the column, adding a note: "This article by Joseph Kraft, long-time columnist-friend of the Kennedy family, ridiculing Indiana, is typical of the propaganda being turned out by pro-Kennedy writers to push the candidacy of Senator Robert F. Kennedy." The *Star* came blasting back with a delightfully sarcastic response:

> Get rid of your horse-and-buggy, your lightning rod, chamber pots, kerosene lamps, bustles and McKinley buttons. Indiana is emerging from antiquity.
>
> The word comes from Joseph Kraft, columnist, whose perception is matched only by the fluidity of his prose.
>
> "For, in Indiana," he beams, "one of the last backwaters in the country has finally entered the mainstream..."
>
> It is the May presidential preference primary, of course, that has focused upon Indiana the eyes of eastern liberals, who usually glimpse our cornfields, barns, hog lots, haystacks and cow pastures only from passing jets. From this lofty vantage point, their vivid imaginations are able to paint the countryside below with stampeding buffalo, Indians on the warpath and musket-shooting frontiersmen.
>
> Now at long last, the light is shining into our ancient darkness. Or as Kraft puts it: "Until very recently, to be sure, the modern America of Kennedy and McCarthy had bypassed the Hoosier state." (We have been lucky, haven't we?) "Indiana had been populated less by immigrant masses from Europe than by migrants from Appalachia—itself a backwater."
>
> Kraft finds one exception to Indiana's general backwardness in Lake County. He doesn't mention whether the remarkable ability of the dead to walk there on election day is what attracted his attention.
>
> Unfortunately, we homespun bumpkins had only, says Kraft, "medium-sized towns"—not big cities with all their wonders, racketeers, air pollution, slums, race riots, super traffic jams, communist cells and monumental graft.
>
> Even so, out here among the covered wagons and the wigwams, grudgingly admits Kraft, the local gentry "fostered cultural pursuits." While we weren't busy getting scalped or eaten by wolves, we had time to produce Booth Tarkington, George Ade, Theodore Dreiser, James Whitcomb Riley, Cole Porter and Hoagy Carmichael.

Kraft mocked Indianapolis mayor Charles Boswell for his refusal to accept federal aid. The *Star* answered: "Shucks, Joe, remember we're just simple country folks.... But dismal as things seem, all is not lost, says Kraft, the prophet from his perch on a mount in the East. For a band of young angels had appeared as if by magic to lead the backward Hoosiers out of the wilderness. By May 7 the tribes will stand at the shore of the Red Sea."

> And if they pull the right lever, a Moses will spring up to lead them through the sundered waters into the Promised Land.
>   Ain't God good to Indiana? Ain't He, fellers, ain't He though?

To some extent the *Star* and Branigin were capitalizing on the resentment that Hoosiers felt toward outsiders. Front-page *Star* editorials told Republicans to cross over and vote for Branigin on the basis of state pride.

> Republican voters who want to help uphold the honor of Indiana and prove to the world that Indiana can't be bought can do so by crossing over in the primary to vote for Branigin. Republican poll watchers can't challenge them; we don't think Democrats will.
>   This is a matter of state pride and state policy to protect us from being subjected to this sort of rich man's invasion every four years.

Kennedy went on to win the primary anyway, running well ahead of Branigin and McCarthy. No longer could Pulliam swing an election with his newspapers. Now the candidates could go to television, buy advertising, and get on the news, where Kennedy's complaints got a wide hearing. In his public statements, Pulliam would not acknowledge that his newspapers had manipulated the news. When Kennedy press adviser Pierre Salinger called for an American Society of Newspaper Editors investigation into the *Star*'s coverage, Pulliam answered:

> Bobby Kennedy is like all spoiled children. When he doesn't get what he wants, he bellyaches about it. The facts are Kennedy and his entourage received more space in the *Indianapolis Star* and the *Indianapolis News* than any other candidate, largely for the reason that he brought his whole family, including his mother, to Indianapolis and they made news and we printed the news. . . .
>   Of course we are opposed to his candidacy because we don't believe men who spend millions of dollars in a primary campaign should be given the nomination for the highest office in our government. Editorially, we have tried to make it clear that Indiana, at least, is not for sale. But in our news columns we have given Kennedy a far better break than he has given his opponents.

His argument seemed to be that the *Star* had to offset Kennedy's money by helping Branigin.

> Senator Kennedy won in Indiana because he had the most money and the largest number of election day workers. He completely dominated the Negro vote. He brought his whole family, including his wife, sisters—and even his mother—to Indiana. As a result, they made more news than either of the other two candidates and we printed it. His statement that he was "completely blacked out of the *Star* and *News*" is ridiculously untrue. He and his entourage received more space than either Branigin or McCarthy. Evidently he thought his stories and picture should be on page one every day.
>
> If Branigin had had one-half the money Bobby spent in Indiana, Branigin would have won hands down. The blunt truth is this primary depended on which candidate had the most money to spend.
>
> During the entire campaign we had no complaints from the Democrats regarding our coverage of the primary—and none from Kennedy until the day before the election when Pierre Salinger made his absurd attack on both the *Star* and *News*.
>
> We editorially opposed Kennedy largely for the reason that we do not trust his judgment in either domestic or foreign affairs; but more importantly, because we do not believe that only millionaires can run for the presidency. If this becomes a fact in American politics, our whole elective system will be destroyed.

Later Pulliam privately and reluctantly acknowledged that he had erred. At a fall meeting with his Indianapolis executives, general manager William Dyer argued with him, saying it should never be allowed to happen again. Puffing on his cigar, Pulliam was silent. Finally he said, "Well, I guess we did go a little too far."

42

The Protesters

TOWARD THE END of the 1960s, the differences between publisher Gene Pulliam and his *Arizona Republic* managing editor, J. Edward Murray, increased. Their fights grew more bitter and antagonistic. Murray had survived for two reasons—his ability as an editor and his willingness to argue with "the Old Man." But they couldn't come to any compromise on the major news stories in those years—the youth protest, the demonstrations, the antiwar rallies, the social and cultural trends.

Pulliam wanted to take a firm stand against the loose and leftist cultural and moral trends of the 1960s. It all went against his grain. He drew national attention in 1969 when his newspapers quit accepting advertising for X-rated movies in an effort to rally support for Phoenix Democrat Dick Smith. Smith had lost his job as a movie theater operator for refusing to show an X-rated film, *I Am Curious Yellow.*

Eugene Pulliam couldn't understand the protests, the radicals who occupied college buildings, the antiwar groups who held mass rallies. He never had time for such nonsense when he was growing up. "Kids don't appreciate a damn thing," he would tell his Indianapolis driver, Tom Jones. He had an activist temperament himself. He stopped by one antiwar rally in Indianapolis in 1967, watched for a few minutes, then started to exhort those who were standing by to protest against the protesters. Occasionally he wrote editorials or made speeches, against the protesters, in his own vigorous style. One editorial, during the nationwide campus demonstrations after the U.S. invasion of Cambodia in 1970, demonstrated his anger and frustration:

Stop it, you anti-Americans. Stop criticizing everything and everybody and every motive and every action except your own. Stop constantly sniping at your government. What in the world is the matter with you? You have the most wonderful nation on earth, a nation that has gone to extraordinary lengths to uplift the poor, feed the hungry, comfort the afflicted, and extend justice to everyone. Yet here you are, applauding the very people who degrade and mock America, who tell you how selfish and corrupt Americans are.

Murray was more sympathetic to the protesters. He came from a different generation, and he had a son who joined in some of the youthful protest. "I thought the paper should be activist, appeal to youth," Murray recalled.

In 1970 Murray hired a young college student, Daniel Ben-Horin, and gave him a column to voice the aspirations of some of the young activists. Ben-Horin thought he toned down his own views in the column, which ran for several months before Pulliam ordered it stopped. Pulliam thought Murray was giving the protesters too much publicity, too much space in the *Republic*. He thought they were just publicity-seekers anyway, and why should they get so much attention? Were they really so significant? When he received the William Allen White Award the same year, he asked in his address:

Have we really printed both sides—or have we succumbed to the lure of printing essentially the sensational? In this troubled era, have we given all the facts—or have we allowed the self-appointed leaders, the noisy publicity-seekers, the quasi-righters-of-all-wrongs—to make the news by over-coverage of their criticisms and condemnations.

Murray, on the other hand, thought Pulliam was trying to ignore real news—and he wanted to move the *Republic* into more interpretative reporting. Until about 1969, he and the publisher would hammer out their differences in the kind of rough-and-tumble arguments they had had so often.

But the gap in their differences had widened by 1970. Pulliam's health was beginning to fail; no longer could he take the arguments with Murray so well. "When I first knew him [Pulliam], he was very vigorous," said *Republic* assistant managing editor Tom Sanford. "He could take a lot of rough-and-tumble. Later it took too much out of him."

Murray found himself getting orders from the new general manager, Mason Walsh, who had been managing editor of the afternoon *Phoenix Gazette*. He could see the end was coming. Some on his staff thought Murray was trying to get fired, looking for ways to make Pulliam angry. "He got suicidal at the end," recalled Bob Early, Jr., later the Managing editor of the *Republic*. "Murray would get bitter over losing arguments, he got antagonistic. He had this concern for the youth movement, but he couldn't explain it well—management would think he was filling up columns with lunatics. He went too far too fast."

"I was surprised Ed stayed ten years," added reporter Ben Avery, who was close to Pulliam. "Gene's really a pretty darn forgiving man. He let Murray get away with a lot."

Ultimately, Murray was fired in May 1971, after he thought Pulliam had invaded his areas of responsibility, canceling the Doonesbury cartoon and firing Ben-Horin. "It came apart when he thought there was too much interpretative reporting, activist reporting," Murray said. "He said we were putting out a good magazine instead of a newspaper. He didn't have the energy and time to devote to news, and we just had a different point of view."

After Murray was fired, morale at the *Republic* plummeted. The new managing editor, former foreign editor, Heinie Milks, was less inclined to argue with Pulliam. Murray had established tremendous rapport with his staff and now he was gone. No reason was announced officially for Murray's firing—it was described as a resignation. Except for Ben-Horin and Murray, Pulliam had seldom fired anyone in his organization. Employees who had been nervous about pleasing the publisher before were doubly so now. Who was next?

Reporters like Don Bolles and Bernie Wynn, who had personal relationships with Pulliam, were not concerned and could understand the conflict between Murray and Pulliam from a more detached perspective. But most staffers only knew Murray, many had been hired by him—he had done battles for them against an eccentric publisher, and now he was gone.

Pulliam at the same time did some odd things that bothered his staff. Bernie Wynn wrote in his political column that state senate majority leader Chet Goldberg had not turned out to be the tiger he had promised to be. Rather, Wynn wrote in 1968, he had emerged as a "pussycat." Pulliam hit the ceiling. Goldberg was a golfing friend, and Pulliam objected to the personal slight. He wrote a front-page retraction:

> In Bernie Wynn's column which appeared in the *Arizona Republic* yesterday, Mr. Wynn unfortunately and unforgivably referred to Senator Chet Goldberg, R-Maricopa, as a pussycat. We apologize to Mr. Goldberg for this very inaccurate and discourteous reference. Everybody who knows Chet Goldberg knows that he is anything but a pussycat. Please accept our apologies, Chet.

Wynn was so angry about the retraction that he refused to write his column. But it was hard for him to stay angry with Gene Pulliam. He had worked for Pulliam at the *Indianapolis Star* in the 1950s. At that time he got in a fight with a lobbyist at the state legislature after he had had one "too many martinis," as he recalled. "It caused a furor," Wynn said. He thought he would be fired. "I got a letter from Gene. He scolded me, said to watch my temper, be careful about drinking. He comes to the rescue of employees like that, tries to give them the benefit of the doubt. So I have to allow him to be wrong also."

After Wynn quit writing the column, Pulliam sent him a note and said let's close the case now, and in a rare admission acknowledged, "Maybe I was wrong."

Wynn started writing the column again. "I can't stay angry with Gene, despite these bouts with him. We feel sentimental about him," Wynn explained. He remembered the personal help the publisher had offered when Wynn was in an auto accident and wound up hospitalized. "He may kick your butt in public one day, but you get in trouble the next day and he'll come to the rescue."

Another *Republic* reporter, Bob Thomas, had a similar experience. He expected to lose his job after punching poet Allen Ginsburg when Ginsburg had called him a name for asking a question at a news conference. Instead of firing Thomas, Pulliam gave him a raise and told him, "I would have done the same thing. Our reporters shouldn't have to take that."

Eugene Pulliam was slowing down more and more in the 1970s. But the changes he was going through were not good for his newspapers, especially in Phoenix, where he played an active role.

No longer was Murray there to boost the staff morale, and Pulliam was becoming increasingly dictatorial and less inclined to listen to arguments.

But when he was willing to fight, his staff gave him grudging admiration for his independence and convictions, even reporters who disagreed with his goals and methods. Tom Sanford, the late assistant managing editor at the *Republic*, decided to remain with Pulliam's newspapers. He had been hired in the early 1950s by Pulliam's then publisher, Simon Casady, who was later fired by Pulliam. "I could never question his motives," Sanford said in explaining why he decided to remain. "I thought they were always high, above board, what he said they were. I might disagree with his methods and thrust, but I never questioned his motives."

Some staffers thought that he was listening to the wrong people more than ever. "He wanted things to stay calm in later years," recalled former *Republic* editorial writer Ed McDowell. "He listened to corporate voices more. He would have thrown them out of his office years earlier."

No longer was he so quick to see through people who wanted to use him and his power. "In his later years, he could be conned a lot more. He lost the ability to see that people were brownnosing," said *Republic* columnist Paul Dean.

Yet he had not lost all of his steam. Sometimes he surprised everyone and came storming back.

43

No Freeway

GENE PULLIAM HAD been a prime mover behind the phenomenal growth in Phoenix and Arizona after World War II. In the ten-year period from 1963 to 1973, manufacturing employment soared 186 percent in the state (from 58,000 to 170,800 jobs), tops in the nation for that period. Personal income rose from $3.3 million to $9.2 million. He encouraged businessmen to relocate in the Valley of the Sun, and his newspapers backed the charter government that was a key attraction for businesses and had generally acted as catalysts for much of the growth. He had suggested and then backed a massive annexation program that kept the suburban areas from strangling the downtown and inner city area.

In one sense, he was uncomfortable with all the power he had accumulated. He tried to let go a little, and began to exercise political influence in more subtle ways. He and other civic leaders organized the Phoenix 40 to encourage younger leadership. In civic affairs he was less inclined to approve every project that came up, but would occasionally make a special move to help. Once he put up $1,000 for the first step of a $24,000 fundraising effort to provide a small town, Allenville, with drinking water. The shantytown had been without water, hauling it from two miles away, because a loan from the federal government had gotten bogged down in red tape.

But in another sense, he was satisfied. He had what he always wanted. He was a patriarchal figure in the 1960s, often a stabilizing statewide influence when the state might have split into warring factions as, for example, over the Central Arizona Water Project. Without the project, most civic and political leaders thought, the state would slide back into economic stagnation. While Democratic

Senator Carl Hayden was keeping the project alive in Congress,
Gene Pulliam was providing a stable point of unity on it in Arizona.
"It would have died a thousand deaths if it weren't for the *Republic*
and *Gazette*," said reporter Walter Meek. "The state would have
split apart on it politically, but Gene provided a good part of the
stability that kept it together."

He never liked the Tucson-Phoenix rivalry, which could have
split the state into feuding groups. When both the University of
Arizona in Tucson, and Arizona State in Tempe, near Phoenix,
sought to have a medical school, Pulliam stepped in and arbitrated.
He worked out a compromise, giving Tucson the medical school
with a promise that ASU could have a law school. Most of his work
was behind the scenes. Only occasionally would he make a public
appeal, for example to the Tucson Chamber of Commerce in 1965:

> Can you remember a factional fight more bitter, more acrimonious than
> the argument over where to locate the medical school? Most of that
> initial white heat has cooled down. Our two cities still face an important
> task, one which will demonstrate just how much we really have
> matured. I'm speaking of the Central Arizona Project, and the
> implications it has for our future. Will Tucson and Phoenix once again
> manage to put aside sectional differences in the interest of statewide
> unity?

Pulliam had ordered his newspapers to tackle some of
Phoenix's problems, like air pollution, in the 1960s, several years
before such issues had become popular nationally. But the
newspapers had never seriously questioned the city transportation
plan which, as far back as 1960, had included the Papago Freeway,
designed to run through central Phoenix. Critics of the freeway plan
came from groups that usually had been frozen out of the Phoenix
power structure—Dr. Gerard Judd, a Phoenix College instructor
who started a citizens organization to oppose the freeway, the
Citizens for Mass Transit Against Freeways; and lawyer James
Walsh, a liberal Democrat, a supporter of Senator George
McGovern in his 1972 presidential race, and a supporter of the farm
workers in their efforts to recall the election of Republican governor
Jack Williams. Judd's group had filed a number of suits, delaying
construction. But he and his supporters had an uphill battle against
the city council, the chamber of commerce, the Arizona Association

of Realtors, the State Highway Department, big bankers, and leading city officials, including Phoenix mayor John Driggs.

City leaders were convinced that the freeway was an essential key for the further growth of Phoenix and that its opponents were blocking all future economic growth. Freeway opponents contended that the highway was poorly planned, would divide the city and be an eyesore, since it would be elevated up to eight stories. Some opponents also argued that the growth in Phoenix was going too far and too fast, without any planning or forethought, damaging the surrounding environment and ruining the natural beauty of the valley.

Gene Pulliam was coming to the same conclusion. He had visited Los Angeles and thought it was a mess. Now, in 1973, he turned against the Papago Freeway and his newspapers turned with him.

Suddenly he began ordering stories on freeways; what had happened in other cities; what the potential impact of Papago would be. Pictures of the smog in Los Angeles and other cities appeared; front-page cartoons mocked the freeway supporters. A bulldozer was pictured sweeping away homes; members of the bulldozer crew were identified as the Phoenix Real Estate Board, the city council, the Phoenix Chamber of Commerce, land speculators, groups that Pulliam had teamed up with in a number of past campaigns.

He ordered frequent editorials on the freeway, telling *Republic* editor Pat Murphy in a memo:

> If we win this fight on the freeway, we've got a perfect example of how a newspaper kept a city on the beauty road instead of the greedy road.

Funds had already been appropriated for the freeway, but the environmental groups now had powerful allies in their lonely and seemingly futile effort to turn the community toward their way of thinking. Now the newspapers and anti-freeway groups demanded a referendum on the project. As the pressure mounted, the city council agreed to put an advisory referendum, which would not be legally binding, on a $56.5 million bond issue that would be tested at the polls.

The influence of the newspapers was to be tested. Could Pulliam take on all the other leaders in Phoenix and tell them what to do? He could and did.

He teamed up with environmentalists and McGovern liberals and took on his old friends, throwing his newspapers whole-heartedly into the fight. The *Republic* and *Gazette* campaigns were typical of Pulliam's old-fashioned style, giving little prominent news space to the opponents. The old kind of bias and one-sided reporting came back. "From the other side of the fence, I thought it was one of the dirtiest campaigns I had ever seen," said Walter Meek, who had left the *Republic* to join the Phoenix city government.

If the style was a reminder of his past methods, his allies in this campaign were not. They were the people he had been fighting for years. Now he was showing them what it was like to have the newspapers on their side. Freeway supporters and civic leaders used all the arguments they could muster. They complained about the company he was keeping. Jim Walsh was a left-wing radical, they would complain, how could he line up with that type? "That's too bad," he replied. The older civic leaders were left shaking their heads, wondering what had happened to the old man. Was he getting senile? He had helped them so much in the past, but now elaborate theories would not explain his actions. Howard Pyle's explanation was still the answer: "Gene has always been his own man. He just thought that way."

For some of his staff, it was a great time. The old man was showing he was his own man, not a part of the small clique of older men who wanted to run the city their own way. "He was in there fighting all the way. I had more fun during that time," recalled former *Republic* managing editor Bob Early, Jr.

> His main concern was that it would divide the north and south side, and make it impossible to unify the city. And the south would become a dumping ground. Then there were the traffic flow problems, air pollution. He gave us a whole list of other cities that were already having problems.

On election day there were pictures of freeways and smog in other cities. The voting ran heavily against the freeway, with 58 percent opposed. And the turnout was 42 percent of the registered voters. It was a dramatic contrast to the 16 percent that had turned out in the city bond election in 1970.

James Walsh, the McGovern supporter, a leader of the opposition and later a state senator, summed up the vote: "There is no question that the newspapers almost singlehandedly killed the freeway."

44

Third Party

WHEN VICE PRESIDENT Spiro T. Agnew was trying to popularize the Silent Majority around 1970, *Esquire* magazine asked, "If the Silent Majority Could Speak, What Would It Say?" To answer the question they featured the ideas and personality of M. Stanton Evans, then the editor of Gene Pulliam's *Indianapolis News*, as well as Paul Harvey and other conservative news commentators in the Midwest.

Evans was certainly a conservative and could speak for the Silent Majority, the over-thirty group that had little sympathy for the youthful protesters of the time. Introducing Evans and the others, *Esquire* writer Tom Ferrell wrote, "There is no doubt, of course, that the Silent Majority is well and truly fed up with antiwar protesters, the cost of living, and long hair...." Evans could articulate the complaints of the Silent Majority. He was comfortable in Indiana. He told *Time* magazine shortly after he joined Pulliam:

> I think my philosophy is pretty close to the farmer in Seymour, Indiana. He believes in God. He believes in the U.S. He believes in himself. This intuitive position is much closer to wisdom than the tortured theorems of some of our Harvard dons.

Evans was a leader in the postwar revival of constructive political theory. Educated at Yale like William F. Buckley, he responded to issues on the basis of thoroughly thought-out conservative principles, schooled in the writings of thinkers like Adam Smith, John Locke, Edmund Burke, Sidney Hook, and Friedrich von Hayek.

His intellectual position didn't get much of a hearing on most college campuses. But it had strong philosophical and theoretical roots, and Evans, magna cum laude and a Phi Beta Kappa at Yale ('55), could easily match his superb debating skills with liberals in arguments. He had worked for conservative publications like *Human Events* and *National Review* before he came to write editorials for Pulliam in Indianapolis. Evans understood and expressed well the resentment many Hoosiers felt for the eastern liberal news media. He had seen it in a number of eastern journalists who came west occasionally to gawk at the odd ways of life in Indiana, explaining to *Esquire* magazine:

> The people of Indiana are self-conscious of themselves as Hoosiers, as midwesterners. A certain hostility toward the East may be assumed. Indiana is generally selected out for reproach by visiting *New York Times* correspondents and people like that, and of course we always argue with them a lot. Robert Gover, the guy who wrote these Kitten books, came out here and did an article in the *New York Times* magazine, a sort of Menckenesque treatment of Indiana, the Sahara-of-the-Bozart type thing, putting down Indiana for corn-fed characteristics, and of course we immediately took issue with this and denounced him, and so forth. Indiana has in some ways become symbolic to people in the East of something they don't like, and vice versa, and there's a natural antagonism.

Gene Pulliam, on the other hand, was anything but ideologically oriented. "He was the most unideological person I ever met," said *Indianapolis Star* editor Jameson Campaigne. He had come to conservative convictions that were very close to Evans' by personal experience and observation, not by reading, studying and thinking. When he wrote or spoke about the left-wing protesters and radicals, he would write more from his heart, less from his head than Evans.

Politically Pulliam was also much more of a pragmatist than Evans. He was interested in political victory, even at the expense of conservative principles which Evans would not compromise. Ultimately, Evans and Pulliam parted company. They differed over whether conservatives should stick with President Nixon, and later, President Ford, or take an uncompromising conservative stance. Pulliam made a number of his conservative editorial writers uncomfortable in these years. He appeared to be erratic and overly pragmatic. He was friendly with Democrats like Hubert Humphrey and muted his editorial criticism of them. Pulliam sometimes thought conservatives like Evans were wrapped up in theoretical ideologies divorced from practical day-to-day realities. They spent too much time unnecessarily fighting the eastern liberal establishment.

Evans was nervous about Pulliam's support of the Nixon administration. He believed Nixon was not really a conservative and should be criticized. Pulliam had similar concerns about Nixon, but he was more inclined to want to rally around those in power. He liked Nixon's foreign policy, his diplomatic moves toward Red China. He favored a flexible, pragmatic approach toward communist countries in the 1950s, faulting Secretary of State John Foster Dulles for a more rigid approach. Nixon was showing the right kind of flexibility. Pulliam thought he deserved popular support to make the trip to Red China in 1971 effective, writing a front-page editorial:

> Mr. Nixon's venture could pay off handsomely for our country, but only if he goes to Peking with the complete backing of his government and his people. It is time to lay aside petty politics by all parties to supply this help he needs. Yakking by politically ambitious nitpickers should no longer be heard in this land.

He had known Nixon since 1952. He had kept in touch with him during the Eisenhower administration, bringing him to DePauw in 1957, sticking with him in 1960 when some conservatives were promoting Senator Barry Goldwater as an alternative candidate. But he had never been able to warm up to Nixon the way he did to Johnson. He wrote in 1968:

> Nixon has a very, very difficult job ahead of him and if he isn't careful he will stub his toe trying to run a Madison Avenue shop rather than a White House government service. As I told Nixon the other day on the telephone, he did not receive a vote of confidence from the people. He got only a chance to show what he could do because the public was fed up with what they had, but it certainly wasn't a vote of confidence and it wasn't a mistake. He has an opportunity to be a great president and also to be a great failure. Frankly, I think he has the courage to do the right thing, unless he takes bad advice.

Privately he complained that Nixon was not a leader, not a Teddy Roosevelt who could use the White House as a pulpit. Why couldn't Nixon work on the unemployment and environmental problems at the same time, he asked a family gathering in Phoenix during Nixon's first term. Why couldn't he set up a job program for cleaning up the environment by hiring the unemployed to work on some projects, a kind of Civilian Conservation Corps?

Of the Nixon advisers, he knew former San Diego newspaper editor Herb Klein the best, and kept in touch with him throughout the first four Nixon years. As Klein was gradually being shoved aside, Pulliam heard about it and wrote Nixon to complain:

> However, the real purpose of this letter is to urge you not to allow anybody to convince you that Herb Klein has lost even one iota of his usefulness to your administration. As a matter of fact, I think he is the most useful man in your administration. He has the respect and confidence of newspapers all over this country. He is dedicated and devoted to you. I have known him even longer than I have known you, and I know of no man who has ever been more sincerely devoted to another man's work and career than Herb Klein has been to yours. I think you would lose the respect and confidence of a whole host of newspapermen if you allowed the nitpicking jealous people in your organization to convince you that Herb is slipping. It is just a damn bit of interoffice gossip that you shouldn't even listen to.
>
> You've always wanted me to be frank and honest with you. That is why I felt free to write you this letter.

Nixon wrote back: "Needless to say, I am in complete accord!" Three years later tapes revealed Nixon's different feelings about Klein. Gene Pulliam felt betrayed. He was through with Nixon.

He also complained that Nixon shifted his position too frequently. "What is your honest opinion about Nixon's chances?" he wrote Gannett newspapers chairman and Associated Press board chairman Paul Miller a year before the 1972 election, adding:

> I think they would be very good if he simply took a definite position on several issues and stayed with them. He jumps around too much to suit me because I don't know today what he is going to do tomorrow. But who could do a better job, God only knows.

Perhaps a lack of alternatives pushed him toward Nixon. He could not agree with more conservative Republicans who were tinkering with third-party proposals.

In 1975, some conservatives began talking about a third-party challenge to President Gerald Ford. To them Ford was a centrist. He had chosen Nelson Rockefeller for vice president and had kept Henry Kissinger as secretary of state. Why not go outside the Republican party and form a truly conservative party?

Ironically, one of the leaders of the conservative third-party program was M. Stanton Evans, who was no longer editor of the *Indianapolis News*. Evans had indicated an interest in doing more writing, and needed to be relieved of some of the administrative reponsibilities as editor. Pulliam made him senior editor, with a column that attracted national syndication. He hired Harvey Jacobs, an Indiana native who had set up a journalism program at New Mexico State University, to be editor.

When Evans joined in the third-party movement, Pulliam was afraid he and the *News* would be identified with it also. He ordered an editorial under his name:

> Realignment and reform go on continuously within the two major parties, with conservative leaders making their voices heard in both party councils. But leading Republican conservatives in particular have not despaired of their party's future and are not seriously considering a third movement, demonstrating the isolation of these third-party leaders.
>
> Leading spokesman for this movement is M. Stanton Evans, former editor of this newspaper and one of the most brilliant writers and thinkers in this country. However, he does not represent the policy of this newspaper and has not made an effort to do so. He is now a syndicated columnist with wide national readership.

Evans left the *News* a few weeks later. Ed Murray, on the left, had lasted ten years with Pulliam. Evans, on the right, had lasted fifteen.

45

Freedom and Nixon

Honors given him by the newspaper profession provided Gene Pulliam with wider opportunities to expound his dread of an ever-expanding federal government. He received the John Peter Zenger Award in January 1966. "Our Natural Enemy, the Government," was his theme and title. He quoted Thomas Jefferson and James Madison and cited a range of dangers to freedom of the press, including the move to guarantee a fair trial by shutting off pretrial news coverage.

> It is very obvious that if the legal profession succeeds in shutting off the flow of pretrial news on the pretext of assuring an impartial trial, other professions, armed with equally convincing sounding arguments, will agitate to reduce the newspaper profession to rewriting handouts and routine releases.

The William Allen White Award in 1970 gave him his next major platform. He scolded Vice President Spiro T. Agnew for his attacks on the television networks and liberal newspapers. It was a sentimental time for him, going back to Kansas to receive the award, remembering his days at the *Kansas City Star*, recalling William Rockhill Nelson and William Allen White.

Pulliam agreed with Agnew's complaints that there was a liberal slant in all television networks, in the *Washington Post* and the *New York Times*. But Agnew was proposing what he had warned against for so long:

If this were a one-time shot, a one-time complaint, we wouldn't need to be too disturbed about what the vice president said. All of us know that much of what he said is true.

Despite all of the disclaimers to the contrary, however, there was at least an implied threat of a crackdown on the network licenses in the vice president's remarks. The public, more wide awake than usual, I think, felt he was sounding a warning to the networks to behave—or else. And we have been told and told again that the vice president spoke with the president's advice and consent.

If Mr. Agnew's remarks had gone unchallenged it is quite possible that the Federal Communications Commission would—before long— have taken some restrictive or even punitive action against the networks; if not now, then at some later date when some other government official lashes out at TV and the press.

Of course government officials have a right to complain, as often and as loudly as they wish, about how bad they think the press and TV are. But if newspapers and TV did not answer these complaints with the truth, and with a reaffirmation of their right to know the truth and to give free expression to it, it wouldn't be so long until network news would be regulated outright.

After that, there would most certainly be an all-out effort by the federal bureaucracy to license and regulate the press.

Pulliam did some detailed research on the federal bureaucracy, aiming at more specific targets. He wrote two long and controversial editorials. The first took up the entire front page of his seven newspapers.

The most serious threat to freedom in America today—including freedom of the press—comes from a federal bureaucracy which seems determined to gain control over every facet of American life.

The editorial was widely reprinted, and he bought space to reprint it in the *Washington Star* and the *Washington Post,* drawing even more attention in national wire service stories. He told the Associated Press:

I'm not promoting anyone for office; I'm not promoting any political party; I'm not asking for anything. I'm just trying to inform the public.

The editorial drew fire in a speech by Health, Education and Welfare Secretary Elliott Richardson. Richardson said the real blame lay not with the bureaucracy, but with the politicians who promised that the government would deliver more than the civil servants could provide. Pulliam's critique, he argued, would only escalate the credibility gap between the government and the people "into a gaping credibility chasm, a void which threatens to separate the people and their government at all levels and on all issues."

"When a bureaucrat is criticized, he immediately cries foul regardless of the charges, circumstances or incidents involved," Pulliam responded. "I don't know any Washington bureaucrat with whom you can argue. All of them know they are right by definition and that you are wrong."

Next, he took on the Federal Communications Commission just before the 1972 election in an editorial, "We Can't Tolerate Government Control of TV."

> Unless the Congress of the United States takes decisive action to halt it, the total takeover of U.S. radio and television by the government will be finalized within the next few years. There will be but one radio and TV system. It will be operated, censored, programmed—in short, completely dominated—by an elite group of Washington bureaucrats.
>
> Television cannot fight this battle alone because it has one hand tied already by severe government restrictions and the power to put TV completely out of business. So it is up to the newspapers to lead this fight and to make every American realize that his own individual freedom is in danger as it never has been before. Do we want a dictatorship of TV or do we want to preserve our system of free enterprise in the communications industry?
>
> A spate of government rulings is eroding the economic base of American journalism. The American communications industry is struggling for its very survival in a web of government regulations. None of these regulations is a decree. None has ever been presented to Congress. Nevertheless they have the full force and effect of law.

There were two ironies in Pulliam's campaign against bureaucracy and federal power. He was supporting the Nixon administration that was plotting to do the very things he had been warning against. Second, the Nixon administration was forcing liberals, who had previously scorned Pulliam's warnings, to take a second look at the potential abuse of the power of the federal government.

In the months before Gene Pulliam's death, Yale University president Kingman Brewster declared that federal grants for higher education did indeed carry potential dangers after all. In the *New York Times* magazine, and later in a book, Columbia journalism professor Fred Friendly wrote how the Kennedy and Johnson administrations, particularly during the 1964 presidential campaign, had used the Federal Communications Commission fairness doctrine to force the suppression of broadcasts that were critical of the Democratic administrations.

Friendly was not the first to discover the story—Pulliam's editor at the *News*, M. Stanton Evans, had written about it ten years before in *The Liberal Establishment*. Now the story got a prominent airing in the liberal *New York Times*. Friendly suggested:

> The facts of the effort are startling enough in themselves after the Watergate story, with its generally accepted assumption that dirty tricks in the Nixon White House were unique. But the story of the fairness doctrine during the 1964 campaign also illuminates—with striking irony—the subtle and fascinating interplay of power politics and regulatory policy.

Time magazine attacked the power and size of the Health, Education and Welfare Department, declaring: "The Beneficent Monster, Rich and Eager to Please, HEW is rapidly growing out of control."

At times, Pulliam expressed doubts about Nixon. He had a hard time even getting to talk to him. Nixon didn't want his advice. Early in the first administration, Pulliam had rebuked him for taking a pay raise from $100,000 to $200,000 when Pulliam thought the president should be setting a symbolic example for cutting down on inflation. Pulliam talked about supporting Washington Democrat senator Henry Jackson rather than Nixon in 1972 if Jackson could get the party's nomination. At least Jackson had some convictions. Pulliam declined to endorse Nixon in 1972. *Arizona Republic* editor Pat Murphy, new on the job, was surprised. He casually asked about it soon after he started work. "Hell no, we won't," Pulliam answered, without offering further explanation.

Nixon visited Phoenix in May 1974, in his first post-Watergate appearance after releasing the White House transcripts. The *Republic* provided sympathetic coverage. Goldwater and Representative John Rhodes had arranged the visit to help Nixon maintain public support as the scandal was unfolding. Gene

Pulliam refused to meet Nixon. He told Murphy, "I don't want that son of a bitch out there putting his arm around me." By summer, when the question of the final and most damaging tapes came before the Supreme Court, Pulliam told Murphy that the newspapers would back the Supreme Court decision. "It is a question of law and a president should not flout it."

When the final tapes did come out in early August, Pulliam was angry. It was clear that Nixon had deceived him about Herb Klein's role. To Pulliam, Klein had been the shining light of the administration, his main contact, a newspaperman who resisted the Madison Avenue style of those who surrounded Nixon during the 1968 campaign. In the June 23 meeting with Bob Haldeman, Nixon had agreed with Haldeman's gloomy assessment of Klein, adding that Klein "doesn't have his head screwed on right." After Nixon resigned, Pulliam acknowledged:

> He fooled me completely. In the first campaign, Ike almost had to kick him off the ticket—that should have told us. I believed in his integrity until a year ago, but he got arrogant and surrounded himself with nincompoops. I didn't see Nixon much—he didn't want to see me. I was invited to dinners though, but I tried not to go.

46

Last Years

"HIS BODY HAS become a cage for his mind," Dr. Hayes Caldwell noted of his eighty-six-year-old patient, Gene Pulliam. Pulliam had only a few months to live. His back had weakened, and he usually walked with two canes. He had to be careful about talking for he might lose his voice if he strained it, and talking to people had always been a favorite activity. He had always had stomach difficulties because of his excess nervous energy, a condition that doctors could not treat medically because it was related to his personality. His Indianapolis physician, Dr. Joseph Walther, said Pulliam had a "migraine personality," the kind of person who was hard-driving, intense, always seeking perfection. "Like most migraine personalities, he'd often have other psychosomatic complaints."

Pulliam depended more and more on television for news, and newspapers and letters had to be read to him. He disliked growing old. "I hope you grow old more gracefully than I have, kiddo," he would tell the author. He grew more short-tempered, taking out his frustrations on the people closest to him.

No longer could he play golf, though he vowed to get back out on the course as soon as he cleared up his troubles. He often went out in a cart and enviously watched his friends play in Phoenix when he arranged games for them.

There were other frustrations. He failed the Indiana driver's license test. Tom Jones, his driver in Indianapolis, had taken him for the test, and Pulliam never said whether he had passed. Even after it was evident that he had failed the test, Jones recalled, he wanted to try it out again, show the world he could still make his own way. He told Jones to pull over and let him take the wheel for a while. He headed south on a one-way northbound street. He then headed back downtown to the Indianapolis Athletic Club where he and Nina kept an apartment. "He burnt rubber," Jones said. "He was doing forty or forty-five down Capitol, switching lanes. I was a nervous wreck. Everybody had been telling him he couldn't drive anymore."

Still, retirement was out of the question. At the *Star* and *News* Christmas dinner in December 1974, he gave a fighting speech, declaring that "I'm going to outlive all of you."

"He knew it wasn't true," said a *Star* reporter, Harley Bierce, who was surprised at Pulliam's vigor at the dinner. "He was saying I'm tough, I'm hanging in there, I'm feeling pretty good. He looked good, considering his age. I guess I had the impression he wasn't well, but he was really with it."

Despite his promise to outlive the others, Gene Pulliam had developed some sense of limits, a feeling that he could no longer save the world. Soon after Nixon's resignation, his Indiana Democrat friend Frank McHale wrote to suggest that he come up with another slam-bang front-page editorial. Now was the time for Pulliam to tell Ford to take himself and his vice presidential nominee, Nelson Rockefeller, out of the 1976 presidential race and devote themselves solely to fighting inflation.

> Now you and I know if the president and vice president are teaming up to run again, the Democrats will not go along with him. Therefore, I thought of you as a real American who has always put the love of country above the love of party.

He was no longer so quick to leap into action. He wrote to his old friend: "The trouble is, I'm not God."

> I agree with you completely, but I can't do a damn thing about this depression and inflation. I don't think your idea about the president would work, but even if I asked him, he wouldn't do it.
> Just the same, I love you just like I always have.

He did want to make contact with the new president about his pardon of Nixon:

Because they are a compassionate people, I sincerely believe the majority
of Americans will approve your Nixon decision. You have done what
you believe to be just and right, so be of good cheer.

He still summoned the energy to meet President Ford at the
Phoenix airport in November the same year. He chided Ford for
planning to leave on an overseas trip two days before Nelson
Rockefeller had been confirmed as vice president, leaving House
speaker Carl Albert in charge of the country. He still had some of the
old fire. "I think you ought to give Congress a good kick in the tail
and get them moving on Rockefeller's confirmation," Pulliam told
Ford. Ford suggested that public pressures on Congress might help.
"I'll be a committee of one to contact newspaper editors and see what
we can do about that," Pulliam answered.

Candidates still came to see him, all the way to Arizona from
Indiana if necessary, seeking his blessing. Indianapolis mayor
Richard Lugar was getting ready to run for the U.S. Senate seat held
by Democrat Birch Bayh and flew to Phoenix in December 1973 to
see the publisher. Pulliam was anxious to see Lugar topple Bayh,
but a team of investigative reporters at his morning newspaper in
Indianapolis was uncovering information that would prove to be a
key factor in Lugar's narrow loss to Bayh.

The reporters—police reporter William Anderson, assistant
city editor Richard Cady, and reporter Harley Bierce—had started to
look into charges of police corruption in August 1973. At first they
planned to spend only a few weeks to check the rumors. They wound
up working six months, joined by photographer Jerry Clark. They
came up with some of the most extensive documentation of police
corruption ever assembled by an American newspaper. But the
reporters were nervous. None of them knew Gene Pulliam well.
They talked frequently with his son, Gene, who gave them a green
light each time. "Do whatever you're big enough to do," the
younger Pulliam would tell them. "But I won't tolerate hatchet
jobs. If you can back it up, this paper will print it."

They still worried. They were assembling explosive material.
How much did the publisher know about their work? They knew
the Pulliams wanted to support Lugar, a conservative-to-moderate
Republican, over Bayh, a liberal Democrat.

"We kept hearing rumors," Bierce recalled. In February, as the first stories were being readied to go to press, they heard the stories would not be printed if they would hurt Lugar's chances in the Senate race. They went to see the younger Pulliam, who said, no, the rumor was wrong, the stories would run. They got nervous again the Saturday before the stories were to run. A call came from Phoenix— the publisher was asking for Lugar's home phone number. What for? No one knew.

The reporters had briefed Lugar on the details of the stories during the past week, giving him a chance to respond. "We had people whose lives we thought were in jeopardy," Bierce said. The reporters even mulled over contingency plans in case the stories were killed. One plan was to fly to Phoenix to present their case to the publisher personally, another to take their information to Congress, or to other newspapers.

The contingency plans, as it turned out, were unnecessary. Gene, Jr., decided to go ahead with the series on Sunday, February 24. He told his father about it the week before. "Well, it won't help his chances, but you have to print it," the elder Pulliam said.

The stories, which would bring a Pulitzer Prize to the *Star*, led to a wider-ranging investigation in 1974. Gene Pulliam's granddaughter, Myrta Pulliam, was added to the team. Republican prosecutor Noble Pearcy, up for reelection in 1974, struck back at the *Star* for the team's stories about his failure to prosecute police corruption. Cady and Anderson were indicted in September for conspiracy to bribe a policeman. Gene, Jr., came back with a front-page editorial the next day:

> Prosecutor Noble R. Pearcy and his chief deputy Leroy K. New have again manipulated a grand jury, this time in a clumsy effort to undermine the credibility of the investigating team and of the series of articles about police corruption and its coverup by the prosecutor's office. Pearcy is running for reelection and we urge the voters of Marion County in November to return him to his private life.

Pearcy was defeated by the largest margin of any incumbent in the history of Marion County. Lugar lost to Bayh by 75,000 votes, running well in other parts of Indiana but losing the race in Marion County. The indictments against the reporters were dismissed by the new prosecutor, James Kelly, who announced there was "no evidence a crime was committed." The informant, Larry Keen, who had testified against the reporters, later acknowledged he had lied to the grand jury. "It was me who set the reporters up," Keen said. "I did it because I was carrying a grudge."

Meanwhile in Arizona Pulliam was meeting a number of candidates for governor—the incumbent Republican Jack Williams could not run for a third term. Among the Republican contenders, an Indiana native, Russ Williams, won the primary. Raul Castro, who had lost to Jack Williams in 1970 by only 5,000 votes, won the Democratic primary.

Castro, a former professional boxer, had come from Mexico, moving to Arizona at a young age and becoming an ambassador and judge. He went to see Pulliam periodically with the thought that the publisher would sympathize with his background—his rise from poverty as an immigrant to a successful career.

Not well known among the influential people in Phoenix, he had aimed his 1970 campaign mainly at minority groups and liberals.

Pulliam gave a luncheon for potential presidential candidate John Connolly in September 1973. He introduced Castro twice as his close personal friend from Tucson, in front of all the prominent figures in Phoenix business and political circles. "I wasn't a good friend. I was out of nowhere," Castro recalled. "I was nothing. Hell, I just came out of the clear blue sky. I was from Tucson."

"He did it very deliberately," Castro added, in reference to the odd double introduction. "He just wanted to make an impression on them. They construed that to be an endorsement. Guys who wouldn't normally say hello to me were introducing themselves to me with the blessing of Gene Pulliam."

"Gene told me he knew he was doing it twice," said *Republic* editor Pat Murphy. "He sort of chuckled about it, saying, 'I know people probably think I'm senile.'" The double introduction was a boost to Castro's subsequent campaign. "Many prominent politicians were saying it meant Gene was going to support Castro for governor in the 1974 election," noted *Republic* political editor Bernie Wynn. Castro won the election. Though Pulliam was neutral in the *Republic* and *Gazette,* privately he gave Castro advice. "I think he wanted a Democratic governor," noted Murphy. "I think he felt it was time to shake up the Republican establishment."

He surprised Castro after the election. The new governor had expected to get orders from the publisher and envisioned a showdown with Pulliam. He wasn't looking forward to it and was a little nervous. But it never came, he noted:

> I think the man was completely unknown. I used to laugh when people would say, "Has Pulliam told you what to do?" I was afraid he'd try to dictate policy. I figured this was where we split the rug. He'd just say use your own judgment. I always expected him to lower the boom. He never did. He could have killed me.

The same year, however, *Republic* investigative reporter Don Bolles found that Pulliam was no longer so quick to back him up as in the past:

> As to libel suits, when I first came to the paper in 1962, Gene's attitude was full speed ahead and to hell with the libel suits. But as he came near the end, his attitude changed. He had a few cases where the lawyers kept pulling him into court and it became a nuisance to him that he didn't want to continue.

Bolles quit investigative reporting for the *Republic* in 1974, soon after Pulliam decided to kill a series on the Arizona criminal justice system. His fight against organized crime had been an uphill battle. Seldom did he get significant public support for his stories:

> The impact of my Mafia series was zilch. I got about 150 telephone calls and letters in response to it, and people still use it for reference, and the State Organized Crime Task Force put it into a book it did, but otherwise, nothing. Emprise changed its name and still is in the racetracks, six years later.

47

Death

GENE PULLIAM DIED the way he wanted to die, and only because it seems even he had to. Martin Anderson, who had joined Pulliam and Charles Marsh after they started General Newspapers and in due course bought the Orlando, Florida, newspapers from the corporation, thought about selling some thirty years later. Before taking the step, he asked Pulliam for his advice and reported the answer: "'Never sell out—not for $30 nor for $40 million. I would never sell, because I am not going back into my grave.' I think that gives you an inkling of his personality and character. He is going to die with his boots on."

And, as Anderson predicted, and as he himself wished, Pulliam died with his boots on.

On the morning of his death, June 23, 1975, he dictated a memo on unemployment to Pat Murphy, editorial page editor of the *Republic*. That afternoon he suffered a massive stroke and was taken to St. Joseph's Hospital. "My God, it's taking a long time to get there," he told his ambulance attendant, still, as always, in a hurry, evoking the days he would tell his drivers to "step on it, kiddo."

On the pad next to his bed, he wrote a reminder to himself: "Goldwater." He died at 3:30 P.M.

Death brought a wide range of eulogies from around the country—President Ford, former President Nixon, AP general manager Wes Gallagher, Gannett chairman Paul Miller, UPI vice president H. L. Stevenson, publisher John Knight, national newspaper union leaders like International Typographical Union president A. Sandy Bevis, and a host of others.

Governor Raul Castro ordered the flags flown at half mast on state buildings in Arizona, and the state's Supreme Court justice Fred. C. Struckmeyer, Jr., declared: "Arizona has lost its outstanding citizen."

"My idea of the classic American patriot," was the summation of House minority leader John Rhodes, who had been part of the original Arizona Republican effort that Gene Pulliam had spurred on in the early 1950s, adding, "He was always the kind of man you could count on to give it to you straight."

"I have lost the best friend a cartoonist ever had," *Star* cartoonist Charley Werner mourned in his cartoon the next day.

In other Arizona newspapers, political observers were speculating about the void left by his death. Who would or could take on his mantle? To whom could the political figures go for advice? Would his wife Nina, the new publisher, follow in his footsteps? One of his editors? Someone else in the *Republic* and *Gazette*? His influence came from something more than his office as publisher of the state's largest newspapers; it stemmed from a dominant and driving personality, and an ineffable something besides. "Who will have the magic influence he had?" asked former Arizona Senate president William Jacquin. "No, I don't think anyone can fill his shoes."

Goldwater, the man he had started in politics and who went on to achieve national renown, declared:

> The loss of Gene Pulliam was not just a personal one for me but for the state of Arizona and the United States.
>
> Gene's coming to Arizona at the time he did sparked the efforts needed after World War II to keep that momentum alive. And it made Arizona one of the truly great states of the nation.

Former Indiana senator William Jenner, another old friend and sometimes foe, believed:

> He represented all that is American. He was a true Horatio Alger, who went from the bottom to the top.

Ralph Gates, the Indiana Republican governor who had been on the receiving end of some of Pulliam's roughest editorials, noted:

I consider him one of the splendid newspapermen in the country. He did much in setting a course for Indiana after World War II.

Former Indianapolis mayor Charles Boswell, who was a preacher's kid like Pulliam, recalled:

Mr. Pulliam brought an evangelistic fervor to this community, as he supported programs and institutions the resulted in vast improvements.

Editorial writers had a hard time summarizing his life—what could you say about this man who had shaped history in two states? He seemed to have walked out of another era of journalism, a latter-day William Rockhill Nelson, putting his firm stamp on Indiana and Arizona at a time when fashion decreed that publishers be more low-key, less flamboyant, less influential. The models he had followed, the old-fashioned individualistic publishers, had died so long ago—Pulitzer in 1911, Nelson in 1915, Hearst in 1951. Most of them had grown up in poverty, begun their climb by grabbing a few pennies on their newspaper routes, then scrambling for that first reporting job and the few dollars a week it brought. They would scrape together enough cash to buy a small newspaper, become the boss, go on to the larger publications. They built up circulation and won a host of enemies with exciting crusades and editorials against local corruption and powerful political figures, wheeling and dealing behind the scenes, refusing to tailor their editorials to advertisers' demands. And at times somehow found the time and energy to head off on foreign reporting trips.

Only a few of that stamp survived after World War II, Colonel Robert McCormick at the *Chicago Tribune* until 1955, Roy Howard of Scripps-Howard newspapers until 1965. His fellow reporter at the *Kansas City Star*, Oscar Stauffer, who founded a substantial media empire in Kansas and several other states, outlived Pulliam. As did John Knight, who with his brother had been the second generation in a newspaper family, and like Pulliam, had built up Knight newspapers into a large chain by 1975.

Ironically a Scripps-Howard newspaperman in southern Indiana best captured the deceased Pulliam among Indiana editorial writers:

Eugene Collins Pulliam was a major figure in Indiana journalism for a half century. His friends—and they were legion—saw him as a champion of conservatism, the very symbol of a strong and free America. His critics, also legion, saw him as a reactionary force who used his newspaper empire to expound a personal ideology and to broker power.

History will have to decide the final place of this colorful, combative Hoosier who died this week at eighty-six, but there's no question that Indiana won't be the same without him.

He was a rough, tough, tenacious gut fighter. Right or wrong, he had the courage of his convictions. He believed in individual liberty. He feared government encroachment into citizens' lives. He abhorred excessive concentration of power in federal hands.

He didn't hesitate to cross swords with those who disagreed with him, pulling his formidable resources into battle with all the subtlety of a dreadnought. Yet he befriended the young and the have-nots of the world and his generosity and loyalty to those in his employ were almost legendary.

He saw a free press as the cornerstone of the liberties he defended with his evangelistic fervor. The proudest moment of his career came only months ago with one of his newspapers, the *Indianapolis Star*, being awarded a Pulitzer Prize for its exposé of police corruption.

Indiana has fostered a rich tradition of distinguished journalism peopled by such figures as Roy Howard, Ernie Pyle, and Kent Cooper. To their influential ranks is now added the name of Gene Pulliam.

William Burleigh, a man who had never met Pulliam, wrote the editorial, having observed his influence in Indiana as a reporter for the Evansville newspaper, and later remarked:

Your question almost answers itself. No young journalist could grow up in Indiana in the 1940s and '50s—as I did—without being acutely aware of the shadow cast by Eugene C. Pulliam. For good or ill, he dominated Indiana journalism. Many, as I am sure you know, thought it was for ill. Perhaps because I never cared for knee-jerk judgments, I did not share that opinion of him. His influence, both on the state and on its newspapers, fascinated me and I suppose I became a Pulliam watcher.

An interesting tribute came from one of his oldest foes, Andrew Jacobs, Sr., a lawyer who had filed a number of libel suits against the *Star* and liked to denounce Pulliam in political speeches. A criminal court judge by 1975, Jacobs wrote to Pulliam's son, Gene, after his father's death:

Your father was a frontal fighter—and I rather liked that kind of father.

Out in Arizona, William Mathews had died six years earlier, and his newspaper, the *Arizona Daily Star*, had been sold to the Pulitzer family. Mathews had been one of the old-fashioned editors, like Pulliam; it seemed fitting that a *Daily Star* editorial also captured some of Pulliam's essence, noting that "his death may mark the last of an era of personal journalism."

Too infrequently in American history there emerges the sort of man, possessed of great will, determination and a little luck, who is able to influence and shape events.

Eugene C. Pulliam, publisher of the *Arizona Republic* and *Phoenix Gazette*, as well as four Indiana papers, belonged to that rare breed. He also belonged to more than two centuries of American journalism history which was perhaps its most glamorous and most powerful.

Mr. Pulliam's contemporaries were such men as William Randolph Hearst, Henry Luce and Col. Robert McCormick. And while such men could disagree as to who should be president and what legislation should pass, they all shared a deep commitment to a free press and to their personal convictions.

Epilogue

GENE PULLIAM HAD left his newspaper stock, the controlling stock of Central Newspapers, Inc., to a three-person trust, rather than to his family. He had seen many newspapers ruined by family stockholders who were not working at the newspapers or by the lawyers and bankers who were acting on behalf of the family. The trust, according to his will, would run until twenty-one years after the death of all his descendants who were alive in 1973. The youngest descendant at the time was a great-grandson, two year old Kelly Quayle, the son of his grandson, Chris, and Linda Quayle. The trustees were his wife Nina, his son Gene, and *Star* and *News* general manager William A. Dyer. If one died, the two others would pick the replacement, who had to be someone working for the newspapers.

He had started a large newspaper family, something like the Ridders, who also had nephews, uncles, nieces, brothers, sisters, and grandchildren, scattered throughout the newspaper business. The family included his brother-in-law, Roy Swank, who died in 1974; his second wife, Martha, who had taken over the *Lebanon Reporter*; and his son Gene, who had joined him at WIRE after a career with the United Press and rose to become publisher of the *Star* and *News* after his death, and had overall responsibility for the *Vincennes Sun-Commercial*. Then too there was his wife Nina, who became president of Central Newspapers after his death, as well as publisher of the Phoenix newspapers, and who had been with his organization longer than any other employee. Nina's sister, Josephine Davidson, had been the editor of the *Arizona Republic* Sunday magazine. Jim Quayle, the husband of his eldest daughter, Corinne, worked for him in Indiana and Phoenix, and purchased the *Huntington Herald-Press* from him in 1964. He returned to the organization in 1973 to become publisher for several years of the Muncie

Newspapers. One of Nina's sisters, Rachel Peden, wrote a popular column on farm life in the *Indianapolis Star* for a number of years. A niece, Corinne Baker, was a secretary at the *Indianapolis News*. All of his ten grandchildren had had some sort of newspaper experience, including several who were establishing careers in the field when he died. Myrta Pulliam, Gene, Jr.'s older daughter, was part of the *Indianapolis Star*'s Pulitzer Prize–winning team of investigative reporters. She also helped establish Investigative Reporters and Editors, Inc., joining the IRE's investigation of organized crime in Arizona after the 1976 murder of *Republic* reporter Don Bolles. Dan Quayle, Jim Quayle's oldest son and the general manager of the *Huntington Herald-Press* when Pulliam died in 1975, was elected to Congress in 1976, and to the U.S. Senate in 1980. Russ Pulliam was a reporter for the Associated Press in New York for five years, later joining the *Indianapolis News* as an editorial writer. Another grandson, Doug McDaniel, became a reporter for the Washington bureau of the *Indianapolis Star*.

A grandson, Chris Quayle, wrote this poem:

And in his native states the flags
In their sad position set
Solemn and reverent on the staff
Where no wind stirred the standard straight
Nor resolved the bloody waves from pure,
Beneath the melancholy constellation,
In humble posture hung—a mute salute
To the youngest herald of an age.

While dry thunder drubbed a double beat,
Sounded off the sterile mountain stone;
And soft lamenting notes drift unhurried,
Complaining in a whisper, across the arid sand.

Index